# Life and Death Decis

Issues of life and death such as abortion, assisted suicide, capital punishment, and others are among the most contentious in many societies. Whose rights are protected? How do these rights and protections change over time and who makes those decisions? Based on the author's award-winning and hugely popular undergraduate course at the University of Texas, this book explores these questions and the fundamentally sociological processes which underlie the quest for morality and justice in human societies. The author's goal is not to advocate any particular moral "high ground" but to shed light on the social movements and social processes which are at the root of these seemingly personal moral questions.

Under 200 printed pages in length, this slim paperback is priced and sized to be easily assigned in a variety of undergraduate courses that touch on the social bases underlying these contested and contentious issues.

**Sheldon Ekland-Olson** is the Audre and Bernard Centennial Professor at The University of Texas at Austin, where he served as the Dean of the College of Liberal Arts and Executive Vice President and Provost. He is the winner of numerous teaching awards, and one of his classes was once listed among the ten Hottest Courses in the Nation. His previous publications include *The Rope, The Chair and the Needle*; *Texas Prisons*; *Who Lives, Who Dies, Who Decides?*; and *Justice Under Pressure*.

## Contemporary Sociological Perspectives

*Edited by* **Doug Hartmann**, *University of Minnesota,* **Valerie Jenness**, *University of California, Irvine and* **Jodi O'Brien**, *Seattle University*

This innovative series is for all readers interested in books that provide frameworks for making sense of the complexities of contemporary social life. Each of the books in this series uses a sociological lens to provide current critical and analytical perspectives on significant social issues, patterns and trends. The series consists of books that integrate the best ideas in sociological thought with an aim toward public education and engagement. These books are designed for use in the classroom as well as for scholars and socially curious general readers.

**Published:**

*Political Justice and Religious Values* by Charles F. Andrain

*GIS and Spatial Analysis for the Social Sciences* by Robert Nash Parker and Emily K. Asencio

*Hoop Dreams on Wheels: Disability and the Competitive Wheelchair Athlete* by Ronald J. Berger

*The Internet and Social Inequalities* by James C. Witte and Susan E. Mannon

*Media and Middle Class Mom: Images and Realities of Work and Family* by Lara Descartes and Conrad Kottak

*Watching T.V. Is Not Required: Thinking about Media and Thinking about Thinking* by Bernard McGrane and John Gunderson

*Violence Against Women: Vulnerable Populations* by Douglas Brownridge

*State of Sex: Tourism, Sex and Sin in the New American Heartland* by Barbara G. Brents, Crystal A. Jackson & Kate Hausbeck

*Social Statistics: The Basics and Beyond* by Thomas J. Linneman

*Sociologists Backstage: Answers to 10 Questions About What They Do* by Sarah Fenstermaker and Nikki Jones

# Life and Death Decisions

## The Quest for Morality and Justice in Human Societies

### Abortion, Neonatal Care, Assisted Dying, and Capital Punishment

Sheldon Ekland-Olson

Routledge
Taylor & Francis Group

NEW YORK AND LONDON

First published 2013
by Routledge
711 Third Avenue, New York, NY 10017

Simultaneously published in the UK
by Routledge
2 Park Square, Milton Park, Abingdon, Oxon OX14 4RN

*Routledge is an imprint of the Taylor & Francis Group, an informa business*

*Library of Congress Cataloging-in-Publication Data*
Ekland-Olson, Sheldon, 1944–
Life and death decisions : the quest for morality and justice in human societies / Sheldon Ekland-Olson.
p. cm. – (Contemporary sociological perspectives)
Includes bibliographical references and index.
1. Life–Moral and ethical aspects. 2. Capital punishment–Moral and ethical aspects. 3. Social justice. 4. Human rights. I. Title.
BD431.E427 2013
179.7–dc23
2012028373

ISBN: 978–0–415–66291–8 (hbk)
ISBN: 978–0–415–66292–5 (pbk)
ISBN: 978–0–203–07182–3 (ebk)

Typeset in Minion
by Keystroke, Station Road, Codsall, Wolverhampton

Printed and bound in the United States of America by Walsworth Publishing Company, Marceline, MO.

# Brief Contents

# Contents

# Preface

This volume is a substantially condensed revision of my earlier book *Who Lives, Who Dies, Who Decides?* The initial volume aimed to provide substantial detail on the historical events defining our struggle to come to terms with deeply important moral issues. This volume sharpens the focus to better identify underlying common themes, and to make the material more useful and accessible to those who would address these issues within a broader context.

Eugenics, abortion, neonatal care, assisted dying, lynching, and capital punishment involve quite distinct questions. The objective here is to identify the common threads that bind these issues of life and death together. We find these threads in the question: How do we justify, through our laws, religions, and customs, our violation of deeply important, perhaps universal, moral imperatives, all the while holding tightly to their importance? The answer we find is that we define life's protective boundaries through an assessment of social worth and we set priorities as we balance competing demands of moral imperatives. We will find evidence for these conclusions throughout the following chapters.

In the process, we will also come across several more general lessons. These are presented in brief detail in the Epilogue. The assessment of social worth flows throughout. We find it in the logic of legal decisions as well as in the emotional empathy generated by rhetoric, visual images, and heart-wrenching stories. Through the power of empathy and constructed logic, we come to believe that chosen pathways are more or less infused with morality or injustice. The inherent dilemmas produced by the imperatives involved pull us first this way, then that. In the end we are left with cyclical change, each side believing deeply in the rightness of positions taken.

# 1
# A Moral System Evolves

## A Single Question

Every society ever known has held to two deeply important moral imperatives:

- Life is sacred and should be protected.
- Suffering, once detected, should be alleviated.

And yet, these imperatives are routinely violated. Illustrations are repeatedly found. Here we will explore the moral landscape of eugenics, abortion, neonatal care, assisted dying, lynching, and capital punishment. We ask a single question. How do we, through our laws, religions, and customs, go about justifying the violation of deeply important, perhaps universal, moral signposts, all the while holding tightly to their importance?

The answer we find is this: We draw boundaries to establish social worth, and we set priorities to resolve dilemmas. In the process, we arrive at understandings calling for, even demanding, actions otherwise seen as deeply disturbing. From time to time, science, technology, and crystallizing events disturb, clarify, and inform our existing understandings. Such occurrences call for renewed resolution of dilemmas and definitions of life's protective boundaries. Along this jagged and often contentious path moral systems evolve. We begin with a movement to eliminate people judged to be "unfit."

## An Exclusionary Movement is Born

The story of Nazi atrocities has been told countless times. It is only more recently that the evolution of the Final Solution has been linked to an international eugenics movement, anchored in the evolutionary theories of Charles Darwin, and legitimized by the U.S. Supreme Court.[1] An exclusionary assessment of social worth provided the cornerstone.

In the formative years of the eugenics movement, no one was more important than the man who coined the term, Francis Galton. Galton was convinced that the means could be found to give "the more suitable races or strains of blood a better chance of prevailing speedily over the less suitable."[2] To Galton, these means were imperfect, but still more humane than the brutal processes of natural selection. In an oft-cited self-reflective passage, Galton noted:

Man is gifted with pity and other kindly feelings; he has also the power of preventing many kinds of suffering. I conceive it to fall well within his province to replace Natural Selection by other processes that are more merciful and not less effective.[3]

We could make life better by minimizing suffering that would otherwise occur. It was our duty to do so.

Galton was convinced that "man's natural abilities are derived through inheritance."[4] He also saw that some of these influences were working toward "the degradation of human nature, and that others are working towards its improvement."[5] We had enormous power—via careful breeding—to influence the makeup of society. We had a duty to humanity to ensure that this power "shall be most advantageous to future inhabitants of the earth."[6] With this rationale, eugenics the scientific investigation became eugenics the progressive social movement. The practical implications of exclusionary differential worth were taking root.

To make matters worse for Galton and those of like mind, birth rates among the less fit were markedly higher. Society was providing a safety net for these less advantaged persons arriving in greater numbers, thus weakening the natural winnowing that would otherwise occur. Eugenicists began to criticize this "indiscriminate benevolence" for the poor, as it produced artificially long life spans for those considered unfit. If left unchecked, these higher birth rates and artificially reduced death rates among society's least capable could mean only one thing—the slow but sure degradation of the populace. The very survival of a thriving, prosperous society was at stake.

Wouldn't it be better to have a society enriched by those who are productive, healthy, emotionally stable, and smart than one stifled by degenerate, feeble-minded, disabled, and criminal citizens? To protect *LIFE*, the lives of the less worthy should be reduced in number. A loosely connected network of individuals and organizations, dedicated to the eugenics cause, began to chart the course toward what they saw as a more secure and prosperous future.[7]

### A Base of Operation

The framing message and assumption of the eugenics social movement was that some lives were more worthy of support and protection than others. Its proponents set about performing research, the fruits of which could be used for the betterment of all. The Station for the Experimental Study of Evolution (SESE) and the Eugenics Record Office (ERO) served as critical early bases of operation.

The SESE and ERO were launched through the efforts of Charles Benedict Davenport, a young professor with entrepreneurial designs. While teaching at Harvard and later at the University of Chicago, Davenport began to seek funding for an independent laboratory. He soon discovered that the recently founded Carnegie Institution of Washington (CIW) had priorities that coincided with his interests. Davenport had just the place for his laboratory—a small summer institute at Cold Spring Harbor, on the northwestern shore of Long Island where he had taught previously. In December 1903, he was awarded a grant from CIW with commitments, as the award put it, to continue indefinitely, or for a long time. The Station for the Experimental Study of Evolution was born.

As Davenport's work moved forward, it soon became clear that he would need a safe repository for his data. He began to search again for funding. In testament to the strength of weak ties[8] and the importance of a tenacious entrepreneurial spirit for the success of any social movement, Davenport thought immediately of his connection to railroad magnate Edward Henry Harriman. Harriman had recently died and left his fortune to his wife, Mary; their daughter (also named Mary) had been a student of Davenport's three years earlier in the summer program at Cold Spring Harbor.

The widow Harriman placed special emphasis on the use of scientific principles to secure a rational, orderly society.[9] Davenport renewed their acquaintance and noted his admiration for her philanthropic endeavors, suggesting that the newly launched endeavor at Cold Spring Harbor would be a good fit for the priorities of Mary's Harriman Foundation. Eventually, Mrs. Harriman offered a financial commitment to Davenport that made the ERO possible. Harry Laughlin, a former teacher and school superintendent from Missouri, was appointed to head it up.

Funding from the Carnegie Institute of Washington and the Harriman Foundation provided not only resources, but also credibility among society's elite. The operation at Cold Spring Harbor was to be taken seriously. It soon became "a meeting place for eugenicists, a repository for eugenics records, a clearinghouse for eugenics information and propaganda, a platform from which popular eugenic campaigns could be launched, and a home for several eugenical publications." The ERO, in short, "became a nerve center for the eugenics movement as a whole."[10] It would be a long-lasting, far-reaching, and in the end a quite troubling legacy.

## Framing the Agenda

The Cold Spring Harbor operation worked hand-in-hand with the American Breeders Association (ABA).[11] Davenport had been elected to the ABA's oversight committee, and in 1906 he helped establish a eugenics committee within the organization. The eugenics committee's charge was to develop methods for mapping traits of families, individuals, and races, with the underlying assumption that some blood lines were beneficial, and some detrimental, to the health of society.

The first president of Stanford University, David Starr Jordan, agreed to serve as the committee's Chair. The committee's purpose was to advance the "interests of the Association that relate to human improvement by a better selection of marriage mates and the control of the reproduction of defective classes."[12] Harry Laughlin was asked to assume the responsibility for producing an early report for Jordan's committee.

Jordan had long-standing interests in these matters. As a young professor at Indiana University, where he later served as president, he became acquainted with Oscar McCulloch, the minister of the Indianapolis Congregational Church where he attended services. Reverend McCulloch, who was a spokesman for what came to be known as the social gospel movement, had been responsible for establishing numerous charitable organizations in the Indianapolis area. In his sermons, McCulloch spoke frequently of the degradation of society and the need for well-planned change.[13] McCulloch had been impressed by Galton's research along with Richard Dugdale's 1877 study of an extended New York family, *"The Jukes": A Study in Crime, Pauperism, Disease, and Heredity*. McCulloch believed that Dugdale's book provided important insights into both the cause of and the remedy for the degenerates who so troubled and damaged the society he aimed to improve.

McCulloch had heard stories of a similar family in his home state of Indiana, so he decided to launch his own investigation. His inquiry extended over the next decade, eventually including some 250 families connected through an extended familial network. From this group, he selected thirty families to investigate in greater depth. In 1888, after eleven years of research, McCulloch presented his findings at the National Conference of Charities and Corrections in Buffalo, New York. There, he introduced the world to *The Tribe of Ishmael: A Study of Social Degradation.*

There were parallels, McCulloch noted, between members of this family and a small, free-swimming, parasitic crustacean. Soon after birth, he wrote: "an irresistible hereditary tendency seizes upon [the crustacean],"[14] leading it to attach itself to a crab and in the process become "degraded in form and function." This behavior, McCulloch went on to note, was learned by its offspring, continuing "in nature as a type of degradation through parasitism, or pauperism." With this vivid parasitic imagery in place, McCulloch continued, "I propose to trace the history of similar degradation in man. It is no pleasant study, but it may be relied upon as fact. It is no isolated case. It is not peculiar to Indiana." Like parasites, generation after generation of McCulloch's Tribe of Ishmael sucked nutrients from society and accordingly became useless dependants.

This energy-sapping degradation, McCulloch concluded, was hereditary, and misplaced charity accelerated its pace. "The so-called charitable people who give to begging children and women with baskets have a vast sin to answer for. . . . So-called charity joins public relief in producing still-born children, raising prostitutes, and educating criminals." For the moment, this preacher of the social gospel, organizer of charitable organizations, and creator of innovative reformatories had apparently become disenchanted with the New Testament's account of the final judgment involving those who were charitable and those who were not.[15] McCulloch closed his presentation with a final three-part admonition. "What can we do? First, we must close up official out-door relief. Second, we must check private and indiscriminate benevolence, or charity, falsely so-called. Third, we must get hold of the children."

Three years after presenting his findings, McCulloch the minister, researcher, and social reformer became president of the National Conference of Charities and Corrections. Shortly thereafter, at the age of 48, he died from Hodgkin's disease.[16] McCulloch's dehumanizing metaphor for the Tribe of Ishmael lived well beyond his lifetime.

## Branching Out

David Starr Jordan, McCulloch's parishioner, as president of Indiana University, had become a well-known academic by the time he was appointed chair of the American Breeders Association's committee. In the same year Oscar McCulloch died, Jordan moved from Indiana to become president of Stanford University. Jordan's position and academic standing made him an attractive draw on the lecture circuit both nationally and internationally. In 1898, he collected many of his writings in *Foot-Notes to Evolution: A Series of Popular Addresses on the Evolution of Life*. In 1902, a speech he gave at Stanford in 1899 was published as *The Blood of a Nation: A Study of the Decay of Races Through the Survival of the Unfit*.[17]

By this time, Jordan's eugenics position had solidified. In *Blood of a Nation* he wrote:

> For a race of men or a herd of cattle are governed by the same laws of selection . . . In selective breeding . . . it is possible, with a little attention to produce wonderful changes for the better . . . To select for posterity those individuals which best meet our needs or please our fancy, and to destroy those with unfavorable qualities, is the function of artificial selection.

Jordan's perspective had been shaped by several visits he made to the Italian village of Aosta, located where Italy, France, and Switzerland converge in a sparsely populated and scenic Alpine valley not far from majestic Mont Blanc. In Aosta, he had observed "feeble little people with uncanny voices, silly faces, and sickening smiles, incapable of taking care of themselves."[18] By 1910, these unfortunates had been segregated by the Catholic Church into an asylum where they were forbidden to marry or have children. In the years ahead, Jordan drew on this lesson of selective breeding via enforced segregation and would become a strong advocate that similar practices be instituted in the United States.

With this background, Jordan accepted the invitation to develop policy recommendations for human eugenics. In 1911, he began to explore, as his ABA committee put it, the "best practical means for cutting off the defective germ-plasm in the human population." The eugenics movement was gaining momentum, now supported by a nationwide network of connections among prominent individuals.

## The Criteria for Exclusion

At the time, the general understanding of heredity was primitive at best. Completely unaware of the structure of DNA or genetic markers, researchers had little more to go on than the early work of Gregor Mendel[19] and the distribution of traits revealed in pedigree studies of familial networks like the Jukes and Ishmaels. These family studies shared a common thread—determining how to separate unfit parasitic individuals from those making more worthy contributions to society.

To identify where the boundaries of social worth lie, Davenport published *The Trait Book*,[20] a detailed listing of individual characteristics, predispositions, and behavioral tendencies. In it, Davenport devised guidelines for field observations, pedigree charts, and surveys. These tools were widely distributed to physicians, teachers, social workers, and parents, and classification schemes were devised to organize the data. Persons found to be feeble-minded, degenerate perverts, epileptics, or paupers were to be identified, isolated, minimized, and, if possible, eliminated.

The feeble-minded were of special concern. At the same time that the Cold Spring Harbor operation was getting off the ground, French psychologists Alfred Binet and Theodore Simon teamed up to create the Simon-Binet Scale, a measurement of intelligence. Jordan's Stanford colleague, Lewis Terman, developed a modified version of the test that became known as the Stanford-Binet test. In 1908, Henry Goddard, a close associate of Davenport and the ERO, translated the work of Binet and Simon into English and introduced benchmarks to differentiate "morons," or persons with marginal intelligence, from "imbeciles" (one category lower) and "idiots" (two categories lower).

Goddard, who served as director of the research laboratory at the Vineland Training School for Feebleminded Girls and Boys in New Jersey, believed that the children in his charge would grow up to have higher fertility rates than others. Thus, he advocated tight controls on their ability to reproduce. As part of the growing network of eugenic cooperation, Goddard routinely made his patients available for family pedigree tracing and assessment and was intimately involved in writing reports for the ERO.

The early family pedigree studies of the Jukes and the Ishmaels were soon joined by other works, including Goddard's widely disseminated and highly influential investigation of the Kallikaks[21] and Arthur Estabrook's re-examination of data on the Jukes.[22] The influence of the eugenics movement in the U.S.A. was clearly broadening, and a relatively small, loose-knit circle of colleagues centered at the ERO in Cold Spring Harbor shaped its agenda. Their aim was to establish a nationwide program of mandatory sterilization grounded in statutory law.

### A Moral Entrepreneur

The legal effort to justify mandatory sterilization was carefully orchestrated. It began with Harry Laughlin's report on the best practical means of cutting off the defective germ plasm in the American population,[23] released in February of 1914. Using this report as a foundation, Laughlin later drafted and released a model law in 1922. Laughlin's 1922 proposed law served as a template eventually upheld as constitutional in 1927 by the Supreme Court in *Buck vs. Bell*.[24] What is less well known is that it also provided the foundation for Germany's first sterilization law enacted in 1933, shortly after Adolf Hitler came to power. In gratitude for Laughlin's pioneering work, Heidelberg University awarded him an honorary degree in 1936. Perhaps more than any other single individual, Laughlin became the moral and policy entrepreneur for mandatory eugenic sterilization. As he drafted his law he drew on efforts from many quarters.

One such initiative came from Pennsylvania, where on March 21, 1905, both houses of its legislature passed an "Act for the Prevention of Idiocy." While the bill had solid support in the Pennsylvania Legislature, the state's governor, Samuel Pennypacker, was vehemently opposed to it. To permit such a mandatory sterilization, the governor remarked, "would be to inflict cruelty upon a helpless class of the community which the state has undertaken to protect." "A great objection," Pennypacker continued, "is that the bill would be the beginning of experimentation upon living human beings, leading logically to results which can readily be forecasted." Pennypacker fundamentally disagreed with the wisdom, justice, practicality, and legality of such a law. He was governor and had veto power; days after the bill was passed, he exercised it. His veto was not overturned. Decades later, his concerns would prove to be well founded.

The outcome in Indiana was quite different. In 1907, Indiana became the first state to have an involuntary sterilization law. The Indiana law was very close in word, procedure, and purpose to the law Pennypacker had vetoed. This time, however, three days after its passage, Indiana Governor J. Frank Hanley signed the bill into law. Discretion was granted to a committee of experts that worked with staff at institutions where targeted individuals were housed. If the committee members judged that procreation was inadvisable they could approve sterilization.

Several of the 119 inmates who were sterilized at the Indiana Reformatory during the first year of the law's existence took exception to the procedure. They wrote letters[25] to Thomas Marshall, Hanley's successor as governor, who would later become Woodrow Wilson's vice president. These letters noted the perfunctory nature of the conversations that led to sterilization decisions and asserted that whatever the law's stated eugenic purpose might be, its consequences were punitive and lacking in procedural safeguards. These letters were received sympathetically by the recently elected governor Marshall, who declared a moratorium.

Between March 1907, when Indiana's legislation was signed into law, and the February 1914 release of Laughlin's recommendations, eleven other states passed statutes similar to Indiana's. Nowhere did the eugenic sterilization movement take deeper root than in California, the adoptive home of David Starr Jordan. In 1909, the legislature enacted the state's first non-consensual sterilization law. There was only one dissenting vote out of sixty-three, and the governor signed the legislation into law. Modified several times over the years and falling into disuse after the revealed Nazi horrors of World War II, it was not until 1979 that California's sterilization statute was finally repealed in a social climate of heightened concern over governmental intrusion into individual lives.[26]

Taking note of these legal developments, Laughlin specified general principles in what he called a "Model Sterilization Law." Its aim was to halt reproduction among the lowest and most degenerate one-tenth of the total population within the next two generations, and included a very precise schedule for the total elimination of defectives within seven decades. In rough approximation, the yearly sterilizations nationwide would rise from 92,000 in 1920; to 121,000 by 1930; 158,000 by 1940; 203,000 by 1950; 260,000 by 1960; 330,000 by 1970; and 415,000 by 1980. The stakes were high, as Laughlin and those who supported his efforts felt the degenerate one-tenth constituted a growing menace to the nation's social welfare. Legal reforms should start immediately.

## The Legal Framework Clarifies

Laughlin's initial 200-page report to the ERO was released in 1914. By 1921, eugenics laws in eight states, patterned after Laughlin's proposed ideas, had been challenged in appellate courts at both the state and federal levels. They did not fare well. All but one ended up overturned, either in whole or in part. This had a dampening effect on the eugenics movement, but Laughlin was learning important lessons. One had come earlier from New Jersey where Governor Woodrow Wilson had signed a mandatory sterilization bill into law in 1911. A year after the law's passage, an appeal was made on behalf of a young epileptic woman, Alice Smith.[27] Much like the concerns Governor Pennypacker had articulated in neighboring Pennsylvania, the New Jersey court noted that if it found the state's intervention legitimate in cases like Alice Smith's, "the doctrine we shall have enunciated cannot stop there." There were other "defects" that might classify people as a perceived burden to the common good. "Racial differences, for instance, might afford a basis for such (a policy) in communities where that question is unfortunately a permanent and paramount issue." Furthermore, in situations where a population might outgrow its resources, why not limit population growth by surgical interference of the sort being advocated?

Alice Smith was not sterilized. In 1918, two similar appellate cases were decided in Michigan and New York.[28] Concerns raised in these and other cases were addressed in Laughlin's 1922 revised model statute. Within two years of Laughlin's revised model statute's release, fifteen states had passed laws that were patterned, to a greater or lesser degree, after Laughlin's recommended language. Among these was a 1924 Virginia law that would soon move to the national forefront.

## A Landmark Case is Contrived

Thanks to the meticulous work of Paul Lombardo,[29] we know how Albert Priddy, Aubrey Strode, and Irving Whitehead, who were long-time friends and close professional associates, crafted the strategy for the successful passage of Virginia's sterilization statute and its eventual affirmation in 1927 by the Supreme Court in *Buck v. Bell*. The story actually began around the time the ERO was getting off the ground in Cold Spring Harbor. Aubrey Strode was a state senator and his efforts led to the 1910 establishment of the Virginia Colony for Epileptics and Feebleminded, which later became known as the Lynchburg Colony. Priddy served as the Colony's first superintendent. Priddy, Strode, and Whitehead made up the first governing board for the Colony, located in Strode's home district.

During the legislature's 1916 session, Strode worked with Priddy to introduce five separate bills related to the treatment of the feeble-minded. The most significant allowed sterilization without explicitly mentioning the procedure. Within five days of that law's effective date, Priddy petitioned the Colony's board for permission to sterilize eight women. With one member absent and one not responding, Whitehead alone approved the request the same day it was received. This quick turnaround soon became the rule as requests to authorize sterilization and subsequent board approval were for the most part routine and perfunctory, with Priddy recommending and Whitehead approving.

Willie Mallory and her eight children were among those confined at the Colony. Mallory and her daughter Jessie were both sterilized after one of the board's rulings. Two months later, Mallory's husband filed suit for the release of his children. The suit also sought US$5,000 in damages related to Mallory's confinement and her forced sterilization. Ultimately, the children were released, but, in the confinement and sterilization case regarding Mrs. Mallory, the jury ruled in Priddy's favor.

Despite the jury's verdict, the judge advised Priddy to discontinue the Colony's sterilizations until the law could be clarified and strengthened. The sterilizations continued, but Priddy's documented rationale for administering them shifted. Instead of referring to the to-be-sterilized women as being of the "moron type," following the Mallory trial the sterilizations were justified as being intended to relieve physical suffering for "pelvic disease" of unspecified origin. While Priddy continued to claim that he could treat his patients as he saw fit, he knew he needed a new law to provide adequate legal cover for his actions.

In 1923 Priddy and Strode crafted new legislation with the support of the General Board of State Hospitals. This time, the team used Laughlin's 1922 revised model sterilization statute as a touchstone. The legislation passed both houses of Virginia's Assembly with only two dissenting votes, but concerns lingered as to whether the statute could withstand an appeal. After all, laws in other states had passed, only to be declared unconstitutional. They needed a compelling, safe case. They chose an 18-year-old woman, Carrie Buck. Whitehead represented Buck, Strode took the case on behalf of the State, and Priddy was the named defendant. Needless to say, it was a close-knit group and a carefully coordinated effort. In retrospect it is hard to argue that Carrie Buck's interests had been defended.

Harry Laughlin was used as an expert witness. He had received correspondence from Priddy that summarized the case, but he never spoke with Carrie Buck or any member of her family. On the basis of Priddy's correspondence, Laughlin strongly supported the claim that Buck was a feeble-minded and otherwise unfit individual. Occasionally repeating Priddy's characterizations verbatim, Laughlin's deposition concluded that the Buck family belonged "to the shiftless, ignorant, and worthless class of anti-social whites of the South."

Carrie Buck had been chosen because of the assertion that she, her mother, and her daughter were all feeble-minded, and that the Buck family had a history of immoral, antisocial behavior. Whitehead could have challenged all of these assertions with substantial, easily available supporting evidence,[30] but he did not. Instead, he called no witnesses in Buck's defense, nor did he cross-examine Strode's witnesses or question in any detail the evidence Strode provided. It was by any standard a shoddy and irresponsible defense.

The County Circuit Court affirmed the decision to sterilize Buck in February 1925. Priddy died a month prior, and at that point his assistant, James H. Bell, took over as the Colony's superintendent. As a result, the case was retitled *Buck v. Bell*. Shortly thereafter, Strode and Whitehead jointly appeared before the Colony's board to celebrate their victory and to discuss their plans for the case's appeal to the next level. Minutes from a board meeting read in part that "Colonel Aubrey E.

Strode and Mr. I. P. Whitehead appeared before the Board—their advice being that this particular case was in admirable shape to go to the court of last resort, and that we could not hope to have a more favorable situation than this one."[31]

Assent from the U.S. Supreme Court was the final step in securing the constitutionality of Virginia's Sterilization Act. The Court heard arguments on April 22, 1927. A week and a half later, on May 2, Justice Oliver Wendell Holmes, on behalf of an eight-to-one Court majority, issued the Court's opinion affirming Virginia's sterilization statute.[32] He grounded the opinion in the common good:

> We have seen more than once that the public welfare may call upon the best citizens for their lives. It would be strange if it could not call upon those who already sap the strength of the State for these lesser sacrifices . . . in order to prevent our being swamped with incompetence. . . . The principle that sustains compulsory vaccination is broad enough to cover cutting the Fallopian tubes.

In his closing, Holmes wrote *Buck vs. Bell*'s most famous sentence: "Three generations of imbeciles are enough." Never before, and never since, has such a strong statement been written by such a respected jurist on the basis of such shoddy evidence. One can only speculate whether it came in some measure from Holmes' own ardent support of the eugenics movement.[33] Carrie Buck was sterilized five and a half months later, on October 19, 1927.

### The Floodgates Open

If ever there was a case that opened the floodgates, it was *Buck vs. Bell*. Prominent theologians and legal scholars continued to support the decision, asserting well into the 1950s that the collective good could not be achieved "if the community may not defend itself, and is forced to permit the continued procreation of feeble-minded or hereditarily diseased children."[34]

According to data collected by the Human Betterment Foundation, twenty-eight states had mandatory sterilization statutes by January 1933. The states with the highest number of sterilizations were spread from coast to coast, with California leading the way with 8,500; Virginia next with 1,300; Kansas and Michigan following with 1,000 each; Oregon next to last with 900; and Minnesota trailing with 700. A dramatic rise in mandated sterilizations occurred in 1929, with another following in 1932.[35] Because of the isolated nature of the institutions and a culture of professional independence among physicians—coupled with spotty record keeping across states and jurisdictions—precise totals and comparisons are all suspect. In all likelihood, the totals were higher. All accounts corroborate a dramatic increase in the number of non-consensual sterilizations following *Buck vs. Bell*.

## Public Health Measures Go Terribly Wrong

Justice Holmes wrote in *Buck* that it would be strange if the state "could not call upon those who already sap the strength of the State for these lesser sacrifices . . . in order to prevent our being swamped with incompetence." In his opinion and in the opinion of seven of his Supreme Court colleagues, the principle supporting public health through mandatory sterilization was secure. (In related personal correspondence, in fact, Holmes also expressed support for "putting to death the inadequate" and "infants that didn't pass the examination."[36]) Some six years later, borrowing heavily from the now legitimized statute Harry Laughlin had crafted, Germany enacted its *Gesetz zur Verhütung Erbkranken Nachwuchses* (Law for the Prevention of Genetically Diseased Offspring) in July 1933. The journey toward Germany's Final Solution had begun.

Following its passage, the ERO's *Eugenics News* reviewed the new German law favorably, stating, "Germany is the first of the world's major nations to enact a modern eugenical sterilization law for the nation as a whole." Parallels to Laughlin's work were noted with pride: "To one versed in the history of eugenical sterilization in America, the text of the statute reads almost like the 'American model sterilization law'."[37] Mandatory sterilization was now grounded in the idea that society's defective outcasts were a burden to society, and could be eliminated for the good of the whole. This underlying logic progressed step-by-step down a long and terrible road.

## An Awakening

In the aftermath of World War II, all agreed on at least one point: the Nazis had engaged in barbaric behaviors. The stark nature of the suffering they inflicted was jolting, but it was rarely mentioned that the Nazis' medical experiments and extermination practices shared roots with events that had taken place in the United States. The war was over, the Allies had won, and it was time to move on.

Shortly after World War II ended, however, Boston physician Leo Alexander published a widely influential article in the *New England Journal of Medicine*.[38] Alexander had been one of the architects of the Nuremberg Code, which was used to prosecute Nazi doctors for their crimes.[39] Alexander expressed concerns about the changing tide of medical thought in the United States. He knew the Nazis' atrocities had not sprung up overnight; instead, they'd been achieved in small, incremental steps. Alexander saw danger signs in the United States. In Alexander's mind, many of his colleagues in the medical field had been infected with a "cold-blooded, utilitarian philosophy" that made them vulnerable to practices like those that had occurred in Germany. Alexander's concerns were rooted in what William Ogburn had labeled cultural lag.[40]

## Crystallizing Events and Cultural Lag

The idea of cultural lag is straightforward:

- Science produces new knowledge.
- New knowledge is fashioned into innovative technologies.
- New technologies, especially those associated with the protection of life and the alleviation of suffering, call for refinements in moral and ethical thinking.
- It takes time to adjust.
- In the interim there is cultural lag.

To people like Leo Alexander, the existing moral and legal frameworks were simply not up to the task. Of particular note was a faulty assessment of social worth. As is often the case, issues were clarified by crystallizing events.

In 1960, Dr. Belding Scribner, working with some colleagues at the University of Washington in Seattle, developed a U-shaped arteriovenous cannula shunt made from a newly developed material, Teflon. This innovative device dramatically improved a patient's chances of surviving end-stage kidney disease. Those who once faced certain near-term death suddenly had years added to their life.

In the beginning, the technology was limited, cumbersome, and expensive. Who should be treated? Were some lives more worthy of saving than others? Who should decide? Answers to the ethical dilemmas and boundaries of relative social worth embedded in these questions provided a new impetus for how health care should be rationed.[41] After three patients had been successfully treated using the newly improved dialysis machine, University of Washington Hospital administrators informed Scribner that he could not accept any new patients. The procedure was simply too expensive, and the facilities too limited.

In short order (January 1962), the Seattle Artificial Kidney Center opened for business. It had three beds, dialysis equipment, and medical personnel on hand. Increased demand for dialysis immediately far exceeded availability. In a 1964 address to colleagues, Scribner noted that some 10,000 "ideal candidates"[42] had died since the shunt's development simply because not enough equipment existed to serve them. Difficult decisions were unavoidable.

Those in charge set up two committees to deal with these decisions. The Medical Advisory Committee, made up of physicians and a psychiatrist, would determine the initial pool of eligible patients. The Admissions Advisory Committee would determine who would be chosen from that initial pool. Random selection and first-come, first-served strategies were rejected. Instead, the role of the admissions committee "was to assess the relative worth of a candidate to their family and the community in terms of the degree of dependence of others upon the candidate's continuing existence, and the rehabilitative potential and moral value or worth of the candidate."[43]

Shortly after the new dialysis center opened and the advisory committees were convened, *Life* magazine sent a young staff writer, Shana Alexander, to Seattle to write about it. Alexander's story turned out to be the longest piece ever published by the magazine.[44] Thirty years later, a conference held in Seattle commemorated Alexander's article as a crystallizing event in the launch of the bioethics movement.[45]

## Social Worth and Rationed Health Care

Alexander's story presented an early glimpse of how uncertain assessment of social worth would dominate moral debates in the years ahead. In this sense, it raised the same question as the eugenics movement. Instead of regulating the ability to have children and thereby protect the health of the broader community, social worth was used to allocate life-prolonging resources. Beyond some vague rationing guidelines, there was little clarity. A doctor remarked in Alexander's article: "We told them frankly that there were *no* guidelines, they were on their own. We really dumped it on them." Piece by piece, a template for assessing differential social worth and the boundaries of protected life began to take shape.

Ambiguities in judgments of relative worth, as well as refinements in the committee's thinking, became evident as their deliberations proceeded. The following details were reconstructed in Alexander's article.

**Minister:** How can we compare a family situation of two children, such as this woman in Walla Walla, with a family of six children, such as patient Number Four—the aircraft worker?

**State Official:** But are we sure the aircraft worker can be rehabilitated? I note he is already too ill to work, whereas Number Two and Number Five, the chemist and the accountant, are both still able to keep going.

**Labor Leader:** I know from experience that the aircraft company where this man works will do everything possible to rehabilitate a handicapped employee . . .

**Housewife:** If we are still looking for the men with the highest potential for service to society, then I think we must consider that the chemist and the accountant have the finest educational backgrounds of all five candidates.

**Surgeon:** How do the rest of you feel about Number Three—the small businessman with three children? I am impressed that his doctor took special pains to mention that this man is active in church work. This is an indication to me of character and moral strength.

**Housewife:** Which certainly would help him conform to the demands of the treatment . . .

**Lawyer:** It would also help him to endure a lingering death . . .

Uncertainty was unavoidable. As the lawyer on the committee noted to Alexander, "I believe that a man's contribution to society should determine our ultimate decision. But I'm not so doggone sure that a great painting or a symphony would loom larger in my own mind than the needs of a woman with six children."

Committee members were also aware that implications of their criteria would soon expand. Successful organ transplants were just around the corner. As the surgeon on the admissions committee noted,

[T]his project will not just benefit one disease—it will benefit all aspects of medicine. We are hoping someday to learn how to transplant live organs. So far, the body will not accept foreign tissue from another person, but eventually we will find a way to break this tissue barrier.[46]

In 1963, one year after that surgeon was interviewed, a spate of medical journal articles appeared that signaled promising success in the use of immunosuppressant drugs and related kidney transplant therapies.[47] At the same time, demand was driving an increase in the supply of dialysis machines. By 1965, an estimated 800 patients were on hemodialysis in some 121 centers spread across the country. Despite this impressive expansion, the demand continued to far outdistance available resources. Estimates put the number of people in need between 60,000 and 90,000, with anywhere from 5,000 to 10,000 people being added to the list each year.[48] Patient selection and access rationing were unavoidable and continued to be driven by assessments of social worth. For many, this was disturbing and offensive.

David Sanders, director of community services at Cedars-Sinai Medical Center, and Jesse Dukeminier, Jr., a professor of law at UCLA, provided a sharp articulation of these objections.[49] With worried introduction, they wrote:

The spectacular recent advances of medical science have created unprecedented legal and ethical problems. . . . Medical science is creating and allocating resources of the greatest value; use of the resource means life, denial means death. . . . If society, with its chief instrument, law, does not tame technology, technology may destroy our sense of ethics—and man himself.

Their critique was harsh. They characterized the Seattle admission committee's decision framework as "a grotesque conceit worthy of Franz Kafka." In practice, the committee was doing nothing other than "measuring persons in accordance with its own middle-class suburban value system." It was simply the "bourgeoisie sparing the bourgeoisie," and creative, contributing nonconformists need not apply. "The Pacific Northwest," the authors wrote, "is no place for a Henry David Thoreau with bad kidneys."

If not social worth, then what? How should the boundaries protecting one life above another be drawn? If all lives are of equal value, why not set up a random selection procedure? Why not operate on a first-come, first-served basis? Why not let market forces determine access and save only those who can pay? While each of these options presented problems, the authors of the UCLA Law Review piece concluded, "Any of these methods is preferable to selection by ad hoc comparative judgments of social worth." Many others disagreed with this conclusion. The debate would endure.

**Stories Told, Doctrines Explored, Conferences Held**

These and related questions were repeatedly explored during the "Decade of Conferences,"[50] a series of gatherings held across the country throughout the 1960s. The conferences aimed to provide useful signposts for blazing a path through "the rapid and awesome advances of contemporary science in controlling the physical and mental processes of human life."[51] These gatherings brought together a stellar array of academic and professional élite.[52] Conference participants grappled repeatedly with ambiguous and troubling dilemmas of who should live and who should die.

Some negative consequences of scientific advances, however, came not from ambiguous forced choices but from flawed judgment and sloppy science. Addressing these issues during a 1966 Reed College conference entitled "Sanctity of Life," physician Henry K. Beecher noted, "One often hears it said these days that moral choices are always among shades of gray, never between black and white. This, of course, is not true."[53] What most concerned Beecher were experiments that were being conducted on humans without their consent—a black-and-white issue. Beecher had set the stage for his damning conference critique in a 1959 article in the *Journal of the American Medical Association*,[54] and the Reed College presentation was largely an update and elaboration on a more recently published piece in the *New England Journal of Medicine*.[55] Both of Beecher's articles would play a role in medical research reforms in the years ahead.

Beecher had ample personal experience to draw upon. As a faculty member at Harvard Medical School, Beecher knew that violations of the Nuremberg Code's first principle—"The voluntary consent of the human subject is absolutely essential"—were occurring all the time, both in research projects in reputable hospitals and universities across the U.S.A. and in clandestine experiments conducted by the CIA on mind-altering drugs and mind-control techniques. In the presentation, he even acknowledged that some of his own practices were not above reproach. Leo Alexander's warning years before—that Americans should be aware of Nuremberg Code violations in their midst—was becoming ever more clear.

Against this backdrop, Beecher documented his concerns. The problem, Beecher told his audience, was that people were being used as pawns in order to achieve a greater good. There were clear dangers in such investigations, and they were likely to increase in the coming years due to increased federal funding, the promise of new knowledge, and academic pressure on investigators to produce results. It was evident to Beecher that in many cases, U.S. researchers were falling into the same patterns followed by German doctors before and during World War II—risking the health or even the lives of their subjects to advance the perceived greater good. Beecher's argument was compelling: tighter controls were needed. First, however, another matter was in need of immediate attention.

Concerns with the ethics of using human subjects in clinical studies led Harvard to establish its Standing Committee on Human Studies, with Beecher as its Chair. Physician Joseph Murray, who later received the Nobel Prize in Medicine for his work on kidney transplants, was one of Beecher's colleagues. Both doctors were aware of the unresolved ethical issues raised by rapid improvements in organ-transplant procedures and the increasing effectiveness of immunosuppressant drugs. They were also convinced that there was an immediate need for clarification.

These issues came to a head late in the evening of December 3, 1967, in Cape Town, South Africa. There, Dr. Christian Barnard removed the heart from the body of Denise Ann Darvall, a woman in her early twenties. Darvall had been critically injured in a car accident earlier that morning. She could be kept alive with "artificial" means, but would die without them. Around 9 p.m. that day, her father granted Barnard permission to remove her heart and kidneys.

Her kidneys were given to a young boy,[56] and the recipient of her heart was a 55-year-old grocer named Louis Washkansky. Barnard's landmark operation drew worldwide attention; while Washkansky survived for only eighteen days, he is still considered the recipient of the first successful human heart transplant. Given the circumstances surrounding Darvall's organ removal and the subsequent transplants, the pressing nature of broader ethical questions loomed large.[57] Similar operations were surely to follow.

Two months before Darvall's heart was transplanted into Washkansky's body, Beecher wrote to the Dean of Harvard Medical School, suggesting that the Standing Committee on Human Studies' charge be expanded. His rationale was clear: "I think the time has come for a further consideration of the definition of death. Every major hospital has patients stacked up waiting for suitable donors."[58]

Shortly after Washkansky's death on December 21, 1967, the Dean of Harvard Medical School heeded Beecher's request and established the Harvard Brain Death Committee. Physicians dominated the committee, but additional members were chosen for their expertise in theology, history, law, and ethics. They set about their task immediately, publishing their recommendations as a special communication to the *Journal of the American Medical Association* seven months, almost to the day, after the committee's formation.[59] These recommendations were widely accepted and formally adopted as the gap between medical technology and moral, ethical, and legal standards narrowed. Still, there was much work to be done.

### Deference to Doctors

Concern about the ethics of medical research (highlighted by the drama of the first human heart transplants[60] and other rapidly advancing medical technologies and procedures) had captured the attention of some in the U.S. Senate—in particular, Sen. Walter Mondale of Minnesota. In 1968, a month after the Harvard Committee began its work, Mondale introduced legislation to establish a Presidential Study Commission on Health Science and Society. Hearings were held in March and April of that year; in them, Mondale summoned a parade of prominent physicians and scientists who testified both for and against establishing such a commission. These experts included Beecher, who spoke in favor of establishing the Study Commission, and Barnard, who addressed a packed hearing room when he voiced his strong opposition.

Beecher reaffirmed his belief that there were limits beyond which medical science, even in search of life-enhancing remedies, should not pass. In Beecher's opinion, these limits needed to be better defined, and the Study Commission would be useful to that end. The major argument of those who opposed the Commission was that government commissions are cumbersome and generally produce needless, counterproductive regulations. As Barnard put it, "I do not think the public is qualified to make the decision. . . . You must leave it in the people's hands who are capable of doing it."[61] Barnard's argument carried the day. The 1968 hearings closed without producing legislation. Trust in those "capable of doing it" remained secure. This would soon change.

In 1969, the stage for further change was firmly set. Theologian James Gustafson organized a conference co-sponsored by Yale Divinity School and the Yale School of Medicine. Sessions were defined around the presentations by Paul Ramsey, a well-known Christian ethicist from Princeton. Ramsey had prepared for the conference by spending the better part of the spring semesters in 1968 and 1969 talking with and observing doctors and scientists at Georgetown University School of Medicine.

Drawing on this experience, Ramsey organized his presentations into four lectures: "Updating Death," "Caring for the Dying," "Giving and Taking Organs for Transplantation," and "Consent in Medical Experimentation." A year after the conference, he published *The Patient as Person* as an extension and elaboration of his lectures. Later, it was noted that Gustafson's conference, along with Ramsey's book, "marked the beginnings of a new and astoundingly influential scholarly practical discipline."[62] Taken together, they might "rightly be called the founding preaching and scriptures of the field of bioethics."[63]

## Four Crystallizing Events

As discussions progressed, trust in and reliance on the common sense of physicians who, as Christian Barnard had put it, were "capable of doing it" began to break down. Other perspectives were needed, and oversight was demanded. Throughout these discussions, *bioethics* became the term of choice. As one observer noted, "The formal birth of bioethics really began by Congressional mandate!"[64] This mandate was precipitated by four separate and disturbing accounts of questionable medical practices.

In 1971, Sen. Mondale and seventeen other congressional co-sponsors reintroduced his 1968 proposal for a commission for the "study and evaluation of the ethical, social, and legal implications of advances in biomedical research and technology." Sen. Mondale was a founding member of the Hastings Center, a nonpartisan bioethics think-tank, and his proposal to Congress, "The Issues Before Us," was published in the first edition of *The Hastings Center Report*. Paul Ramsey, seen by many as the cornerstone scholar for the fledging field of bioethics, wrote an accompanying insert urging physicians, scientists, and legislators to give these issues the serious attention they deserved.

Months later, on October 8, 1971, the *Washington Post* ran a front-page story with the headline, "Pentagon Has Contract to Test Radiation Effect on Humans." The lead paragraph stated:

For the past 11 years, the Pentagon has had a contract with the University of Cincinnati to study the effects of atomic radiation on human beings. The prime purpose of the study, according to the contract, has been to "understand better the influence of radiation on combat effectiveness."

The head of the University of Cincinnati research team, Dr. Eugene Saenger, was quoted reaffirming his belief in the legitimacy and value of the project:

There is a need to investigate the effects of radiation on human beings to give support to the military. . . . These are tough problems that should not be swept under the rug, and I personally think the work we are doing is damned important.

All the patients who were receiving the radiation treatment had cancer. They were poor, had little education, and were unable to pay for medical care. All had come to the hospital seeking help. There was little or no hope that the full-body radiation treatment would help them personally, but researchers believed that by monitoring the radiation's effects, they would learn something valuable to help military personnel on the battlefield or citizens in the event of an atomic attack. The full extent to which similar radiation experiments were being conducted across the country would not come to light until years later.[65]

One thing, however, was immediately clear. There were strong parallels between this research and the practices and rationale German doctors had for conducting medical experiments during World War II. In Cincinnati, as in Germany, experiments were designed to shed light on how to protect military personnel under life-threatening conditions. In both instances, medical research that was known to create painful, and even lethal effects was performed on patients for the purpose of advancing knowledge, rather than to improve their health. In both instances, no wealthy and privileged people were being studied. In Cincinnati, as in Germany, one could see the question clearly: If patients of less social worth are going to die anyway, why not use them for the greater good?

The *Washington Post*'s revelation of the Cincinnati radiation experiments captured the attention of a few legislators. It also caught the eye of Martha Stephens, a young assistant professor of English at the University of Cincinnati, and some of her colleagues in the Junior Faculty Association (JFA). After reading the *Post* article, Stephens approached the director of the university's medical center to get further details. Her request was met with resistance initially, but one afternoon Stephens walked into the director's office and saw a large stack of documents on his desk.[66]

"Here they are, if you really want them," the director told her. She walked out of the office with more than 600 pages of double-spaced transcript. Over the holidays, she read the material and began writing a report to her colleagues on the JFA. It was a sobering experience. She read profile after profile that doctors had appended to their reports. "I could readily see . . . that one patient had died six days after radiation, and others on day seven, day nine, day ten, fifteen, twenty, twenty-two, and so on." "It was clear," Stephens concluded, "that these tests would have to be brought to an end and that any of us on campus who could help must do so." Stephens' seven-page report, addressed to "the campus community," was released in a press conference held by the JFA on January 25, 1972, a little less than four months after the initial story had emerged.

At the same time, Massachusetts Sen. Edward Kennedy was working with Sen. Mondale and others to revive congressional interest in more effective regulation of medical experiments involving humans. Kennedy asked one of his aides to work with Stephens and her colleagues. The medical community was challenging the JFA report, and Kennedy wanted to find out more. The JFA's conclusions were confirmed. Soon after, Sen. Kennedy and Ohio Governor John Gilligan met with the University of Cincinnati's president, Warren Bennis, and the three reached an agreement to stop the research. Momentum for reform was beginning to build. It was further energized by three revelations that appeared in the months immediately ahead.

The first revelation came the same month Martha Stephens and her colleagues released their JFA report. Again, there were charges of serious wrong being done to people on the margins of society. In a 1966 *New England Journal of Medicine* article, Henry Beecher wrote about a research project in an institution for mentally retarded children. The study was directed "toward determining the period of infectivity of infectious hepatitis." A later account was more specific: "The experiments typically involved injecting some of the unit residents with gamma globulin and feeding them the live hepatitis virus (obtained from the feces of . . . hepatitis patients)."[67] At the same time, a "control" group was "fed the live virus without the benefit of gamma globulin, to ascertain that the virus was actually 'live,' capable of transmitting the disease, and to measure the different responses." The institution was Willowbrook, an overcrowded, squalid, and poorly tended institution located on Staten Island in New York.

In many ways, Willowbrook was a legacy of institutions for the feeble-minded that had been established in the heyday of the eugenics movement. The conditions and practices within the severely underfunded and badly deteriorated walls of Willowbrook had remained out of the public's view for nearly thirty years, but in November 1971 this began to change. Local newspapers began running stories. A Willowbrook doctor began organizing parents and staff to protest the abysmal conditions of the facility and the mistreatment of children that went on there— an effort that got him fired. The same doctor approached a friend and local television reporter, Geraldo Rivera, about documenting the "horror" at Willowbrook.[68] In particular, he wanted Rivera to see one section where "there are sixty retarded kids, with only one attendant to take care of them. Most are naked and they lie in their own shit."[69] Rivera's report on the conditions in Willowbrook was aired in early January 1972, and it immediately captured national attention.

As bad as the conditions at Willowbrook were, there was more to come. On July 25, 1972, another troubling story broke in the *Washington Evening Star*. The headline read, "Syphilis Patients Died Untreated." The story was picked up nationwide and the next day, the *New York Times* ran a parallel article: "Syphilis

Victims in the U.S. Study Went Untreated for 40 Years." The lead sentence left little doubt:

> For 40 years the United States Public Health Service has conducted a study in which human beings with syphilis, who were induced to serve as guinea pigs, have gone without medical treatment for the disease and a few have died of its late effects, even though an effective therapy was eventually discovered.

If appalling institutional conditions, researchers intentionally infecting young children with hepatitis, and radiation studies performed on impoverished cancer patients had awakened the conscience of some in Congress, the account of the Tuskegee syphilis experiment scarred the souls of the men and women on Capitol Hill. It is hard to imagine a more dramatic, inescapable example of the country's racist legacy than what took place in Macon County, Alabama over a forty-year period between 1932 and 1972.[70]

Taken together, these three revelations of highly questionable medical research left little doubt: some lives were deemed less worthy than others, and thus they were less likely to be protected. They could be used for the benefit of others—even if it meant inflicting harm, suffering, and death.

It could no longer be easily argued, as Dr. Christian Barnard and others had done during Sen. Mondale's 1968 hearings, that the common sense and professional judgment of physicians involved in research should be trusted. By November 1972, the House of Representatives' Science Policy Committee reported, "Never before have the issues [of medical research] been given such wide publicity or discussed so frankly as has been the case in recent months."[71] A later, more thorough account reported, "More than any other experiment in American history, the Tuskegee Study convinced legislators and bureaucrats alike that tough new regulations had to be adopted if human subjects were to be protected."[72]

Sen. Mondale's repeated calls for action were further energized by one additional account of ethically questionable science—the use of newly aborted fetuses—in the *Washington Post* on April 10, 1973, just months after the landmark Supreme Court abortion decisions. The story prompted a phone call from Eunice Shriver, sister of John F., Robert, and Edward Kennedy and the primary benefactor of the Kennedy Institute at Georgetown University, to the Institute's director, Dr. André Hellegers.

A visiting colleague at the Kennedy Institute, self-described as a recently appointed professor in the fledging field of bioethics, was having lunch with Dr. Hellegers at the time of Shriver's call. "As we were eating lunch, a waiter called him to the phone. After ten minutes, Dr. Hellegers returned, saying in his British-tinged Dutch accent, 'That was Eunice Shriver. She wanted to discuss what should be done to stop the fetal research that was reported in this morning's *Post*.'"[73]

The article, "Live-Fetus Research Debated," led with the sentence, "The possibility of using newly delivered human fetuses—products of abortions—for medical research before they die is being strenuously debated by federal health officials." "Most scientists feel," the *Post* article continued, "that it is both moral and important to health progress to use some intact, living fetuses—fetuses too young and too small to live for any amount of time." The fetuses often lived for an hour or so, but they could not live longer without aid, primarily because their lungs were still unexpanded. But with artificial life support, the article noted, the fetus might be kept alive for three to four hours.

In the article, a well-known genetics researcher threw his support behind the research. "I do not think it's unethical. It is not possible to make this fetus into a child, therefore we can consider it as nothing more than a piece of tissue. It is the same principle as taking a beating heart from someone and making use of it in another person." Others quoted in the article shied away from such a bold analogy; instead, they turned to alternative comparisons that drew the boundaries of life worthy of protection quite differently. Using a not-yet-dead but soon-to-die fetus for medical research was more like experimenting on a person without his or her consent. Dr. Hellegers noted, "It appears that we want to make the chance for survival the reason for the experiment." When a colleague retorted, "Isn't that the British approach?" Hellegers responded, "It was the German approach. 'If it is going to die, you might as well use it.'" Hellegers was deeply concerned. The boundaries of protected life were important and were being breached. The live fetus should be included inside the protected human community whether it was inside or outside the uterus.

Three days later, a second article about the controversy appeared in the *Post*. In it, representatives from the National Institutes of Health (NIH) were quoted as stating that the organization does not now support, nor would it in the future, research on "live aborted human fetuses anyplace in the world." These assurances had been made before a gathering of more than 200 Roman Catholic high school students organized by, among others, 17-year-old Maria Shriver, Eunice Shriver's daughter. The students were not convinced. Referring to a federal advisory group who supported the continuation of "planned scientific studies" of fetuses under "carefully safeguarded" conditions, one student asked, "Why are they drawing up guidelines if they don't intend to use live fetuses?"

As it turned out, the student's skepticism was justified. A third *Post* article appeared two days later, reporting that the NIH was in fact funding fetal research, and that some researchers were conducting their investigations in Finland and other countries where live fetuses and fetal tissue were more accessible. Still, the NIH appeared to be increasing restrictions on such research.

These new regulations led one advocate of continued fetal research to worry aloud: "What I fear is that the new NIH action may make the situation so rigid that all research in this area may now be foreclosed." This would be a mistake, the advocate believed. "Rather than it being immoral to do what we are trying to do, it is immoral—it is a terrible perversion of ethics—to throw these fetuses in the incinerator, as is usually done, rather than to get some useful information."

The Cincinnati, Willowbrook, and Tuskegee experiences, coupled with the fetal research examples, galvanized powerful bipartisan support. Years later, Albert Jonsen, the "fledging" bioethicist who had been lunching with Hellegers when he took Eunice Shriver's call, had become the leading historian of the bioethics movement. He later wrote, "The Tuskegee scandal cried out to liberals as a blatant violation of civil rights and an example of racism. The fetal research question, with its abortion implications, aroused conservatives in the prolife camp."[74] The stage was set for the first-ever piece of legislation calling for a government body to set forth fundamental ethical principles.

## The Search for Common Principles

Public Law 93-348, a historic piece of legislation, became law when President Richard Nixon signed it in July 1974. Congress had established the National Commission for the Protection of Human Subjects of Biomedical and Behavioral Research, and its first order of business was to develop recommendations on fetal research.

Five months later, the Commissioners issued their report: under carefully specified conditions, fetal research could continue. One well-respected member of the Commission, however, was not willing to consider the fetus less than human and submitted a strongly worded dissent. Professor David Louisell found two of the Commission's recommendations of particular concern.

1. Recommendation #5 dealt with research on the fetus in anticipation of abortion. Given the Supreme Court's recent abortion decisions, Louisell knew he was on thin ice, legally speaking, in asserting that a fetus still in the womb retained human rights. To him, it did not matter; he called to mind Abraham Lincoln's response to the Dred Scott decision, a ruling that declared people of black African descent to be non-citizens. Louisell argued that as with the Dred Scott decision, it was not necessary to extend the findings in Roe to other situations. Even if the Court had excluded the unborn from the fully protective boundaries of personhood, he reasoned, the idea should not be extended to other contexts. Louisell could see no legal principle that would justify, let alone require, passive submission to such a breach of our moral commitment.

2. To Louisell, Recommendation #6 was even more troubling. It spoke of the "nonviable fetus ex utero." Up until that time, a fetus ex utero would have been seen simply as an infant. In his judgment, "all infants, however premature or inevitable their death, are within the norms governing human experimentation generally. We do not subject the aged dying to unconsented experimentation, nor should we the youthful dying."

In Louisell's mind, these recommendations were misguided, "insofar as they succumb to the error of sacrificing the interests of innocent human life to a postulated social need." He continued,

> For me the lessons of history are too poignant, and those of this century too fresh, to ignore another violation of human integrity and autonomy by subjecting unconsenting human beings, whether or not viable, to harmful research even for laudable scientific purposes.

Fetal research was only one aspect of the Commission's report. In addition, the Commission was charged with identifying "the ethical principles which should underlie the conduct of biomedical and behavioral research with human subjects." In February 1976, some two years after they had been sworn in, the Commission members convened to address this task. They gathered at the Belmont House, in Elkridge, Maryland, about a forty-five-minute drive from the nation's capital.

## The Belmont Report and the Georgetown Principles

In 1977, after the twenty-seventh meeting of the Commission, a group of commissioners, consultants, and staff convened at the San Francisco home of Albert Jonsen. The group's aim was to produce a set of guidelines and principles that would be "succinct, easily comprehensible, and relevant to research practice."[75] By the close of the meeting, three principles for medical research were settled upon:

1. Respect for persons (autonomy).
2. Beneficence.
3. Justice.

By design, these principles and associated guidelines were general in nature and broad in scope, having been gleaned from the specific problems the Commission had addressed. Committee member Tom Beauchamp, a philosophy professor from the Kennedy Institute, took responsibility for writing what was initially referred to simply as the "Belmont Paper." While working in this capacity, Beauchamp began collaborating with a colleague, Jim Childress, on what became a highly influential book, *Principles of Biomedical Ethics*.[76] On June 10, 1978, the Commission finally approved the *Belmont Report* for release.

There was some disagreement on specifics between these two documents, but in the end the *Belmont Report* and Beauchamp and Childress' book *Principles of Biomedical Ethics* were written simultaneously—each influencing the other. By design, both aimed to identify important elements of a "common morality," principles "shared by all morally decent persons," which were "woven into the fabric of morality in morally sensitive cultures."[77] Taken together, these overlapping works became highly influential benchmarks for bioethics, providing a "common coin of moral discourse." A later observer writing in the *Hastings Center Report* remarked, "The Babel of information formerly thought to be relevant to an ethical decision has been whittled down to a much more manageable level through the use of principles."[78]

Still, questions and criticisms emerged.[79] The enunciated principles of autonomy, beneficence, and justice did not provide straightforward guides to action. What did they mean in particular situations?[80] Lacking an explicit ethical road-map, specific decisions became works in progress. Checklists were developed to assist physicians and ethics committees.[81] Life is inherently valuable and should be protected. The alleviation of suffering and aversion to its creation are deeply seeded in our makeup. There is virtually no disagreement on these statements. Most would also agree that respect for the dignity and autonomy of the individual should be honored. Justice, accomplished through a sense of equality, opportunity, and just desserts should command respect.

When these broad principles are applied within specific circumstances, however, disagreements emerge. Who should decide? Given the core importance of the imperatives involved, competing social movements are spawned, issues are framed, power is exercised, and laws are crafted and protested. Within this emotion-laden, dilemma-balancing, boundary-drawing, situational-ethical matrix, justifications for violating otherwise binding moral imperatives emerge. These are the issues before us. We begin with abortion.

# 2

# The Early Moments and Months of Life
## Should the Baby Live?

When it comes to abortion and the protection of life, religions have evolved beliefs, legislatures have passed laws, courts have articulated findings, and people have made choices. Politicians have taken positions, waged campaigns, and won and lost elections. Scholars have worried over the fine points of philosophical and legal arguments. Activists have produced statistics, argued for the rights of the disabled, underscored the importance of privacy and choice, organized right-to-life demonstrations, bombed clinics, and murdered abortion providers. Where should the protective boundaries of life be placed?

Some have argued that they should extend even prior to conception.

[E]ach and every marital act must of necessity retain its intrinsic relationship to the procreation of human life. . . . We are obliged once more to declare that the direct interruption of the generative process already begun . . . [is] to be absolutely excluded as lawful means of regulating the number of children. Equally to be condemned, as the magisterium of the Church has affirmed on many occasions, is direct sterilization, whether of the man or of the woman, whether permanent or temporary. . . . Similarly excluded is any action which either before, at the moment of, or after sexual intercourse, is specifically intended to prevent procreation—whether as an end or as a means.[1]

Through this rationale, the Catholic Church has argued that even contraceptive measures should be banned. In fact, not so long ago, throughout much of the United States, they were.

### From Comstockery to the Right to Privacy

In the early 1870s, U.S. postal inspector Anthony Comstock became the quintessential moral entrepreneur.[2] In Comstock's mind, explicit advertisements for various birth control measures threatened the public good and perverted public discourse. Moved to action, Comstock drafted model legislation prohibiting such material; in March 1873, Congress passed a federal law, an "Act for the Suppression of Trade in, and Circulation of, Obscene Literature and Articles for Immoral Use." The Act would eventually become known simply as the Comstock Law. Within a few years, a majority of states had passed similar laws. One of the stricter versions came in 1879 in Connecticut, Comstock's home state. According to that law, even married couples were vulnerable to a jail term for the use of methods to prevent pregnancy.

These laws gave rise to counter-crusades and counter-crusaders, perhaps none more famous than Margaret Sanger.[3] Sanger is credited with founding the American Birth Control Movement, which eventually evolved into the Planned Parenthood Federation of America. Driven by a sense of injustice at the repression of women, Sanger and others committed to the increased availability of birth control methods challenged the legitimacy of the Comstock Law. For Sanger and those who agreed with her, the case was clear: people (and, in particular, women) should be able to plan their families effectively, and the government had no business intervening in these private decisions. In the 1930s, as the severe economic consequences of the Great Depression were hitting the hardest, these arguments became ever more persuasive.

As demand for access to contraception grew, the market responded. Eventually, the Pill—at last, a convenient and reliable oral contraceptive—hit the market. An early version of the Pill was approved by the Food and Drug Administration for the U.S. market for the regulation of menses in the late 1950s; in 1960, it was submitted to the FDA again for approval as a birth control pill. This approval, along with numerous other birth control drugs that followed, marked a dramatic improvement in both the effectiveness and the convenience of birth control options. Given this increased effectiveness and convenience—as well as the profit potential at stake— challenges to state limitations on contraception gained momentum.

A version of the 1879 Comstock statute remained on Connecticut's books as late as the 1960s. Estelle Griswold, executive director of the Planned Parenthood League of Connecticut, and the group's medical director, Lee Buxton, a member of the Department of Obstetrics and Gynecology at Yale Medical School, gave a married couple information and medical advice about preventing conception, and found themselves arrested, tried, and convicted. Griswold and Buxton appealed their conviction, and eventually their case was argued before the Supreme Court in March 1965 in *Griswold v. Connecticut*.[4] A little more than two months later, the birth control prohibitions of a Connecticut statute, grounded in almost century-old legislation, were declared unconstitutional.

For most, this was an easy case. All nine Supreme Court justices—even those who dissented—agreed that the anti-contraception statute was foolish; "silly" and "asinine" as Justice Potter Stewart put it. Nowhere in the Constitution, however, is birth control or contraception mentioned. Where should the justices look? In the penumbras, or shadowed implications of general constitutional principles, was the answer. "[T)he Bill of Rights," Justice William O. Douglas argued in the majority opinion in *Griswold*, "have penumbras, formed by emanations from those guarantees that help give them life and substance." In particular, the Court found protections of individual autonomy embedded in the implications of the First, Fourth, Fifth, Ninth, and Fourteenth Amendments. The common collection point, Douglas argued, was the right to privacy, which included the decision to use contraceptive measures. Laws prohibiting such practices were thus unconstitutional.

In a Massachusetts case decided some seven years later,[5] this right was extended, for reasons of equity, to unmarried persons as well. In this particular case, an abortion rights activist, William Baird, while lecturing on contraception to an audience at Boston University, exhibited contraceptive articles. At the end of the lecture he gave a package of Emko vaginal foam to a young woman in the audience. These actions violated Massachusetts' law. Baird's convictions were appealed, and the Supreme Court's rationale for overturning the conviction was straightforward:

> If under *Griswold* the distribution of contraceptives to married persons cannot be prohibited, a ban on distribution to unmarried persons would be equally impermissible. . . . If the right of privacy means anything, it is the right of the individual, married or single, to be *free from unwarranted governmental intrusion into matters so fundamentally affecting a person as the decision whether to bear or beget a child* [italics added].

New England had been the region of the country with the most stringent Comstock laws, and these laws were now dead. The boundaries of protected life did not extend prior to conception. In addition, the stage was set to restrict governmental intrusion even further. Privacy was now said to extend to the decision to "bear or beget a child." Legal scholars would continue to argue about whether privacy could be found in the penumbras of constitutional language, but for most citizens the articulated restrictions on governmental intrusion into matters of contraception seemed quite reasonable. There were realms of individual autonomy and dignity into which the government should not intrude. Of course, the next question was unavoidable: Was the decision to terminate pregnancy in the same category? Here, there was far less consensus.

While privacy and the right to choose are important, few argue that they are absolute. How far does the right to privacy extend, and where does the autonomy and sanctity of the newly forming life with associated protections begin? At what point does state intrusion become compelling? These and other questions would dominate political landscape in the years ahead.

### Potential for Life, Potential for Suffering

The Court's conclusions about privacy and the use of contraception were not reached in a vacuum. A broad-based civil rights movement designed to establish more equitable standing for women and women's rights was gaining momentum. Supreme Court justices were clearly aware of these events, and they were also aware of heightened concerns about the potential quality of life for the yet-to-be-born. These concerns were intensified during the tumultuous 1960s.

In 1962, Sherri Finkbine was the host of a Phoenix-based edition of the popular children's show *Romper Room*. She was also the mother of four children under the age of 7 and pregnant with what would be her fifth child. Early on in her pregnancy, she had taken a drug her husband had purchased over the counter during a trip to Europe in order to help her sleep and deal with morning sickness.

The morning sickness pill contained thalidomide. When Finkbine became aware that thalidomide had been linked to deeply troubling birth defects, she went to her doctor for advice. He was resolute: Finkbine should have an abortion. As Finkbine later recalled, "In talking it over with my [obstetrician], he said, 'Sherri, if you were my own wife and we two had four small children, and you really wanted a fifth child, I'd say start again next month under better odds.'"[6]

At that time in Arizona, early-term abortions were available if a woman's physician recommended that the abortion was appropriate and necessary to protect the mother's health and a three-member therapeutic abortion board at a hospital concurred. While her doctor recommended that Finkbine should not go to the local Catholic hospital where her last baby had been born, he was confident that approval would be a formality at a local public hospital. It was, and the procedure was scheduled for the following Monday morning.

Fearing that other pregnant women might unwittingly take a drug that could cause devastating birth defects, Finkbine decided to call a friend who worked for the local newspaper to relate her story and alert others to the dangers of thalidomide. An article about Finkbine's situation ran in the paper: "Baby-Deforming Drug May Cost Woman Her Child Here." After reading the story and realizing that their approval of Finkbine's, as well as other therapeutic abortions, might violate a strict reading of Arizona law, hospital doctors and administrators immediately canceled Finkbine's procedure.

The national wire services picked up the story and newspapers across the country as well as the international press ran features. Finkbine and her husband received thousands of letters, some of which included death threats. The Finkbines were forced to seek and secure FBI protection. Eventually, Finkbine had to travel to Sweden to receive an abortion, by then in the fourth month of her pregnancy. The tending physician reported that the fetus was so seriously deformed it would not have survived. In the aftermath, both Sherri and her husband lost their jobs, Finkbine being told by the vice president of the NBC affiliate that she was no longer fit to handle children.[7] By all accounts, this heart-wrenching, widely publicized case marked an important turning point. As one author, echoed by many others, put it, the refusal to grant a legal abortion in these dramatic conditions marked a point "when a diffuse dissatisfaction with the law began to crystallize into an organized movement to change the law."[8]

Further impetus for change came after a rubella (also known as German measles) pandemic swept across Europe and throughout the United States between 1964 and 1966. A rubella infection during the first three months of pregnancy can lead to serious birth defects or stillbirth. Testimony at Senate hearings[9] held in 1969 indicated that the rubella outbreak had been responsible for some 20,000 newborns with birth defects and nearly 30,000 fetal deaths. The issue came to a head in 1966 when a member of the California Board of Medical Examiners, an organization that had taken a strong stance against abortion, initiated proceedings to revoke the licenses of nine prominent, well-respected San Francisco physicians who had performed abortions for women who had been exposed to rubella. The procedures clearly violated a nearly century-old California statute rooted in Comstock-era legislation.[10] Faced with the loss of their licenses, the physicians, who came to be known as the "San Francisco Nine," questioned the law's legitimacy based on their professional responsibilities. "We do not believe that violation of an archaic statute is unprofessional conduct."[11]

### Interest Groups Compete

The widespread publicity of Finkbine's experience with thalidomide, the threat of birth defects resulting from the rubella outbreak, and the move to prosecute nine highly respected physicians for terminating pregnancies galvanized efforts for reform. In the aftermath, the Society for Humane Abortion (SHA) was founded in San Francisco. SHA soon became a well-organized mouthpiece collectively arguing for a woman's unbridled right to choose. SHA's argument was straight-forward: "The termination of pregnancy is a decision which the person or family involved should be free to make as their own religious beliefs, values, emotions, and circumstances may dictate."[12] Hearings about legalization of abortion were held by the California legislature in 1964. As a counterbalance to the pressure for reform, the Catholic Church began a strong lobbying effort in opposition to abortion in any form.

Given the competing interest groups—professional, personal, and religious—it's not surprising that the 1964 hearings ended in no formal action. The heated, divisive political climate surrounding abortion reform in California was mirrored in New York, Colorado, Illinois, and other states. It became increasingly clear that those calling for abortion for any reason, as well as those adamantly opposed to abortion under any circumstances, were both in opposition to leaving the decision up to doctors and hospital committees. Organized efforts to advance the interests of physicians and therapeutic abortion committees began to take shape. The California Committee on Therapeutic Abortions (CCTA) was formed as a result of these meetings and discussions.

The CCTA launched an initiative to educate the public and solicit support for legislation that included provisions for physician discretion and the establishment of therapeutic abortion boards. The bill was named for Anthony Beilenson, its sponsoring state senator from Beverly Hills, and in 1967 the Beilenson Bill was passed. As a result, physicians and abortion boards could take into consideration both the physical and mental health of the woman, and also consider whether the pregnancy was the result of rape or incest (including cases of statutory rape when the woman was under the age of 15). In order to also address the issue of potential birth defects, such as those associated with thalidomide and rubella, all initial versions of the bill included provisions for the consideration of "fetal indications."

Given that much of the impetus for reform had emerged from the rubella outbreak and the thalidomide scare, these latter provisions were to be expected. Last-minute negotiations with the governor and his advisers, however, led to the deletion of this portion of the bill. In the end, California Governor Ronald Reagan, who later became known for his adamant anti-abortion stance,[13] signed the legislation without the provisions for "fetal indications." The Beilenson Bill became law.

## A Bolt from the Blue

Even as the Beilenson Bill was being crafted, debated, and passed, an abortion case was winding its way toward the California Supreme Court. A young unmarried woman had become pregnant, and she and the father of her child had seen Dr. Leon Belous on television advocating for change in California's abortion laws. Belous, a physician specializing in obstetrics and gynecology, was a member of the board of directors of the CCTA. The couple contacted Belous to seek his assistance in securing an abortion.

After an examination confirmed her pregnancy, the couple pleaded with Belous for assistance. There was no immediate threat to the woman's health, so a therapeutic abortion could not be justified. Nevertheless, the couple told the doctor they would secure an abortion one way or another—even if they had to go to Tijuana to get it. Belous insisted that he did not perform abortions, but out of concern for the woman's health and safety, he gave them the telephone number of an acquaintance who performed abortions in a neighboring city. He also gave the woman a prescription for antibiotics and instructed her to return for an examination if she decided to go through with the abortion.

The abortion was performed, and soon after, the abortionist's office was raided by the police. During their search of the doctor's office, the police discovered notebooks containing the names of other patients and physicians, including Belous. On the basis of this information, Belous was arrested.

Belous was convicted in a jury trial in 1967, the same year the Beilenson Bill was passed. He received a US$5,000 fine and two years' probation. He appealed the decision to the Supreme Court of California. As a precursor to the U.S. Supreme Court's *Roe v. Wade* decision, the California court overturned Belous' conviction, finding the wording of the law too vague and uncertain to pass California constitutional muster. They also noted the recent finding in *Griswold,* as well as several of their own decisions that protected "right of privacy" or "liberty" in matters related to marriage, family, and sex.

As a final consideration of the state's duty to balance protection of the mother's rights with those of the unborn, the court held that "there are major and decisive areas where the embryo and fetus are not treated as equivalent to the born child" and that "the law has always recognized that the pregnant woman's right to life takes precedence over any interest the State may have in the unborn." With these conclusions, the Supreme Court of California became the first in the nation to strike down an abortion statute,[14] and it did so in a classic case of abortion on demand. The scene would soon shift to the U.S. Supreme Court.

Throughout the 1960s, opposition to perceived injustices and the illegitimacy of intrusive state action was strong. It was in this climate that the National Organization for Women (NOW) was launched. NOW, which eventually boasted more than half a million members, soon became a rallying point for the women's movement. While a woman's right to choose to terminate a pregnancy was not originally one of the group's central concerns, it soon became a cornerstone for NOW's initiatives. One of NOW's founders, pioneering feminist Betty Friedan, joined forces with activist-author Lawrence Lader and prominent New York physician Dr. Bernard Nathanson to found the National Association for the Repeal of Abortion Laws (NARAL), eventually known as NARAL Pro-Choice America, in 1969.

As one activist reported in an interview:

> [W]ithout that right, we'd have about as many rights as the cow in the pasture that's taken to the bull once a year . . . if you can't control your own body you can't control your future.[15]

The personal, professional, and association networks embedded in and bridging across such organizations as the American Law Institute (ALI), SHA, CCTA, NOW, and NARAL mobilized resources in a nationwide social movement to liberalize abortion laws. By 1972, some sixteen states had enacted liberalized abortion statutes based largely on the Model Penal Code of the American Law Institute.[16] Four states had statutes that permitted abortion on demand as long as it was performed by a licensed physician. Many abortion activists were ready to declare that their mission had been accomplished. Except for the political clout of the Catholic Church, right-to-life advocates had yet to gather steam.

This would unexpectedly change following the Supreme Court's *Roe v. Wade* decision in 1973. As sociologist Kristin Luker has noted, the mobilizing impact of *Roe* came like a bolt from the blue. More people joined the prolife movement in 1973 than in any other year, most reporting they were moved to do so the day the decision was handed down.[17] If the law of the land did not protect life, they believed, the law of the land was unjust and illegitimate. It needed to be changed, ignored, or intentionally disobeyed.

When *Roe v. Wade*, from Texas, and *Doe v. Bolton*, from Georgia, were originally scheduled for argument before the Supreme Court in the fall of 1971, there were only seven sitting justices. (For reasons of failing health, two justices had retired in September of that year.) As a result, Chief Justice Warren Burger set up a committee to screen cases and recommend which were controversial enough to be postponed until a full nine-member court could be convened, and which could move forward easily with only seven justices participating. Having heard mainly from those who favored the liberalization of abortion laws, and influenced by the searing impact of birth defects caused by the thalidomide tragedies and the rubella pandemic, Burger and the remaining justices thought that the abortion cases before them could be decided quietly, on narrow grounds.

In a note written several years later to then Chief Justice William Rehnquist, Justice Harry Blackmun recalled his participation on this committee.

> I remember that the Old Chief appointed a screening committee, chaired by Potter, to select cases that could (it was assumed) be adequately heard by a Court of seven. I was on that little committee. We did not do a good job. Potter pressed for *Roe v. Wade* and *Doe v. Bolton* to be heard and did so in the misapprehension that they involved nothing more than an application of *Younger v. Harris*. How wrong we were.[18]

## Landmark Cases Take Shape

Blackmun's original draft of a possible decision in the *Roe* case, written in 1971, ran to some seventeen pages and concentrated on the relatively narrow question of whether the wording of the Texas statute was too vague. A related case from Georgia, *Doe v. Bolton*, was heard at the same time. While the *Roe* case hinged on a law firmly rooted in late nineteenth-century legislation, the case from Georgia directly reflected recommendations made much more recently—1959—by the ALI. Both cases raised issues of privacy, and, perhaps purposefully, had incorporated the wording from *Eisenstadt v. Baird*: "If the right to privacy means anything, it is the right . . . to bear or beget a child."[19]

Clearly, this wording had implications for abortion cases. Given the ensuing discussion among the justices that followed Blackmun's narrowly drawn initial draft, the Court decided to reargue both cases later, when the Court was at full strength. Eventually, the *Roe* decision (three times longer than Blackmun's original draft) would be the lead case. The Court purposefully released both of its decisions on January 22, 1973. Chief Justice Burger, who had been President Nixon's first appointment to the Court, feared that the decisions might be politically embarrassing to the president. He delayed submitting his short concurring opinion until two days before President Nixon was sworn into office for his second term—thus effectively delaying the release of the *Roe* and *Doe* decisions until after Inauguration Day.[20]

A few months after the *Roe* and *Doe* decisions were released, a well-respected Yale law professor named John Hart Ely sowed the early seeds of questioned legitimacy in an article that would be one of the most widely cited pieces in the history of the *Yale Law Journal*.[21] For Ely, it was not so much what was decided, but who made the decision. "Were I a legislator," Ely wrote, "I would vote for a statute very much like the one the Court ends up drafting."[22] The Supreme Court, however, should not be in the business of drafting legislation. The Court needed to decide on constitutional grounds, not on personal values or policy preferences. This, Ely argued, had not been done. "*Roe* was a bad decision because it was a groundless intrusion by one branch of government into matters best left to the jurisdiction of another."

The majority of justices on the Court, of course, disagreed with Ely. In fact, the Court had anticipated much of Ely's argument in *Roe*:

> We forthwith acknowledge our awareness of the sensitive and emotional nature of the abortion controversy. . . . Our task, of course, is to resolve the issue by constitutional measurement, free of emotion and of predilection. We seek earnestly to do this.

In the years that followed, many others began to assess the decision in much the same way as Ely had, and by the 1990s the abortion debate had gained significant intensity. Disagreements became part of what some saw as a cultural war.[23] A symposium on the topic written by a group of influential scholars was published in 1996 in the ecumenical journal *First Things*.[24] The editors of *First Things* worried aloud about what they saw as the Supreme Court's abuse of power, wondering whether "we are witnessing the end of democracy."[25]

In even more dramatic terms, they continued:

> Law, as it is presently made by the judiciary, has declared its independence from morality. Among the most elementary principles of Western Civilization is the truth that laws which violate the moral law are null and void and must in conscience be disobeyed. . . . What is happening now is the displacement of a constitutional order by a regime that does not have, will not obtain, and cannot command the consent of the people.[26]

This left the editors wondering "whether we have reached or are reaching the point where conscientious citizens can no longer give moral assent to the existing regime." These are very serious assertions. As might be expected, such claims generated a great deal of controversy, even among contributors to the symposium.[27] For citizens who were more removed from the academic fine points, the case was clear. Driven by an allegiance to a higher law that they found in biblical scripture, withdrawal of legitimacy was complete. An unjust law was no law at all. Violence followed.

## A Clash of Absolutes?

Prior to *Roe* and *Doe*, abortion laws dated mainly from the latter half of the nineteenth century. In the intervening years, of course, countless medical advances had been made. When the earlier laws criminalizing abortion were enacted, antiseptic techniques and antibiotics were not widely used or available. It could be argued—indeed, it *was* argued—that the real focus of these early laws criminalizing abortion were designed to protect not the unborn, but the lives of the women who carried them. Medical procedures had vastly improved since the late 1800s, and abortion during the early months of pregnancy was now safer than childbirth—suggesting a minimal need for state intervention. At the same time, abortion during the final stages of pregnancy continued to involve serious risks and therefore suggested a greater need for regulation of procedures, facilities, and physician qualifications.

With this understanding, the Court constructed a sliding scale for justifying state intervention. For reasons of maternal health and safety, the state had compelling reasons to regulate abortion in the later stages of pregnancy, but there were fewer compelling reasons in the early months. The Court developed a parallel sliding scale as it turned to the life-defining boundaries surrounding the embryo, fetus, or unborn child. The question then became how to segment what was in truth a continuum.

Two polar-opposite positions for protecting life's boundaries were proposed by the lawyers arguing *Roe*:

1. No protections, with abortion on demand.
2. Full protection for the unborn child, from the moment of conception.

The Court rejected both options. The right to privacy was broad enough to include a mother's decision to terminate her pregnancy, but there were limits. With abortion on demand set aside, the Court turned to whether the protective boundaries of life were fully present at the moment, more accurately during the process, of conception. There was no crystal-clear answer: the boundaries of protected life were hazy. The Court decided not to decide.

> When those trained in the respective disciplines of medicine, philosophy, and theology are unable to arrive at any consensus, the judiciary, at this point in the development of man's knowledge, is not in a position to speculate as to the answer.

Instead, the Court turned to the *potential* for life. In its contraception decisions, it had concluded that the potential for life inherent in the act of intercourse did not open the door for governmental intrusion. Conception, however, solidified the potential for life. As advances continued to be made in the understanding of conception both inside and out of the womb and at the cellular and molecular levels, it came to be understood as a process rather than a moment. That, along with prenatal assessments of the potential quality of life, would provide grist for the mill among bioethicists, politicians, and legal scholars in the years ahead.[28]

The nine-month gestation period was divided into trimesters. During the first trimester, when health risks of an abortion were low, there was no compelling reason for state intervention. On this basis, the attending physician, in consultation with the woman, should be free to determine—without interference from the state—whether the pregnancy should be terminated.

When it came to the potential life the mother was carrying, the point of compelling state interest came with viability, the point at which the fetus was capable of "meaningful life outside the mother's womb." Given the level of medical technology available at that point in time, this probabilistic point was said to be somewhere between six and seven months after conception. After this point, state regulations designed to protect the interests of the unborn child could go so far as to prohibit abortion, except when necessary to preserve the "life or health" of the mother.

Still, the boundaries for the legitimate protection of lives of both mother and fetus remained hazy. Did the mother's well-being include her mental as well as her physical health? How threatening or debilitating did the threat have to be? These issues were more directly addressed in the companion case from Georgia, *Doe v. Bolton*. Threats to the mother's health included "all factors—physical, emotional, psychological, familial, and the woman's age—relevant to the well-being of the patient." The boundaries for considering the health of the mother were wide, extending even to her family.

And so the stage was set. The shifting boundaries of protected life were divided into three-month increments determined by potential. For the fetus, it was the increasing potential for a viable, meaningful life. For the mother, it was the increasing potential threat to her health and life, broadly defined. The Supreme

Court had found the right to privacy in the penumbras of the Bill of Rights and the Fourteenth Amendment, but it did not find full protections for the fetus. Instead, the Court was persuaded that "the word 'person,' as used in the Fourteenth Amendment, does not include the unborn."

## The Power of Empathy

This exclusionary conclusion about the legal standing of the fetus would not be viewed with such steely-eyed detachment by a significant portion of the population. For many, it became a clarion call for action; these newly aroused advocates campaigned with increased vigor. They pointed to ultrasound images to build empathy for the fetus. Poster-sized pictures of late-term abortions were carried to the streets to demonstrate the humanity of the unborn child and generate disgust at what the Supreme Court had wrought.

Perhaps the most compelling example of the power of images to generate empathy is the conversion of Dr. Bernard Nathanson, the co-founder of the National Association for the Repeal of Abortion Laws (NARAL). In his self-reflective book, *The Hand of God,* this former director of the largest abortion clinic in the United States wrote, "When ultrasound in the early 1970s confronted me with the sight of the embryo in a womb, I simply lost my faith in abortion on demand."[29] Nathanson's conversion had evolved over a period of years, but in the early 1980s he worked with a colleague to videotape (using ultrasound technology) what happened during an abortion of an 11- to-12-week-old fetus. He reported being "shaken to the very roots of my soul."

Nathanson's grainy videotape was edited and made into a film, *The Silent Scream.* Its explicit purpose was to generate empathy for the human qualities of the developing fetus in the womb. It began with a voice overlay: "Now we can discern the chilling silent scream on the face of this child who is now facing imminent extinction." *The Silent Scream* was shown to President Reagan, who had recently published an article entitled "Abortion and the Conscience of the Nation." The president was so moved that he provided members of Congress with copies of the film. News accounts and editorials appeared, and screenings were held in churches across the country.

For many, *The Silent Scream* was mind-opening and conscience-prodding. It was praised for raising public awareness of the evils of abortion much like Harriet Beecher Stowe's *Uncle Tom's Cabin* had done for slavery. The film was also vilified as being visually misleading and scientifically inaccurate.[30] Accepted or not, the intended spoken and visual message of the film was clear: Fetuses were persons, well within the communal boundaries of protection. They were human beings, fully deserving of all the protections a moral community can offer. How could we tolerate what *The Silent Scream* called the tearing apart of a baby, limb from limb?

## Protests and Rescue Missions

Protests and disruptive actions escalated. By 1979, a group of people involved in the pro-life movement had become disenchanted with the willingness to compromise among many prolife organizations. Led by Paul and Judie Brown, this group splintered off and founded the American Life League (ALL). One year later, Joseph Scheidler, a former Benedictine monk widely considered to be the godfather of the early activist anti-abortion movement, organized the founding of the Pro-Life Action League (PLAL). For members of ALL and PLAL, abortion equaled murder. Thus framed, the call for confrontational politics among these highly energized activists intensified.

The stated mission of the PLAL was to save unborn children through "non-violent direct action." In pursuit of this mission, the group published a manual, *Closed: 99 Ways to Stop Abortion*, around the same time as the release of *The Silent Scream*. This how-to guide began with the sentence, "This book is based on the equation that abortion equals murder." It outlined a collection of methods for protesting and preventing abortion, tactics based on the premise that:

> No social movement in the history of this country has succeeded without activist[s] taking to the streets . . . not only to save lives, but to garner public attention, bring the media into the struggle, and shake politicians into recognizing the determination of anti-abortion supporters.

The strong framing message was straightforward: life is sacred and should be protected. It begins at conception. *Roe* was illegitimate, unjust, and immoral. As one icon of the anti-abortion movement put it, "The bottom line is that at a certain point there is not only the right, but the duty, to disobey the State."[31] This argument was taking hold among a broader public, reflective of a national network of aroused organizations and people.[32] Energized by their success, they expanded their moral crusade.

## Violence Increases

In 1984 to 1985, the same years in which *The Silent Scream* and *Closed: 99 Ways to Stop Abortion* were released, violence in the anti-abortion movement escalated across the country. On Christmas Day, 1984, three clinics in Pensacola, Florida were bombed by a small group of young activists who identified with the Old Testament story of Gideon, the slayer of those who offered infant sacrifices to Baal, and referred to their protest efforts as the Gideon Project.[33] One of the suspects, soon arrested, claimed his actions had been "a birthday gift for Jesus," and that the graphic images and films he had been exposed to at his church had helped motivate him to violence.

Such increasingly aggressive and violent militancy did not go unnoticed. Criminal charges were lodged, arrests were made, lawsuits were filed, and counter-demonstrations were planned. Among pro-life moderates, disillusionment and a sense of betrayal set in. As one angry advocate of non-violent pro-life strategies put it, "The work we're doing, it totally shoots it down. There are a lot of minds and hearts to win over. Blowing up clinics only hardens hearts."[34] Less moderate anti-abortion religious groups joined forces, organized more clinic blockades, and created new organizations.

In the early years of the anti-abortion cause, the Catholic Church had been the dominant force. When Protestant fundamentalists joined the cause, they moved center stage. One adherent, a young, charismatic Pentecostal minister named Randall Terry, had become closely aligned with the efforts of Joseph Scheidler's PLAL. In 1986, Terry split with the group and, with others, formed Operation Rescue. This new operation was far more confrontational, taking seriously the admonition from Proverbs 24:11: "Deliver those who are being taken away to death, and those who are staggering to slaughter." In 1987, the first major Operation Rescue clinic blockade took place in Cherry Hill, New Jersey. More than 200 people were arrested. A subsequent assessment suggested that the activities in Cherry Hill had been transformative: "Clinic sit-ins and blockades were no longer small, isolated local events; they had suddenly become the most important form of political expression in the entire national debate over abortion."[35]

It was not until the following year, however, at the 1988 Democratic National Convention in Atlanta, Georgia, that Operation Rescue received nationwide attention. A large protest was organized there, and again several hundred arrests ensued. Just as Supreme Court justices had found justification for the right to privacy in the penumbras of the U.S. Constitution, Terry found justification for his activities in his interpretation of Scripture. As he remarked in an interview conducted shortly after the demonstrations:

> Interviewer: How do you justify violating the law in your fight against abortion?
>
> Terry: Easily. When God's law and man's law conflict, Scripture clearly teaches that man is not to obey that law. Some examples are when the three Hebrew children were thrown into the fire, when the apostles were jailed for preaching the Gospel, and when the stone was rolled away from the Lord's tomb. That was in defiance of a man-made law. God never gave the government a blank check to do what it wants to do. It is a heresy to teach Christians to obey a law which runs counter to His law. [36]

By 1991, Operation Rescue had focused its confrontational tactics and organizing influence on three abortion clinics in Wichita, Kansas, in what came to be known as the Summer of Mercy. The group paid special attention to a Wichita clinic run by Dr. George Tiller, known to many in the pro-life movement as "Tiller the Baby Killer." Tiller advertised the fact that he would perform elective abortions as late as the second and third trimesters nationally, since few other providers did. Entrances to Tiller's and two other Wichita clinics were blocked and between 2,500 and 3,000 arrests made.

Eventually, a federal judge issued decrees designed to protect abortion providers and seekers.[37] When the local Wichita police refused to enforce the decrees, the judge asked federal marshals to step in, but President George H.W. Bush counter-manded the judge's orders. After a siege of seven weeks of protests, orders, counter-orders, and substantial publicity, some 25,000 to 35,000 (estimates varied) people gathered in Wichita State University's stadium to underscore their common cause and celebrate their commitment to "Hope for the Heartland." The anti-abortion cause had clearly become a political force to be reckoned with.[38]

In 1992, prompted by events in Wichita and similar protests in other cities, the bipartisan Freedom of Access to Clinic Entrances (FACE) Act was proposed in the U.S. Congress. While this bill was being debated, a case involving the judge in Wichita who had called in federal marshals to enforce his decree had reached the Supreme Court for a second hearing. On behalf of the Justice Department, John Roberts, Jr. argued the case for the Bush Administration.

Since actions of protestors were even-handed, Roberts argued, attempts to prevent abortion were not discriminatory. Needless to say, lawyers for NOW and women's health clinics disagreed. They believed that a nationwide, systematic conspiracy existed that was designed to intimidate abortion providers and to prevent women from exercising their civil rights. The Supreme Court, in another split vote, sided with Roberts and the Justice Department: abortion clinics and their clients would have to look elsewhere for protection.[39]

**Taking Lives to Save Lives**

Two months later, on March 10, 1993 (shortly after the twentieth anniversary of *Roe)*, Dr. David Gunn became the first abortion provider to be murdered by anti-abortion extremists. Gunn, who provided abortion services in clinics in Alabama, Georgia, and Florida, was confronted that day outside his Pensacola, Florida office by protesters carrying posters reading "David Gunn Kills Babies." As he got out of his car, Gunn was shot three times by a man dressed in a gray suit who shouted, "Don't kill any more babies." The previous Sunday, the same man, Michael Griffin, had asked his congregation to pray for Gunn's soul and conversion.

Griffin had grown up in Pensacola. Like members of the Gideon Project, he had been influenced by what his attorneys characterized as the relentless rhetoric and graphic images shown to him by his minister, a local anti-abortion extremist and former Ku Klux Klan member.[40] The minister was the regional director of Rescue America, an organization that had evolved from Operation Rescue.

A few months after Gunn's murder, Dr. George Tiller, the major focus of the Summer of Mercy demonstrations, was wounded in a botched attempt on his life as he was leaving work one evening. Shelley Shannon, Tiller's admitted assailant and a participant in the Summer of Mercy, was a sympathizer with Michael Griffin. She, too, had become convinced that more drastic action was called for. Like others, Shannon turned to her God's word and prayer for support.

> I am glad for those who are publicly refusing to condemn Michael Griffin. I'm sure there will be more of these works. Mine is clear. This morning in bed it seemed God asked, "Is there any doubt?". . . . Again He asked, "Is there

any doubt?" I could recognize some fear and other things. The third time He asked, "Is there any doubt? No, Lord. Please help me do it right."[41]

A short time later, referencing Isaiah 6:8 ("Then I heard the voice of the Lord saying, 'Whom shall I send? And who will go for us?' And I said, 'Here am I. Send me!'"), Shelley Shannon decided to act. The shootings of Gunn and Tiller drew substantial public attention and concern. The FACE legislation had failed to pass Congress in 1992, but following the actions of Griffith and Shannon in 1993, the bill was reintroduced and supported by a bipartisan coalition of senators and representatives, including presidential candidate and Kansas Senator Bob Dole. This time, FACE passed.[42] On May 26, 1994, President Bill Clinton signed FACE into law, finally securing protections for those seeking abortions and those providing services by making it a federal crime to use force, the threat of force, or physical obstruction to injure, intimidate, or interfere with persons obtaining or providing reproductive health services.

Reported incidents of clinic protest activities, as recorded by the National Abortion Federation, began to taper off. The number of blockades had been eighty-three and sixty-six in 1992 and 1993, respectively. In 1994 there were twenty-five, and in 1995 the total was five. There would be an increase in picketing and peaks of more threatening activity in later years, such as the increase of anthrax threats in 2001, but there was a sense among supporters and opponents alike that the FACE Act was having an impact. Yet problems remained: four murders and eight attempted murders occurred in 1994 alone.

## The Army of God

For a small, highly motivated minority, commitment to lethal action continued apace. The injustice and illegitimacy of existing laws were clear. They were witnessing a holocaust, and they were no longer going to stand idly by. One such group called itself the Army of God, which counted Shelley Shannon among its members. Shannon's letters and diary, along with her testimony and evidence presented at her trial, shed important light on how violence was spreading like a virus among a small, isolated, and loosely connected group of extreme adherents to the anti-abortion cause. In particular, the Army of God's manual—found buried in Shannon's backyard following her arrest—brought increased and unintended attention to this shadowy organization.

The history of this organization remains clouded, but folklore indicates that the original version of the manual was drafted by some of the Operation Rescue protesters while they were jailed after protests at the 1988 Democratic Convention in Atlanta. In a later edition of the manual, the religious footing for the group's violent response to increased federal regulations was starkly stated in an explicit warning: "We, the remnant of God-fearing men and women of the United States of Amerika, do officially declare war on the entire child killing industry."

Neal Horsley, a central figure in the Army of God,[43] wrote "Understanding the Army of God" shortly after a clinic bombing in Birmingham, Alabama, that killed an off-duty policeman and seriously injured a woman:

If all the previous evidence did not make it clear, the bomb in the Birmingham clinic should prove to all that the Army of God has entered this warfare. . . . Do not expect this war to end until legalized abortion is repealed. . . . People enraged by the war being waged in this nation against God's children will continue to engage in terrorist actions. Because the government of the USA has become a godless and apostate body, the people who rise up in arms against such idolatry deserve the name "The Army of God."[44]

Among the Army faithful, a sense of injustice was deep, legitimacy for the government was withdrawn, and a demonizing sense of *us vs. them* was complete. Destructive and lethal violence followed. Fellow travelers in the Army of God, including its chaplain, Michael Bray, systematically advocated this violence. Bray had written *A Time to Kill*, a book which argues that it is justifiable to kill abortion doctors.

Similarly, Eric Rudolph, who had become widely known after hiding in the woods of North Carolina for some five years before being captured and facing four trials in four separate jurisdictions for his violent activities, wrote,

I am not an anarchist. I have nothing against government or law enforcement in general. It is solely for the reason that this government has legalized the murder of children that I have no allegiance to nor do I recognize the legitimacy of this particular government in Washington. . . . Because I believe that abortion is murder, I also believe that force is justified in an attempt to stop it.[45]

It was Paul Hill, however, a former Presbyterian minister, who provided the most extensive exposition of the position taken by this loosely connected group of admitted terrorists. Following several days of protests in late July 1994, Hill shot and killed Dr. John Britton and his armed escort, seriously wounding the escort's wife in the process. Hill, who admitted to the killings, was convicted and sentenced to death. While awaiting execution, he collected and expanded his writings into a manuscript, *Mix My Blood with the Blood of the Unborn.*

Hill was executed before he was able to finish his book. Subsequently, one of Hill's friends and confidants, Rev. Donald Spitz, put the unedited manuscript online.[46] Its grounding principle was succinctly stated: "It is certain that the innocent should be defended with the means necessary, and since the unborn are innocent, it is equally certain that they should be defended with the means necessary."

On September 3, 2003, Hill became the first person to be executed for killings associated with abortion clinics. His last recorded words were an appeal to the Golden Rule:

Two of the last things I'd like to say, if you believe abortion is a lethal force, you should oppose the force and do what you have to do to stop it. May God help you to protect the unborn as you would want to be protected.[47]

Other clinics were bombed, and other doctors who performed abortions were killed and assaulted,[48] but with Paul Hill's execution, justification of taking life to protect life had come full circle. This former Presbyterian minister called on a higher law to justify killing those whom he charged with killing babies; then he, in turn, was executed. Both life-ending actions were justified by invoking the imperative, "Life is sacred and should be protected." The rationale differed only in how the protective boundaries of life were defined.

Some six years later, on May 31, 2009, the killing continued. George Tiller, who had escaped Shannon's murder attempt following the Summer of Mercy, was shot to death while attending church. His assailant used the defense of justified homicide. Following Tiller's murder, Randall Terry released the following statement:

> George Tiller was a mass-murderer. We grieve for him that he did not have time to properly prepare his soul to face God. I am more concerned that the Obama Administration will use Tiller's killing to intimidate pro-lifers into surrendering our most effective rhetoric and actions. Abortion is still murder. And we still must call abortion by its proper name; murder.
>
> Those men and women who slaughter the unborn are murderers according to the Law of God. We must continue to expose them in our communities and peacefully protest them at their offices and homes, and yes, even their churches.[49]

More direct justifications for Tiller's murder appeared on outlets for the Army of God, one of which was titled "A Just End to a Violent, Wicked Man."[50] Tiller was best known, revered, and reviled for his willingness to provide late-term therapeutic abortions, cases where the fetus was, some would note, mere inches from life.

## Partial-Birth Abortion

In 2005, John Roberts, who had argued before the Supreme Court on behalf of anti-abortion protestors involved in the Summer of Mercy,[51] became Chief Justice of the U.S. Supreme Court. Two years later, he joined four of his colleagues in a decision that upheld the Partial-Birth Abortion Ban Act of 2003, signed into law by President George W. Bush. This Act outlawed a subset of late-term abortion procedures that had so troubled and outraged those demonstrating in Wichita in 1991.[52] The boundary where abortion became infanticide was clarified.

Phrases can become powerful political tools. "Partial-birth abortion" was not a medical term, but a phrase of political art. It evolved from a description of a medical procedure outlined in Dallas in September 1992 by Dr. Martin Haskell, the physician owner of a women's health center in Cincinnati, Ohio.[53] He had performed more than 700 abortions using what he called dilation and extraction (D&X) procedures, thought to be easier and safer than the more commonly used dilation and evacuation (D&E) methods.

Haskell's practice precisely illustrated what so troubled the organizers of the Summer of Mercy. In an interview, he related, "Prolife activist Randall Terry recently said to me that he was going to do everything within his power to have me tried like a Nazi war criminal."[54] When talking with his colleagues that day in Dallas, however, Haskell had other risks in mind. Specifically, he was interested in reducing the medical risks inherent in late second-trimester and early third-trimester abortions, offering details on a safe, quick, outpatient procedure he had developed. Haskell's presentation was laced with technical descriptors, but these were of little interest to those who stood in opposition. When describing the technical details, however, he also highlighted the human qualities of the fetus.

> The surgeon introduces a large grasping forceps. . . . When the instrument appears on the sonogram screen, the surgeon is able to open and close its jaws to firmly and reliably grasp a lower extremity . . . and pulls the extremity into the vagina . . . the surgeon then forces the scissors into the base of the skull. . . . Having safely entered the skull, he spreads the scissors to enlarge the opening.
>
> The surgeon removes the scissors and introduces a suction catheter into this hole and evacuates the skull contents. With the catheter still in place, he applies traction to the fetus, removing it completely from the patient.[55]

In an interview conducted a year following his presentation, Haskell was asked, "Does it bother you that a second trimester fetus so closely resembles a baby?"[56] He responded, "I really don't think about it. Sure it becomes more physically developed, but it lacks emotional development. It doesn't have the mental capacity for self-awareness. It's never been an ethical dilemma for me." [57]

Later in the same interview Haskell was asked, "Does the fetus feel pain?"[58] Admitting some ignorance, he likened the fetus to a pet.

> I'm not an expert, but my understanding is that fetal development is insufficient for consciousness. It's a lot like pets. We like to think they think like we do. We ascribe human-like feelings to them, but they are not capable of the same self-awareness we are. It's the same with fetuses.[59]

In all likelihood, the physicians listening knew that such procedures constituted only a small proportion of abortions performed and were most likely to be used only when there was a direct threat to the mother's health or life. For these people, Haskell's presentation was helpful. For anti-abortion activists, however, it was a jarring offense against life. Unwittingly, a doctor who was skilled and experienced in performing abortions had just handed anti-abortion activists all the ammunition they needed. D&X abortions involved the intentional killing of a partially born human being, in many cases occurring beyond the point of viability of twenty-four to twenty-eight weeks (alluded to in *Roe).* Unlike the embryos or fetuses aborted in the first trimester, the late-term fetus had easily identifiable human qualities and was clearly capable of experiencing pain.

This became evident in testimony given at a later congressional hearing by a self-described pro-choice nurse who had attended the D&X abortion of a 26.5-week-old fetus.

The baby's little fingers were clasping and unclasping, and his feet were kicking. Then the doctor stuck the scissors through the back of his head, and the baby's arms jerked out in a flinch, a startle reaction, like a baby does when he thinks that he might fall. The doctor opened up the scissors, stuck a high-powered suction tube into the opening and sucked the baby's brains out. Now the baby was completely limp. I was really completely unprepared for what I was seeing. I almost threw up as I watched the doctor do these things.[60]

Actions taken during late-term abortions might be labeled D&X for clinicians, but for others they were the destruction of a small, vulnerable human being. The procedures were a repulsive abomination.

The National Right to Life Committee (NRLC) was the first to take up the charge on a national scale. One of its first steps was to distribute cartoon-like sketches drawn by an Oregon activist, Jenny Westberg,[61] later refined into color representations for the internet,[62] and based upon Haskell's description of D&X procedures. Their message was clear: the life of a small, vulnerable baby was being taken. The last of the sketches showed the instant when the suction catheter was placed in the infant's skull.

These images drew the attention of Keri Harrison, who drafted an early version of the partial-birth abortion ban legislation. To Harrison, the argument was simple:

To think that a human being would actually hold a little baby in his or her hand, and then kill it—that's what got me. If you're holding that child in your hand, and knowingly killing the child, you can't argue any more that it's not really a human being. You just can't do it.[63]

Anti-abortion activists knew they needed a dramatic phrase to capture the procedure. It had to be a phrase that would be accurate and compelling, but not connect their efforts with the alienating fringe elements of the anti-abortion movement. "Late-term abortion" was too ambiguous and all-encompassing. It also left the sense that the procedure was fully covered by the *Roe* and *Doe* decisions. In D&X procedures, the fetus was moved into the birth canal, making it in many ways similar to a premature birth. If the cervix dilated a little more, the child would emerge through the birth canal without assistance.

Harrison later recalled that after throwing around terms with Rep. Canady and an NRLC lobbyist Douglas Johnson, the three finally came to agreement. "We called it the most descriptive thing we could call it."[64] The fetus was indeed just inches from being born. "Partial-birth abortion" was decided on as the phrase to frame their message.

### Protecting Health as Well as Life

With that, the Partial-Birth Abortion Ban Act of 1995 was drafted. It was passed in Congress in December, but did not carry enough votes to override a presidential veto.[65] When explaining his veto, President Clinton did not refer to "partial-birth abortions," but rather noted his long-standing opposition to late-term abortions except where necessary to protect the life or health of the mother. Had the bill included an exception for serious health consequences, consequences including "serious physical harm, often including losing the ability to have more children,"[66] President Clinton remarked, "I would sign it now."

Concluding his remarks, the president wanted all to know he understood and agreed with "the desire to eliminate the use of a procedure that appears inhumane. But to eliminate it without taking into consideration the rare and tragic circumstances in which its use may be necessary would be even more inhumane." Both Congress and President Clinton wanted to protect life and alleviate suffering. They disagreed on where the boundaries should be drawn and how the dilemma involving competing values should be resolved.

Why had supporters of the bill not included a health exception? Those opposing the health exception recalled the language of *Roe's* companion case, *Doe v. Bolton*, wherein the Court had defined health broadly to include "all factors—physical, emotional, psychological, familial, and the woman's age—relevant to the well-being of the patient." This was no boundary at all, as anyone could conceivably claim a health exception. Opening the door to the health exception would be opening the floodgates to a disregard for life: partial-birth abortions on demand.

Advocates for exceptions, by contrast, focused on circumstances where debilitating deformities or severe brain damage in fetuses are not detected until late in pregnancy. Some of these birth defects preclude meaningful life for the yet-to-be-born infant. In addition, in some cases, not permitting a late-term abortion represented a threat to the health and physical well-being of the mother, including her ability to have children in the future. While the law might be useful for general policy, it is ham-handed in individual cases and should not intrude. These difficult, often tragic decisions should be left to the people who are most directly involved.

President Clinton's veto was issued on April 10, 1996, to the immense relief of those committed to respecting the autonomy of mothers, families, and their physicians to make these intensely personal decisions. Those concerned with what they saw as the taking of life just inches away from birth—and in fact an emerging culture that de-emphasized the sanctity of life—were incensed by it. They did not plan to let the issue drop. In an impassioned speech in which he urged his colleagues to override President Clinton's veto, Illinois Rep. Henry Hyde foresaw profound societal consequences.

> It is not just the babies that are dying for the lethal sin of being unwanted or being handicapped or malformed. We are dying, and not from the darkness, but from the cold, the coldness of self-brutalization that chills our sensibilities, deadens our conscience, and allows us to think of this unspeakable act as an act of compassion.[67]

Hyde was not alone. A week after his veto, President Clinton received a letter of protest signed by the Catholic archbishops of Chicago, Philadelphia, Washington, Baltimore, Boston, Los Angeles, Detroit, and New York, along with the president of the National Conference of Catholic Bishops. They wrote with "deep sorrow and dismay." They found the President's veto "beyond comprehension for those who hold human life sacred." These religious leaders were convinced that the president's action would ensure "the continued use of the most heinous act to kill a tiny infant just seconds from taking his or her first breath outside the womb."

As for the mother's health, they found the president's assessment too broad, noting,

> If a woman is "too young" or "too old," if she is emotionally upset by pregnancy, or if pregnancy interferes with schooling or career, the law considers those situations as "health" reasons for abortion. In other words, as you know and we know, an exception for "health" means abortion on demand.

The president's decision was taking:

> our nation to a critical turning point in its treatment of helpless human beings inside and outside the womb. It moves our nation one step further toward acceptance of infanticide. Combined with the two recent federal appeals court decisions seeking to legitimize assisted suicide, it sounds the alarm that public officials are moving our society ever more rapidly to embrace a culture of death.

The Partial-Birth Abortion Ban legislation was reintroduced in the next session of Congress. The new bill was very close to its original form, and the lobbying, hearings, and outcome were repeated. Once again, the health exception was not included, and once again, President Clinton issued a veto on October 10, 1997. Again, among supporters of the ban, there was an outcry of dismay, sorrow, and disgust. Those seeking to maintain and strengthen respect for the health, autonomy, and integrity of mothers, fathers, their families, and physicians breathed yet another sigh of relief. While passage of the bill had garnered more support, it was still a few votes shy of what was needed to override the presidential veto.[68]

National public opinion polls painted a mixed picture. One review of all major public polling found "wide variation in support for partial-birth abortion bans, ranging from 77 percent in one poll . . . to 49 percent in another." The review continued,

> When not providing respondents with specific legislative details about the timing of the procedure or the life of the mother exception, and indicating a doctor is involved, the survey question yields net opposition to the ban; only 43 percent favor banning the procedure while 51 percent are opposed.[69]

Some thirty states passed legislation that in one way or another banned partial-birth abortions. Wording used in these statutes reflected a coordinated, national agenda focused on the D&X procedures that Haskell had outlined. For the most part, these statutory bans did not ban all late-term procedures, but rather focused on D&X and the location of the unborn at the moment of termination.

## A Strange and Strained Argument

Court challenges to these state statutes came quickly. The first to reach the Supreme Court, *Stenberg v. Carhart*,[70] was from Nebraska, where the statutory ban had been challenged just two days after its passage. On June 28, 2000, in the midst of a closely contested presidential campaign, the Supreme Court handed down an aggressively argued five-to-four decision that declared the Nebraska law unconstitutional for two reasons. The first, which was the most obvious, was that the Nebraska statute lacked an exception for protecting the health of the mother. Five of the Court's nine justices found that this omission violated precedents set out in *Roe, Doe,* and *Casey.* Second, the definition provided by Nebraska legislators for the term "partial-birth abortion" procedures was deemed to be too ambiguous.

There had always been potential confusion between D&X and D&E procedures. Recall that Haskell had noted the connection between the two when describing how the fortuitous location of a foot allowed the fetus to be easily pulled into the birth canal. The Nebraska statute focused on D&X procedures, but included the following language:

> deliberately and intentionally delivering into the vagina a living unborn child, *or a substantial portion thereof,* for the purpose of performing a procedure that the person performing such procedure knows will kill the unborn child and does kill the unborn child [emphasis added].

What did "substantial portion" mean? A foot? Two legs? The torso? In his oral argument before the Court, Nebraska's attorney general pointed to legislative debate for clarification. During the debate, one senator had asked the bill's sponsor, "[Y]ou said that as small a portion of the fetus as a foot would constitute a substantial portion in your opinion. Is that correct?" The sponsoring senator had agreed. "Yes, I believe that's correct."

This being the case, D&E and D&X procedures shaded into one another. Surely, protected life should not depend solely on the chance location of a foot. What happened if a D&E turned into a D&X while the abortion was taking place? The majority of the Court concluded that too much overlap existed. This overlap left physicians at risk of prosecution and women with too few acceptable options, creating a "substantial obstacle" and an "undue burden" on their choices—a violation of the Court's findings in *Casey.*

When it came to defining the protective boundaries of life, this was a strange and strained argument. Nebraska's law was unacceptable because it did not specify clearly where the fetus was when life was taken. Justice Scalia's dissent, which referred to D&X procedures as live-birth abortions, berated the majority's rationale, noting that overturning Nebraska's ban on "this visibly brutal means of eliminating our half-born posterity is quite simply absurd." Justice O'Connor disagreed, concurring with the majority. She noted that if the statute had been limited to D&X procedures and included a health exception, "the question presented would be quite different." Given the question posed, however, their reasoning was sound in O'Connor's mind.

Sound or absurd, the vote was five to four, and Nebraska's statute banning partial-birth abortions was overturned. Given that statutes in more than two dozen other states had similar wording,[71] the impact was felt across the country. Those working to ban partial-birth abortions were dealt a serious setback. But the battle to determine when early life was fully protected was not over.

Proponents for the ban took lessons from the Supreme Court's assessment of Nebraska's law. On December 12, 2000, some six months after Nebraska's *Stenberg* decision, the Supreme Court certified the election of George W. Bush. While his administration would soon be consumed with other matters, President Bush was far more sympathetic; indeed, he was committed to banning partial-birth abortions.

### The Political Landscape Shifts

By October 2003, after carefully considering the Court's assessment of the Nebraska statute, authors crafted new federal legislation to ban partial-birth abortions. Hearings were held, amendments considered, revisions made, and votes taken. The Partial-Birth Abortion Ban Act of 2003 did not contain a health exception for the mother, but it did clarify various other issues. It passed both houses of Congress by wide margins.[72] On November 5, 2003, President Bush signed the Act into law. At the signing ceremony, Bush grounded his support in reverence for all young lives, remarking,

> The best case against partial-birth abortion is a simple description of what happens and to whom it happens. It involves the partial delivery of a live boy or girl, and a sudden, violent end of that life. Our nation owes its children a different and better welcome. The bill I am about to sign protecting inno-cent new life from this practice reflects the compassion and humanity of America.

During the signing ceremony, President Bush may or may not have been aware of experiences like the one Gretchen Voss wrote about a few months later in the *Boston Globe*.[73] In the article, Voss wrote about having an ultrasound and watching the images flicker across the screen with her husband, Dave. "As images of our baby filled the black screen, we oohed and aahed like the goofy expectant parents."

The technician's expression, however, was telling. It soon became evident that something was wrong. A few minutes later, the expectant parents met with their doctor and received terrible news. The ultrasound image had shown that the fetus had an open neural tube defect. The extent of the problem was not clear, and the Vosses were advised to go to another hospital in Boston for further diagnosis. The news they received there was no better.

Instead of cinnamon and spice, our child came with technical terms like hydrocephalus and spina bifida. The spine, she [the doctor] said, had not closed properly, and because of the location of the opening, it was as bad as it got. What they knew—that the baby would certainly be paralyzed and incontinent, that the baby's brain was being tugged against the opening in the base of the skull and the cranium was full of fluid—was awful. What they didn't know—whether the baby would live at all, and if so, with what sort of mental and developmental defects—was devastating. Countless surgeries would be required if the baby did live. None of them would repair the damage that was already done.

For Gretchen and Dave, the Partial-Birth Abortion Ban Act of 2003 did not reflect life-affirming compassion. Instead, it was a callous, misguided attempt to prohibit humane responses to deeply personal tragedies.

President Bush's attempt to ban partial-birth abortions threatens all late-term procedures. But in my case, everyone said it was the right thing to do—even my Catholic father and Republican father-in-law. . . . Though the baby might live, it was not a life that we would choose for our child, a child that we already loved. We decided to terminate the pregnancy. It was our last parental decision.

Later, after her husband's brother had left a tearful message on their answering machine, Voss wrote that she found her husband "kneeling on the floor in our bathroom, doubled over and bawling, his body quaking."

There were no truly satisfying answers. Still, proponents on both sides pressed forward. The question now became whether the new federal statute—lacking an exception for the mother's health—would clear the constitutional hurdle any better than Nebraska's law.

## Legal Details

The bill's drafters had gone to great lengths to ensure it would, but the omission of a health exception seemed to fly in the face of the Nebraska ruling. Nonetheless, the omission was intentional, and the drafters' reasoning was blunt.

Congress finds that partial-birth abortion is never medically indicated to preserve the health of the mother; is in fact unrecognized as a valid abortion procedure by the mainstream medical community; poses additional health risks to the mother; blurs the line between abortion and infanticide in the killing of a partially-born child just inches from birth; and confuses the role of the physician in childbirth and should, therefore, be banned.

The bill's proponents had gone to great lengths to develop the factual basis for this conclusion through sworn testimony, and they felt their well-developed findings deserved the Court's deference. There was no need for a health exception.

The second problem the Supreme Court had found with the Nebraska statute was the meaning of the phrase "substantial portion" of the fetus outside the womb. How much was enough? Also of concern was the chance that what started as a common D&E procedure might unintentionally become a partial-birth, D&X. To deal with these issues, Congress included quite specific wording. The term "partial-birth abortion" means an abortion in which the person performing the abortion deliberately and intentionally vaginally delivers a living fetus until, in the case of a head-first presentation, the entire fetal head is outside the body of the mother, or, in the case of breech presentation, any part of the fetal trunk past the navel is outside the body of the mother for the purpose of performing an overt act that the person knows will kill the partially delivered living fetus.

Clearly, there were now specific anatomical landmarks for the protected boundaries of life. In the case of head-first presentation, the fetus' head must be completely outside the mother's body. In the case of a breech presentation, the fetus' head must be pulled outside the mother's body beyond its navel. There was no rationale provided for these markers, nor were reasons given for why this type of abortion was more gruesome and inhumane than the D&E *in utero* dismemberment. The lines, however, had been drawn.

It remained for the courts to decide. The day President Bush signed the Act, cases were brought almost simultaneously to the U.S. district courts in northern California, southern New York, and Nebraska. Citing well-known precedent, all three district courts struck down the law, finding the Partial-Birth Abortion Ban Act of 2003 unconstitutional. There was continuing concern about whether the Act imposed undue constraints on a woman's choices, but more importantly, the courts found the omission of any consideration given to exceptions for the woman's health to be unacceptable.

As U.S. Attorney General Alberto Gonzales appealed these rulings to the relevant circuit courts, the outcome was the same each time: all found the Act unconstitutional. In the Nebraska case, the circuit court noted that the drafters' claims notwithstanding, "If one thing is clear from the record in this case, it is that no consensus exists in the medical community." In this situation, "the Constitution requires legislatures to err on the side of protecting women's health by including a health exception." The conclusion followed, as night follows day: "Because the Act does not contain a health exception, it is unconstitutional." By the end of January 2006, a total of six district and circuit court opinions had relied on the Supreme Court's findings in *Stenberg* and other supporting cases to find that the Act signed into law by President Bush was unconstitutional.

Still, the attorney general appealed the case to the Supreme Court, which agreed to hear the Nebraska case combined with a case from California in February 2006. It had been seven years since the original Nebraska case had been decided, and two of the justices who had ruled on that case were no longer on the Court. Justice Alito had replaced Justice O'Connor, who had voted to strike down the Nebraska law. John Roberts, the attorney who had argued before the Supreme Court on behalf of the Summer of Mercy protesters, had replaced Chief Justice Rehnquist, who also upheld the earlier Nebraska law as constitutional. With these two new justices siding with the majority, the Supreme Court, again voting five to four, found the new law overcame the shortcomings of the earlier Nebraska statute. The Partial-Birth Abortion Ban Act of 2003 was found to meet constitutional standards.

Justice Anthony Kennedy, who had written a dissenting opinion when the Nebraska law was overturned, wrote this time for the majority. The concerns regarding overlap in D&X and D&E procedures, which were so evident in the Nebraska law, had been remedied. Intentional action was required, and the protected boundaries of life had been specified. Whether a head-first or breech delivery was involved, the anatomical markers were clear.

But what about protection of the mother's health, which was totally missing? Courts at all levels, including the Supreme Court, had previously underscored its importance numerous times. The circuit courts had ruled that in such uncertain circumstances, legislatures should "err on the side of protecting women's health," but Kennedy and his colleagues were more willing to tolerate uncertainty. They wrote, "The Act is not invalid on its face where there is uncertainty over whether the barred procedure is ever necessary to preserve a woman's health." In such circumstances, the decision continued, remedies should be sought in an "as-applied challenge." Thus, threats to the mother's health would have to be decided on a case-by-case basis, and she and her doctor would have to ask for an exception to the law before proceeding with D&X procedures.

This, certainly, was a new twist. In her dissent, Justice Ruth Bader Ginsburg found this "piecemeal" approach "gravely mistaken" in that it jeopardized the woman's health and put the physician in an "untenable position." The single remaining woman on the Court and three of her male colleagues found the majority's reasoning inappropriate and condescending. It reflected, Ginsburg noted, "ancient notions about women's place in the family and under the Constitution—ideas that have long since been discredited." Citing *Casey*, she reminded her brethren that they had previously found the "destiny of the woman must be shaped . . . on her own conception of her spiritual imperatives and her place in society." Further, Ginsburg noted, the means "chosen by the State to further the interest in potential life must be calculated to inform the woman's free choice, not hinder it."

Ironically, the majority of the Court had grounded their reasoning in concern for the mother's mental health:

> It is self-evident that a mother who comes to regret her choice to abort must struggle with grief more anguished and sorrow more profound when she learns, only after the event, what she once did not know: that she allowed a doctor to pierce the skull and vacuum the fast-developing brain of her unborn child, a child assuming the human form.

Thus, the majority of Court members felt that these procedures should be banned to protect the mother from her own faulty, poorly informed judgment.

The tension remained. This time, however, the razor-thin five-to-four majority fell on the side of banning not the taking of life late in pregnancy, but specifically the procedures used and the location of the fetus at the time of the abortion.

## Adapting to a Strange and Strained Decision

The Partial-Birth Abortion Ban Act of 2003 was now the law of the land. Like the earlier decision in *Stenberg*, this was a strange and strained decision that did not demand exceptions for the mother's health—although it expressed paternalistic concern for her mental anguish. The newly established legal boundary for protected life depended on whether the unborn child had been intentionally drawn out of the birth canal past its head or beyond its navel when its life was ended.

Women, their physicians, and supporting hospital abortion policies adjusted to follow the Act's guidelines. A few months later, the *Boston Globe* reported,

> In response to the Supreme Court decision upholding the Partial-Birth Abortion Ban Act, many abortion providers in Boston and around the country have adopted a defensive tactic. To avoid any chance of partially delivering a live fetus, they are injecting fetuses with lethal drugs before procedures.[74]

In three major Harvard-affiliated hospitals, the article continued, such alternatives had become policy as physicians responded to the ban by making the injections beginning at around twenty weeks' gestation.

While the Partial-Birth Abortion Ban Act of 2003 established anatomical markers for the protected boundaries of life, it did not provide a quality-of-life rationale for why these markers were chosen. In 2011, a number of states turned to the capacity of the fetus to feel pain to address some remaining concerns. If the fetus is capable of feeling pain, it exists in the realm of protected life. As one commentator put it, "The purpose of this type of bill is to focus on the humanity of the unborn child. . . . Fetal pain is something that people who are in the middle on the abortion issue can relate to."[75] Advocates set the time around the twentieth week of gestation.

If a threshold based on a capacity to feel pain is established, and a child is protected once it emerges from the birth canal past the navel (if breech) or to the neck (if head-first), then the protected status of a fully born infant's life would appear to be settled. The law has long held that infants born alive are considered people, fully entitled to the protections of the law. As the twentieth century drew to a close, however, U.S. Rep. Charles T. Canady grew increasingly concerned about changes in the legal and cultural landscape, and the emergence of what he and others saw as a "culture of death."[76]

As he introduced legislation fashioned from these concerns—the Born-Alive Protection Act of 2000—Canady explained his reasoning. "The principle that born-alive infants are entitled to the protection of the law is being questioned at one of America's most prestigious universities." Princeton University bioethicist Peter Singer, Canady noted, was arguing "that parents should have the option to kill disabled or unhealthy newborn babies for a certain period after birth." This was based on Singer's view, Canady continued, that "the life of a newborn baby is 'of no greater value than the life of a nonhuman animal at a similar level of rationality, self-consciousness, awareness, capacity to feel, etc.'" For Singer, Canady noted, "killing a disabled infant is not morally equivalent to killing a person. Very often, it is not wrong at all." The purpose of his bill, he told his congressional colleagues, was "to firmly establish that, for purposes of federal law, an infant who is completely expelled or extracted from her mother and who is alive is, indeed, a person under the law."

After some minor amendments were worked out, President George W. Bush signed the all but unanimously passed Born-Alive Infant Protection Act into law on August 5, 2002. Almost three decades had passed since the *Roe* and *Doe* decisions, and some forty states had passed related born-alive legislation. Why was so much effort needed to resolve such a seemingly obvious question?

### Lives Worth Living, Protecting, and Supporting

Concern about the moral standing of infants was raised shortly after *Roe*, when genetic researcher James Watson, writing with his colleague, Francis Crick, was quoted as remarking, "If a child were not declared alive until three days after birth. ... The doctor could allow the child to die if the parents so chose and save a lot of misery and suffering. I believe this view is the only rational, compassionate attitude to have."[77] Some years later, American University professor Jeffrey Reiman joined the fray, articulating his rationale in his 1999 book *Abortion and the Ways We Value Human Life*.[78] "Killing children or adults is wrong," Reiman wrote, "because of properties *they* possess; killing infants [is wrong], because of an emotion that *we* naturally and rightly have toward infants." For many, the implications of his distinction were elusive.

Reiman elaborated, explaining that it was all a matter of empathy and assessed social worth. We might love, identify with, and desire to protect infants, but infants "do not possess in their own right a property that makes it wrong to kill them." It followed that while empathy and emotional attachments should be honored, "there will be permissible exceptions to the rule against killing [infants] that will not apply to the rule against killing adults or children." In particular, Reiman continued, "I think (as do many philosophers, doctors, and parents) that ending the lives of severely handicapped newborns will be acceptable." Reiman left blurred the exact boundary that, in his opinion, separated less-protected infancy from fully protected childhood and adulthood. He was also unclear on the precise meaning of the term "handicapped newborns." Fully protected life depended on when and whether the infant possessed self-awareness and other attributes of "personhood" or "human-hood."[79] Reiman was not alone.

It was Peter Singer who drew attention to the protective boundaries of early life more thoroughly, provocatively, and carefully than anyone else. In 1985, Singer and his colleague Helga Kuhse released a book entitled *Should the Baby Live? The Problem of Handicapped Infants*. The book began bluntly with a provocative, intentionally jarring, and directly stated claim: "This book contains conclusions which some readers will find disturbing. We think that some infants with severe disabilities should be killed."

This assertion was grounded in the belief that a patient's level of suffering must be taken into account and weighed against a physician's duty to prolong and protect life. In some circumstances, the most humane course of action, according to Singer and those who agreed with him, was to terminate an infant's life with care and compassion. Some lives, some moments, and some manifestations of life were seen as more worthy of protection and support than others. While some might want to deny this, and think it to be morally wrong, or believe it had deeply troubling ethical implications, for Singer and Kuhse there was ample evidence for the need for merciful killings in certain circumstances. Such actions could be justified and should be defended. Their argument was built by first reviewing the cases of two babies, both of whom had been born with Down's syndrome. In both instances, the parents decided to let their child die. The first case occurred in 1980 in Derby, England, and the second in Bloomington, Indiana, in 1982.

In the Derby case, the mother was overheard by one of her sisters saying tearfully to her husband, "I don't want it, Duck," shortly after the birth of her child. Once the doctor heard of her wishes, he acted accordingly, writing in the baby's records, "Parents do not wish baby to survive. Nursing care only." The doctor also prescribed a pain-killing drug to ease the child's suffering. Two days later, the infant became restless, struggling for breath, perhaps because of the painkiller. Early in the morning of the baby's third day of life, he died in the arms of a nurse.

A member of the hospital staff who was troubled by the circumstances of the baby's death reported the doctor's actions to an advocacy organization. Members of the organization went to the police, and the doctor was charged with murder. (The charge was later reduced to attempted murder, as it was learned that the baby had developed pneumonia, making it unclear whether the baby had died from the pneumonia or the drug prescribed.) After a brief trial, the judge outlined several examples he felt might help the jury work through the legal and ethical issues defining the line between lawfully letting a patient die and unlawful murder. Ultimately, the jury believed that the doctor was not attempting to kill the child, but instead trying to alleviate his suffering. Whatever the rationale, two hours after deliberations began, the jurors returned with a verdict—not guilty.

In the Bloomington case, the child also had a physical complication frequently associated with Down's syndrome—a blockage in its digestive tract. In order for the baby to survive, it would need to have a relatively simple operation (with a high probability of success) in order to remove the blockage. The operation would not affect the underlying mental handicap inherent with Down's syndrome, but the child could be expected to lead an otherwise normal life. The child's mother and father were in their early thirties and had experience working with children with this condition. Both parents were of the opinion that such children never had a minimally acceptable quality of life. They also had other children at home, whom they wanted and needed to support. After consulting with their physicians, they decided not to go through with the operation.

Doctors and administrators at the hospital where the child was born contacted a local judge and asked for intervention, but the judge sided with the parents. Since the baby was then three days old and close to death, they decided not to appeal the judge's ruling.

A local prosecutor asked a judge to order intravenous feeding to keep the baby alive, at least temporarily, but the judge refused. The prosecutor then took his pleas for intervention to the state's Supreme Court, which also supported parental autonomy and denied the request. As the case became increasingly publicized, a number of families called the hospital and filed petitions with the Court offering to adopt the baby, requests that were also denied. By the infant's sixth day of life, the prosecutor, accompanied by a law professor from Indiana University, flew to Washington, D.C. seeking emergency intervention from the U.S. Supreme Court, but while they were en route the infant died.

Word spread immediately about the Bloomington case, producing an outcry. Commentator and columnist George Will, the father of a child with Down's syndrome, wrote a column about the case a week after Bloomington's "Baby Doe" had died. Will stated unequivocally, "common sense and common usage require use of the word 'homicide'." In addition to his consternation and condemnation of what had happened, Will wanted his readers to know of and learn from the childhood joys experienced by his son:

> Jonathan Will, 10, fourth-grader and Orioles fan (and the best Wiffle-ball hitter in southern Maryland), has Down's syndrome. He does not "suffer from" (as newspapers are wont to say) Down's syndrome. He suffers from nothing, except anxiety about the Orioles' lousy start.
>
> He is doing nicely, thank you. But he is bound to have quite enough problems dealing with society—receiving rights, let alone empathy. He can do without people like Infant Doe's parents, and courts like Indiana's asserting by their actions the principle that people like him are less than fully human. On the evidence, Down's syndrome citizens have little to learn about being human from the people responsible for the death of Infant Doe.[80]

As compelling as Will's story was, not all parents of children with Down's syndrome agreed. Some of their children had not been so fortunate. A couple in Santa Barbara, California, identified with the Bloomington parents: "After much agonizing thought, prayer and discussion with family, friends, clergymen and other doctors," they had made "the same painful decision."[81] In their case, however, the doctors did not go along with their wishes. They knew how to successfully replace the baby's missing esophagus and decided to proceed with the surgery, with or without the parents' consent. They obtained a court order and the surgery was performed. The outcome was not good.

> Our baby has endured a great deal of pain, suffering and misery during his 18 months on Earth, due to the nature of his deformities, surgical procedures, and complications arising from them.
>
> He is not well today and is unable to eat orally. The doctors have told us there is a good probability that our son will suffer from lifelong problems. . . . It is indeed difficult to stand by and watch this occur.[82]

## Regulations Emerge

George Will had helped craft President Ronald Reagan's successful campaign for office, and subsequently he remained close to the Reagan Administration. A week after Will's column appeared, President Reagan issued memoranda to relevant federal agencies requesting that policies be devised to prevent a case like the Bloomington baby's from ever happening again.[83] The president grounded his orders in a 1973 law that forbade agencies receiving federal funds from withholding services to handicapped citizens. In a communication with his attorney general, Reagan noted, "Our nation's commitment to equal protection of the law will have little meaning if we deny such protection to those who have not been blessed with the same physical or mental gifts we too often take for granted."

Note should be taken of how rapidly the rhetoric surrounding these matters was shifting. It was common through the 1950s to use the terms *moron, imbecile, idiot,* or even *monstrosities at birth,* to characterize children not "blessed with the same physical or mental gifts we too often take for granted."[84] Medical technology had greatly enhanced the life chances of many of these infants and deepened our understanding of the underlying genesis of birth defects. By the 1980s, medical technology and greater sensitivity to civil discourse were changing both the probability of death and the rhetoric used to discuss these children. Eventually, the dehumanizing monster reference disappeared from legal and moral discourse, but disagreements over the boundaries of protected life for otherwise imperiled infants remained.

Initial regulations in keeping with Reagan's orders were hurriedly constructed, and then revised almost immediately in the oxymoronic "Interim Final Rule," which took effect on March 22, 1983. The rule called for posters to be displayed in "a conspicuous place in each delivery ward" stating that failure to feed and care for handicapped infants was a violation of federal law. The posters also stated that "any person having knowledge that a handicapped infant is being discriminatorily denied food or customary medical care" should contact the "Handicapped Infant Hotline."

A great deal of confusion and suspicion followed. Critics began referring to the absurdity of "Baby Doe squads" being dispatched from the nation's capital to hospital delivery wards all across the nation in response to anonymous phone calls. A pediatrician practicing in New Mexico reported,

> Because of the fear I had in being "reported," I recently spent one agonizing hour trying to resuscitate a newborn who had no larynx, and many other congenital anomalies. The sad part was that both the parents in the delivery room watched this most difficult ordeal. It was obvious to me that this was in no way a viable child but I felt compelled to carry on this way out of fear someone in the hospital would "turn me in." I am sure that you who sit in Washington are not faced with such difficult decisions at two o'clock a.m.[85]

The regulations also failed to recognize that not all handicaps were as minor as those faced by Jonathan Will or Bloomington's Baby Doe. What about a child born with most of his brain missing? What about a child with an intracranial hemorrhage who might never breathe without a respirator and might never have the capacity for cognition? What about a child missing a substantial portion of her digestive tract, leaving her without the ability to digest food?

For many, such handicaps raised questions about whether the child in question had a life worth living, prolonging, and protecting. Sometimes it might be best to let an infant die, or to even hasten its death as peacefully and comfortably as possible. The intention to let life go can be profoundly different from the intention to destroy it. The boundaries of tolerable suffering—like the boundaries of protected life—would have to be more carefully drawn. Otherwise, forced, tragic choices between protecting life and alleviating suffering could not be avoided.

### Nagging Uncertainties—Who Should Decide?

As the Baby Doe regulations were being revised yet again, this time allowing specified exceptions,[86] a young baby girl known as "Baby Jane Doe" was born on October 11, 1983, in Port Jefferson, Long Island, New York. She was the first child of a young couple who had been married for about a year. Baby Jane Doe had numerous interrelated physical and mental defects, including spina bifida; kidney damage; microcephaly, a condition associated with incomplete brain development; and hydrocephaly, a condition that causes fluid to accumulate in the brain, sometimes causing brain damage.

Baby Jane's physicians advised her parents that several operations could potentially help their child with the manifestations of spina bifida and to reduce the fluid in her skull. If performed, these operations might lengthen her life from a matter of weeks or months to perhaps twenty years or more. However long her life would be, however, Baby Jane Doe would likely be severely mentally handicapped, epileptic, paralyzed, and subject to frequent infections. After consulting with their religious leaders and attending physicians, Baby Jane's parents decided to forgo the operations and ensure only that their baby girl was made comfortable and kept free from infection. Given the many uncertainties the child faced, the physicians agreed.

The course of treatment would have been set had it not been for a Vermont lawyer named Lawrence Washburn, Jr. Washburn, a dedicated pro-life activist and a total stranger to the family, filed suit with a New York judge who had been the Right-to-Life party's candidate when he ran for office the previous year.[87] The judge appointed a guardian who stated at the subsequent hearing that he thought the physicians and parents were wrong, arguing instead for immediate treatment. The judge agreed and so ordered. The parents took the case to New York's Court of Appeals. With the appellate judges labeling Washburn's lawsuit "distressing and offensive," the court found that the parents had made "these decisions with love and thoughtfulness, and that strangers, however whimsical or well-intentioned, cannot subject them to this outrageous kind of proceeding."

As the case wound its way through the courts, publicity followed and the parents agreed to an interview on *60 Minutes*. Interviewer Ed Bradley asked the infant's mother, "How do you feel when someone else who didn't know you, didn't know the child, had no connection with your family went to court to make a decision about your child's life?" With obvious emotion, she responded,

> I think it is unbelievable. They don't have any right at all. They don't know our child. They don't love her. We are her parents. We are the only ones who can make this decision for her. . . . It is very hard to understand his [Washburn's] concern about our daughter's life when after all the court proceedings have ended, he would no longer be around, or heard from, or there to care for our daughter.

Washburn, who still had not met the parents or their struggling child, was unmoved. He responded in a subsequent interview that he remained convinced about the rightness of his actions, believing that profoundly mentally handicapped children were "*l'enfants bon Dieu* [the children of the good God] . . . they are given to us because it is our call to heroism, to greatness, to have a child like this."[88] The case was taken to the U.S. Supreme Court, where the justices declined, without comment, to review it. The New York Court of Appeals decision stood firm. Other issues, however, remained unresolved.

In a related case, the U.S. Supreme Court did agree to review the case of *Bowen v American Hosp. Ass'n.*[89] In it, the basic rationale for the Baby Doe guidelines came under review. In *Bowen,* the Court concluded that some three years after Baby Jane Doe had been born, "concerned and loving parents had chosen one appropriate medical course over another." They had made an informed decision that was in the best interests of the infant. Like the New York Court of Appeals had before it, the U.S. Supreme Court once again affirmed parents' right to decide what was in the best interest of their handicapped children. Absent evidence of abuse, the Court instructed, the government should stay out of these matters.

## When Doctors Say No

The cases that so bothered George Will, President Reagan, and Lawrence Washburn led to the Baby Doe Regulations, a set of regulations initially grounded in civil rights-era legislation prohibiting discrimination against the handicapped. Subsequent revisions to the regulations clarified that justification of governmental oversight must be based on evidence of child abuse and neglect. Whatever the justification might be, these regulations had evolved from cases in which parents refused consent for treatment of their newly born infants. What if parents wanted treatment for their child and their physicians refused to give it?

This question had been raised in the *Bowen* case but dismissed as being too remote a possibility for serious consideration. Justices writing in the majority opinion chided their dissenting colleagues for "speculating about nonexistent hypothetical cases in which a hospital might refuse to provide treatment requested by parents."

The idea that doctors might refuse to treat infants with parental pleas to do so seemed far-fetched. As medical technology continued to advance and medical care became more and more expensive, however, the possibility became increasingly and, for many, distressingly real. On October 13, 1992, in Falls Church, Virginia, a baby girl was born lacking a significant portion of her brain. While she was still in her mother's womb, the condition—anencephaly—had been detected. The early indicators of the condition were severe enough that both the obstetrician and neonatologist involved counseled the mother to terminate her pregnancy.[90] They knew that the child's care would be quite expensive, and that life would be profoundly limited—perhaps not worth living.

The mother disagreed, and the child was born. Much of her brain, skull, and scalp were missing. Her brain stem supported her autonomic functions and reflex actions, but lacking a cerebrum, she remained permanently unconscious. The child was unable to see or hear, lacked all cognitive abilities, and was unaware of and otherwise unable to interact with her environment. There was no known medical treatment that would improve her vegetative condition.

Such infants generally die within a few days after birth due to breathing difficulties or other complications. When the baby's breathing became labored, however, her doctors placed her on mechanical ventilation, in part to allow them time to explain the baby's prospects to her mother (the child's father was only marginally involved in her life).

Within a few days, the baby's physicians were urging the mother to discontinue the artificial ventilation. Because all known treatments would serve no therapeutic or palliative purpose for her, they recommended that her child, soon to be known to the outside world as Baby K, be provided with nothing more than nutrition, hydration, and warmth, and that she be allowed to die.

Baby K's mother once again disagreed with her doctors. She firmly believed that all life is sacred and must be protected—including her anencephalic daughter's life. She knew her child's situation looked hopeless, but she believed God could work miracles. She wanted everything possible done, including using the ventilator.

Given Baby K's profoundly limiting birth defects, her physicians remained firm that continuing that level of care was morally and professionally inappropriate. For one nurse who cared for Baby K, the answer was clear:

> I find it appalling to care for her each day. It is cruel and inhumane to keep her "alive." Animals are euthanized for far less problems and yet this is a human being who really has no voice and no rights other than her mother demanding she be kept alive.[91]

The impasse with Baby K's mother continued, and eventually, the hospital sought to transfer the infant elsewhere. No other hospital would accept responsibility for her care, with costs estimated at about US$1,400 per day. About a month after her birth, Baby K's condition stabilized somewhat, and her mother agreed to have her transferred to a nearby nursing home only after securing an explicit agreement that if an emergency occurred, the hospital would readmit her daughter.

Over the next few months, Baby K was transferred between the nursing home and the hospital three times. Following her second readmission, which occurred when the infant was six months old, the hospital, now joined by the baby's father, sought to legally resolve the issue of whether the hospital was obligated to provide emergency medical treatment to Baby K that it deemed medically and ethically inappropriate. The appellate court found that it was, noting that it was "beyond the limits of our judicial function to address the moral and ethical propriety of providing emergency stabilizing medical treatment to anencephalic infants."[92]

Parents had the right to request emergency medical treatment for their children, but Baby K's parents disagreed with one another about her care. In such circumstances, the court found priority should be given to the decision "in favor of life." Baby K lived to be 2 years old, but disagreements about whether her short, vegetative life had been worthy of the heroic, expensive, and ultimately futile support measures it received would continue for many years.

The same issues emerged again in a case involving a young mother and her infant son Emilio Gonzales, who died on May 19, 2007 at the age of 19 months in Austin, Texas. Emilio was born with Leigh disease, a rare disorder that causes the breakdown of the central nervous system and related motor skills. By the time he was 17 months old, Emilio was in an intensive care unit. He was not vegetative, as Baby K had been. He was, however, losing his motor skills. He was deaf and blind, and his brain was shrinking. Emilio's conditions were getting worse day by day.

Medication to reduce Emilio's pain caused him to spend most of his time asleep. He was kept alive with hydration, nutrition, and a respirator; his doctor estimated that removal of the respirator would lead to death within minutes or hours. While Emilio's life could be prolonged, there was no known treatment for the degenerative effects of Leigh disease. In this sense, continued treatment was futile.

Eventually, as Emilio's condition worsened, tending physicians sought to remove the respirator. It was inhumane, they felt, to do otherwise, but the child's mother disagreed. She wanted to spend more time with her son. She did not want the timing of her son's death determined by physicians.[93] Eight years earlier, the state of Texas had passed an Advance Directives Act. This legislation, signed into law by then-governor George W. Bush, combined and revised three existing laws into a single law. There were a number of provisions, including a new standard for living wills and definitions of terminal and irreversible illness, but the legislation became best known as the Texas Futile Care Law.[94] If a patient requested treatment which the physician believed was futile, a seven-step process outlined in the law should be used to resolve the dispute.[95] These steps were patterned after those listed in a report released in that same year by the American Medical Association.[96]

This was just the type of situation that confronted Emilio Gonzales' mother and health care providers. The various steps specified in the law, including seeking alternative remedies (such as a transfer to another hospital), had been followed. For her part, Emilio's mother remained firm in her beliefs:

I believe there is a hospital that is going to accept my son . . . I just want to spend time with my son . . . I want to let him die naturally without someone coming up and saying we're going to cut off on a certain day.[97]

Advocacy groups seeking to strengthen rights for the disabled developed petitions and wrote to the governor, pleading for a stay of execution for young Emilio.

The Texas legislature, which convenes every other year, was in session, so a revised law was drafted. As the debate wore on, young Emilio's condition worsened and he died in his mother's arms while the legislature was still in session. The revised legislation, which foundered in the 2007 legislative session, was reintroduced in 2009, but failed to emerge from committee hearings.[98]

## Dealing with Futility and Uncertainty

As the short lives of Baby K and Emilio Gonzales illustrate, the meaning of futile treatment can become as contentious as it is unclear. In one sense, there is absolute clarity. Unless a dramatic breakthrough occurs, we will all eventually die—no exceptions. In this sense, all medical treatment is futile. At the same time, until death occurs, nothing is futile. Any person can fight for the next moment of life.

Futility involves both objective and subjective judgments. What is the time horizon sought to extend the life in question—a year, a month, a day, or a moment? What quality of life is desired—restoration of function, an acceptable sense of self, a level of consciousness, or the absence of pain and suffering? What are the chances that the desired outcome—whatever that might be—can be achieved? If there is a very high probability (scientists like to talk in terms of five nines—99.999 percent) that the procedure or treatment will not accomplish the ends sought, is the treatment technically futile? After all, even using the five-nines criterion, a chance that something might work still exists: the improbable might become real.

"[H]ope is what human beings summon up to seek a miracle against over-whelming odds. It is possible then to say in the same breath, 'I know this is futile, but I have hope.'"[99] A sense of futility only occurs when all hope of an acceptable quality of life has been extinguished. In the meantime, why not try? Making such decisions is never an easy task.[100] There are uncertainties, even in such clearly debilitating conditions as anencephaly, Leigh disease, spina bifida, hydrocephaly, and microcephaly. In each individual case, how extensively will the patient's mental capacities be diminished? How long is each child's life likely to last? How much suffering will each child endure?

There are also uncertainties of intentions, evident in the doctrine of double effect—intending good, knowing that harm will follow—which has been widely discussed by philosophers and lawyers. Are drugs being administered to hasten death, alleviate suffering, or both? When there is a single-minded intention to let life go, or even to hasten its end, this decision may reflect care, palliative healing, virtue, compassion, and justice. Or it could reflect neglect and abuse, or a judgment that individual interests be set aside for the greater good.

Finally, there are uncertainties about who should decide. After all, no one knows what the infant's wishes are. "[I]t is nonsensical in general secular terms to speak of respecting the autonomy of fetuses, infants, or profoundly retarded adults, who have never been rational. There is no autonomy to affront."[101] Attention then turns to those closest to the infant. How much weight should be given to assessments of quality-of-life preferences when compared to the inherent value of life, regardless of individual interests and preferences? Mothers, fathers, relatives, doctors, nurses, surrogates, lawyers, government officials, and judges all have some say. They also often have competing preferences, interests, and intentions.

Consensus-generating boundaries of protected life and tolerable suffering remain elusive. This is nowhere more apparent than in what came to be known as assisted dying.

# 3

# The Boundaries of Tolerable Suffering

Speaking at the International Conference on Euthanasia and the Future of Medicine in October 1988,[1] U.S. Surgeon General C. Everett Koop was worried. He had been disappointed with the outcome of the Baby Doe cases, but his worries went far beyond. Pointing to a much-cited article written in the 1920s,[2] influential in shaping the tragedy of Nazi Germany, he saw a "euthanasian ethic" beginning to infuse the culture. "We've had 'Baby Doe,'" Dr. Koop noted, "and, as sure as I'm standing here tonight, we're going to have 'Granny Doe,' too." The danger resided in the rhetoric being used to frame the debate. The surgeon general saw modern society replacing "its fundamental human values with a counter-framework outfitted with a new and fuzzy vocabulary that permits the healer to become killer." "We're snared," Koop continued, "in a marshland of new euphemisms and circum-locutions." What particularly confounded and angered him was the phrase "quality of life." He had no idea "what anyone else's 'quality of life' was, is, or will be. No idea at all." Nor, in his opinion, did anyone else.

For those who disagreed with Dr. Koop, the counter-point was obvious. If only the patient herself could determine what made the quality of life bearable and if the individual determined that life was filled with unbearable pain and suffering, and she wanted to let life go, why should these wishes not be honored? In addition, if life was void of higher brain functions—including losing awareness of surround-ings, the ability to relate to others, and even the ability to experience suffering and judge the quality of life–why should efforts to prolong life be continued? Why *shouldn't* there be a right to die? If medical help was needed to end life to avoid suffering, why shouldn't physicians provide it?

## Troubling Cases in Troubled Times

These issues had been around for a very long time. They had come once again to the fore in the troubled 1930s. In early November 1935, the same year the Voluntary Euthanasia Society—the first organization of its type—was founded in London, a story about euthanasia ran in the *London Daily Mail*. A physician, described in the article as a kind-eyed, elderly country doctor, reported:

> Five times have I taken a life . . . The first case was a newborn child, clearly doomed to imbecility. . . . In the second case, the child was born without a skullcap. The third case was that of a farmer suffering from an incurable and

agonizing disease. He died clasping my hand, and murmuring, "God bless you, doctor." The fourth case was a man suffering from the same disease and unable to eat, drink, or sleep. He was in agony beyond the torment of the damned. He also died with a smile on his face and with his hand in mine. The fifth case [had] the same disease. I had no hesitation in ending his life.

When the story appeared in the U.S. a week later in the pages of *Time,* readers learned that despite the fact that the doctor's actions were illegal, his conscience had "never stabbed him." He would do it again if necessary and was ready to face "any tribunal in the land."

Earlier that same year came the widely publicized murder conviction of May Brownhill.[3] "Mother May" had tended her son Dennis, "an imbecile," for thirty years. She was scheduled for an operation and didn't want Dennis to be without care during her recuperation. Brownhill admitted, "I did put Dennis to sleep with 100 sleeping tablets, and before I left him I did turn on the gas." Brownhill was convicted of murder and sentenced to hang, but her story "stirred the well of British sentiment to its depths." Two days after her conviction, Brownhill was pardoned and reportedly driven home in a limousine.

These and similar cases formed the foundation for much debate in Britain. In a speech delivered in the House of Lords, the royal physician, Lord Bertrand Dawson, spoke of euthanasia as a mission of mercy, a matter best left to the conscience of individual physicians. Lord Dawson argued that the act of dying should be made more peaceful, even if it involved shortening a life. Dawson spoke from experience.

Late in the evening on January 20, 1936, in just such a mission of mercy, Dawson had hastened the death of King George V. He noted in his log, "The King's life is moving peacefully toward its close."[4] Dawson had injected the dying king with three-quarters of a gram of morphine and one gram of cocaine because, he said, "It was evident that the last stage might endure for many hours, unknown to the patient but little comporting with the dignity and the serenity which he so richly merited and which demanded a brief final scene." Dawson had chosen to perform his act of mercy late in the evening, to ensure the announcement would be carried "in the morning papers rather than the less appropriate evening journals." The King deserved to die with dignity. The next morning, a headline read, "A Peaceful Ending at Midnight."

Dawson was not alone. Not quite four years after the king's death, on September 23, 1939, famed neurologist and psychoanalyst Sigmund Freud died following a battle with cancer at the age of 83. Dr. Max Schur, Freud's former student, friend, and personal physician, recalled in a book published a little more than three decades after the fact[5] that Freud had only one wish in his final days. Two days before his death, he told Schur, "My dear Schur, you certainly remember our first talk. You promised me then not to forsake me when my time comes. Now it is nothing but torture and makes no sense any more." Schur reassured his friend and patient that he did recall their earlier conversation. "When he was again in agony," Schur continued, "I gave him a hypodermic of two centigrams of morphine. He soon felt relief and fell into a peaceful sleep. I repeated this dose after about twelve hours. He lapsed into a coma and did not wake up again."

Efforts to craft permissive euthanasia legislation in Britain during the trying years of the Great Depression were ultimately unsuccessful. Nonetheless, most commentators suggest that in America and throughout Europe—including Britain and Scandinavia—the euthanasia movement was gaining momentum.[6] Germany led the charge. The German euthanasia initiative was launched with a decree sent by Adolf Hitler to Dr. Karl Brandt, his personal physician, and Philipp Bouhler, Director General of the Foundation for Welfare and Institutional Care. The decree was backdated to September 1, 1939 in order to correspond to the outbreak of war. It read, in part, "patients considered incurable according to the best available human judgment of their state of health, can be granted a mercy death."[7] While the phrase "granted a mercy death" implied carrying out a patient's request in the face of suffering, the practice of euthanasia in Germany became something quite different. Instead of compassionate alleviation of suffering, it was imposed to rid society of those considered a burden.

The German euthanasia program began with killing first children, and then adults, in Poland. Grounded in Germany's early eugenics law, the initial criteria for euthanasia included anyone diagnosed with "serious hereditary diseases." This list grew steadily, eventually including a wide range of people seen more broadly as "useless eaters," a term meant to refer to anyone who could be considered to be draining society of resources and contributing little. In *Buck v. Bell*, Justice Oliver Wendell Holmes referred to such people as those who "sap the strength of the State." Mercy death techniques perfected in this German euthanasia initiative were eventually used in a much broader genocidal holocaust. In later years, those opposed to assisted dying would repeatedly point to the Nazi experience as a dangerous precedent.

### The Stages of Suffering

Religious traditions have long justified the endurance of suffering as a way to achieve personal or spiritual growth. Much discussion of this interpretive framework transpired in the years following World War II. Among the most poignant and influential was a small volume published in 1946 in German by the Austrian neurologist and psychologist Viktor Frankl titled *Man's Search for Meaning*.[8] (The book was translated into English in an expanded form in 1959.) Frankl had been incarcerated in German camps for three years during World War II. Frankl's account was influential in part because it so clearly and concisely addressed the connection between the meaning and quality of life and the significance of suffering. "If there is a meaning in life at all," he wrote, "then there must be a meaning in suffering. Suffering is an ineradicable part of life." As personal and private as suffering is, Frankl noticed some general patterns.

For example, he found that prisoners in concentration camps seemed to adjust in stages. The first phase, Frankl recalled, was "shock." This was accompanied by confusion and denial—a "delusion of reprieve." "We clung to shreds of hope and believed to the last moment that it would not be so bad." Denial and the delusion of reprieve became difficult—perhaps impossible—to sustain in the face of over-whelming evidence. A singular defining moment would sometimes bring to a close this first stage of shock, denial, confusion, and disgust.

For Frankl, this moment came when a fellow prisoner at the camp scoffed at Frankl's concern over a manuscript he was writing. The manuscript contained his life's work, Frankl responded; couldn't he understand how important this was? "A grin spread slowly over first piteous, then more amused, mocking, insulting, until he bellowed one word at me . . . a word that was ever present in the vocabulary of camp inmates: 'Shit!'" At that moment, Frankl recalled, "I saw the plain truth and did what marked the culminating point of the first phase of my psychological reaction: I struck out my whole former life."

Inmates' second stage of adjustment to suffering entailed separating from their former life and dealing more realistically with their current predicament. This assessment, however, generated depression and thoughts of suicide "born of the hopelessness of the situation." Paradoxically, for some, this hopelessness also meant that "there was little point in committing suicide, since, for the average inmate life expectation, calculating objectively and counting all likely chances, was very poor."

Whether an inmate was suicidal or simply waiting for the death that was likely to arrive soon, the second phase was, Frankl noted, "a phase of relative apathy, in which he [the inmate] achieved a kind of emotional death." Having encountered undeniable suffering, the prisoner

> did not avert his eyes any more. By then his feelings were blunted, and he watched unmoved. . . . Disgust, horror and pity are emotions that our spectator could not really feel. . . . By means of this insensibility the prisoner soon surrounded himself with a very necessary protective shell.

Protected by a shell of insensibility, some prisoners coped by retreating "from their terrible surroundings to a life of inner riches and spiritual freedom." These inmates drew upon what Frankl called "tragic optimism." With tragic optimism, they found value and meaning in the worst situation. Rather than collapse under the enormity of their suffering, they drew strength from what good they could find in life. To Frankl, this inner strength and sense of purpose—whatever its source—determined the shifting boundaries between tolerable and intolerable suffering.

A decade after Frankl's account appeared in English, psychiatrist Elisabeth Kübler-Ross expanded further our understanding of the shifting boundaries of tolerable suffering. As a teenager, Kübler-Ross had worked in Poland and Russia with people who had recently been released from Nazi concentration camps. Later, as a trained psychiatrist, Kübler-Ross joined a group of U.S. physicians conducting interviews with people who had been recently diagnosed with terminal cancer. Her goal was to shed insight on what many tended to avoid—the experience of death and dying.

Kübler-Ross wanted patients to become teachers. She wanted to learn from them about the final stages of life, including all their anxieties, fears, and hopes. From these conversations and stories came her 1969 book *On Death and Dying*, an influential and instant bestseller. The five stages of coping with death contained in Kübler-Ross' model—denial, anger, bargaining, depression, and acceptance—are similar in many ways to those proposed by Frankl. These stages continue to frame our understanding of grief, and have become almost like a mantra, more than forty years after their publication.

Subsequent researchers, and there have been many,[9] have criticized the stages and suggested refinements, including adding, dividing, or substituting stages. Some, including Kübler-Ross herself, have questioned the inevitability of these stages, noting that grief does not always occur in a regular fashion; in fact, some stages frequently occur simultaneously and not always in the same order. Criticisms and refinements notwithstanding, if ever there was a book that framed subsequent thinking on a topic, *On Death and Dying* was it.

Whatever the number, content, duration, intensity, or sequence of stages, there is widespread agreement that the experience of and tolerance for suffering shifts over time. These shifting cognitive–emotional, semi-regular stages add yet another element of uncertainty when defining the boundaries of tolerable suffering and the right to die. When should the decision be made?

### Please Let Me Die

One illustrative tragedy involved a gas-line explosion on a rural East Texas road in the summer of 1973. Donald Cowart (known as Don or Donnie to his friends and family) was looking to buy a piece of property. He and his father visited one particular rural area, unaware of a pipeline leak filling the surroundings with explosive gas. When the two men started their car to leave, the ignition set off an explosion, injuring both men. Don's father, Ray, died on the way to the hospital. Don survived, but he was no longer the person he had been.

He was no longer a self-sufficient, independent athlete and former Air Force pilot hoping to launch a career with a commercial airline. His appearance had been dramatically altered, and he had lost the use of his hands, legs, and eyes, as well as some of his hearing. He needed assistance in every aspect of his life. Dealing with painful treatments, he endured constant, excruciating pain in order to save a life he no longer wanted. He wanted to end his suffering and repeatedly pleaded, "Please let me die!"[10] It was not to be. His mother, his lawyer, and most of his doctors wanted to save his life, even if he did not. Paternalism, defined as "non-acquiescence to a person's wishes, choices, or actions for that person's own benefit,"[11] was paramount. Cowart's autonomy was secondary to what his caretakers perceived as beneficence.

Donald Cowart (who now wanted to be known as Dax) was moved from Parkland Hospital in Dallas to the burns center at the University of Texas Medical Branch in Galveston, where his treatments and pleas for relief intensified. At that time, the Texas legal landscape vis-à-vis assistance in dying was in transition.[12] In its 1973 legislative session, the Texas Legislature passed a new penal code with wide-ranging provisions, including sections outlawing both attempted and assisted suicide. Cowart's accident had occurred in July, 1973, and the new code took effect on January 1, 1974.

While legal guidelines were shifting, Cowart's preferences were crystal clear. A thirty-minute film entitled *Please Let Me Die*, which was produced while Cowart's treatments were progressing, documented his wishes extensively. Cowart wanted his treatments stopped. If he refused to undergo the cleaning and removal of dead tissue procedures, which were like "alcohol was being poured over raw flesh," he would be removed from the bed, placed on a stretcher, and treated anyway. The cleaning was a painful process that continued "seven days a week, week after week, after week." Anticipating right-to-die cases to come in the years ahead, Cowart argued,

> Something should be done in the future so a person who did not want the care could be left alone and would not have to undergo the painful treatment. Like, I am having to undergo this painful treatment regardless of my feelings.

Dax Cowart's pleas were not the rants of a deranged patient, as he was twice judged to be competent. How, then, could his wishes be denied? His mother's love and concern for her son's relationship with God were part of the answer. When asked about it, Ada Cowart replied, "As a mother it was hard for me to say that I could give up a child."[13] In addition, she believed God had a plan, remarking,

> When Donnie wanted to discontinue treatment there were a number of things that kept going through my mind. I had prayed that he would never be killed instantly. . . . Had I believed it was God's will for him to want to die, I think I could have accepted that.

She realized her son was rational, but she also wondered whether he would change his mind. If the treatments were stopped, it would be too late. She had already lost a husband and did not want to lose a son. She intended to do everything in her power to ensure that she didn't.

Cowart's doctors and lawyer agreed with his mother. As professionals, they were driven by their sense of what was right. These commitments transcended particular cases. Cowart's lawyer, Rex Houston, was a long-time friend of the family. He was also representing Cowart's mother, and as a lawyer he had fiduciary responsibilities. On behalf of Dax, Houston sued the oil company that was responsible for the gas leak. Houston's rationale for keeping Cowart alive was straightforward.

> My reason for that was that Dax was a single man, 26 years of age. He had no dependants. He had no surviving children. He had no wife. He had no one dependent upon him. His lawsuit, were he dead, had no great value to it, because he had nobody surviving who was dependent upon him.

With a living plaintiff, the lawsuit, Houston continued, "had tremendous value. . . . Here you have a person who has lost both hands and both eyes. . . . It [the lawsuit] has almost any value you can imagine." An out-of-court settlement was soon reached, yielding Cowart a large sum.

Even with the lawsuit settled, other paternalistic interests worked to keep Cowart alive. Like lawyers, physicians are compelled by professional ethics. "The deepest ethical principle restraining the physician's power," physician and bioethicist Leon Kass has written,[14] "is neither the autonomy and freedom of the patient nor the physician's own compassion or good intention." Instead, "it is the dignity and mysterious power of human life itself ... the purity and holiness of the life and art to which the physician has sworn devotion." For Kass, "a person can choose to be a physician but cannot simply choose what physicianship means."

One of Cowart's tending physicians seemed to reflect this paternalistic approach, reporting that he was deeply troubled by the case.

> I have a very difficult problem in terms of deciding not to treat a patient, because in my opinion when you do not treat a patient, you are in a sense killing that individual. I have the knowledge and the means of caring for this patient so that he does survive, and you are asking me not to do this. . . . Why am I in medicine? . . . For me I cannot change my way of treating patients.[15]

Another physician saw things differently:

> I wanted to rehabilitate the world, and especially Don Cowart. That wasn't necessarily his priority. The difference now is that I am more comfortable with people choosing to not necessarily achieve the level of function that I think is possible for them, especially if it causes them acute discomfort or really may interfere with their quality of life.[16]

Cowart understood exactly what was going on and how he had been put in such a subordinate position:

> It's just a result of the doctors having the power. The doctors' interest has been to preserve life and also to benefit the patient on their own terms rather than the patient's. My case was an example of where the two are not the same.[17]

Reflecting more generally on the lessons that might be taken from what had happened to him, Dax was also clear about the remedy.

> Today it is insane for anyone to require that person to undergo cancer chemotherapy or whatever if that is not that person's wishes. . . . [I]f we force people to undergo treatment, what we're doing is putting the individual at the mercy of whatever medical or scientific technology comes into being in the future. We may preserve . . . "life," but what is left of the patient may be only a shell. No quality of life left. No ability to function—even think. If you define life as just the fact that the individual is not decaying, it's not any life that anyone I know would have an interest in maintaining.[18]

Dax Cowart survived, but his consternation and outrage continued. Ten years after *Please Let Me Die* was made, the follow-up film *Dax's Case* was released. By that time, Cowart had a thriving legal practice. He remained adamant in his belief that the end result did not justify the means.

> I suppose this would mean then that if the only way an individual's life could be saved would be with treatment that would be as equally painful as being boiled in hot oil or being skinned alive then we should go ahead and use that treatment. I totally disagree.[19]

Cowart was alive and happy, but he remained firm in his belief and quick to note, "My own life could have turned out much differently than it has. I could be stuffed away somewhere in a back room . . . not going out and not living the happy life that I am now."

Cowart's pleas to stop treatment never went to court. The impact of his experiences, in this sense, was limited. The issues that had so troubled those involved—respect for the autonomy of patient wishes, the legal right to end one's treatment, the delegation of authority to others, the standing of professional responsibilities, the meaning of beneficence, the redemptive power of suffering, and the unyielding protection of the sanctity of life—would wind their way through moral debates and legal proceedings in the years ahead.

## When Life Becomes Vegetative

A case involving a young woman incapable of expressing any wish whatsoever became a legal cornerstone for the position Dax Cowart so adamantly sought—the right to determine one's own destiny. In mid-April 1975, a little over a year and a half after Cowart's accident, a young New Jersey woman spent the evening celebrating a friend's birthday. In the early hours of the next morning her mother received a phone call. "Mrs. Quinlan, this is the nurse from Newton Memorial Hospital. Your daughter was admitted to the intensive care unit. She is unconscious."[20]

After ingesting a combination of Valium and alcohol that evening, 21-year-old Karen Ann Quinlan had become disoriented, and her friends took her home. Initially, they figured she was simply drunk and had passed out, but later they found that she wasn't breathing. She was revived and taken to the hospital, where she slipped into a "persistent vegetative state."[21]

As one of the coiners of that phrase would later explain,[22] human beings have internal regulation mechanisms that control body temperature, breathing, blood pressure, heart rate, chewing, swallowing, sleeping, and waking. They also have highly developed brains, which are uniquely human. The brain controls one's interaction with the outside world, including the capacity to talk, see, feel, sing, and think. Karen Ann Quinlan was a young woman with the capacity to maintain survival functions—the regulation mechanisms—but she no longer had a functioning mind that was capable of receiving or projecting information. Was hers a life worthy of living, a life worth prolonging?

After much anguish, prayer, and consultation, her parents decided that Karen would say, no. Karen's doctors disagreed. She was not dead by any acceptable criteria, and as doctors they had the professional, legal, and moral responsibility to do whatever they could to maintain her life—including the use of a respirator to assist her breathing. Several months later, Joseph and Julia Quinlan went to court to ask that their daughter's respirator be removed. The trial court denied their request, so Joseph and Julia appealed to the Supreme Court of New Jersey.

The New Jersey High Court listened carefully, weighing competing values and interests. Most importantly, Quinlan was alive—there was no disagreement about this point. There was also no disagreement that her life was of very limited quality. The Court summarized, "As nearly as may be determined, considering the guarded area of remote uncertainties characteristic of most medical science predictions, she can *never* be restored to cognitive or sapient life." There was no evidence of parental neglect. On the contrary, the Court found that there was "a high degree of familial love which pervaded the home of Joseph Quinlan and reached out fully to embrace Karen."

With the facts of the case in hand, and the character and motives of the parents assessed, New Jersey's Supreme Court turned to constitutional and legal issues. Of primary concern was the recently established right to privacy. In the cases leading up to and concluding with *Roe v. Wade* in 1973, this right was always balanced with compelling state interests. In the case of Karen Ann Quinlan, the Court found, there were none.

In a unanimous opinion, the seven judges had

> no hesitancy in deciding . . . that no external compelling interest of the State could compel Karen to endure the unendurable, only to vegetate a few measurable months with no realistic possibility of returning to any semblance of cognitive or sapient life.

It was no different than a similar choice that might be made by "a competent patient terminally ill, riddled by cancer and suffering great pain; such a patient would not be resuscitated or put on a respirator . . . and *a fortiori* would not be kept *against his will* on a respirator."

Although the court's conclusions were clear and unanimously grounded in the facts of the case and the relevant constitutional issues, the justices were also aware that problems remained. Of particular concern were the implications of rapidly evolving medical technology and treatment. What was ordinary? What was extraordinary? What implications did this ambiguity have for the clarity of professional, legal, and moral standards that governed the decisions physicians had to make? What was the resulting risk of malpractice litigation or criminal prosecution? In this arena, the Court noted, there was a "paucity of pre-existing legislative and judicial guidance as to the rights and liabilities" of those involved.

The judges aimed to clarify. They stated and then restated their findings, specifying what they had decided. Their goal was to shield any participant from civil or criminal liability, including charges of homicide, suicide, or assisted suicide, should the decision be made to take Quinlan off the respirator. In a later interview, Julia Quinlan recalled returning home after the decision had been made; that night, she and her husband had very little to say to one another. "It was a quiet evening. What do you say to one another when you know you are going to lose someone you love?" [23]

As the weeks went by, both Julia and Joe noticed that their relationship with the doctors was deteriorating. They felt shunned as they walked the hospital hallways. After one particularly unpleasant meeting, hospital officials even refused to comply with and carry out the Court's decision. Ultimately, however, on May 17, 1976, they were forced to begin weaning Quinlan off the respirator. The process took five days. When the process was complete on May 22, Julia recalled,

> Karen appeared tired but peaceful. She no longer had to struggle . . . I cannot put into words what a stressful week that was. We had no indication of how she would respond to the process. She could have died. . . . We had no idea how long she would survive.

In fact, their daughter would live for another nine years and twenty days. Around 5:30 on the evening of June 11, 1985, Joe and Julia, along with their priest, Fr. Tom Trapasso, were visiting Karen in her room. They had ordered a pizza for dinner, and once the pizza arrived, Joe and Fr. Trapasso went to get it. Julia decided to stay. "When I was alone with my daughter, I held her twisted hands in mine and prayed the Memorare." Julia sensed that death was near. She called Joe and Tom back into the room. "As we stood around her bed I continued to hold her hands, while Joe wiped her forehead. Suddenly, she was gone."[24]

The compelling faith, love, and sadness, as well as the profound parental connection, so vividly present in this final moment of life, were hardly evidence of an emergent culture of death. Valuing life, and letting life go, are not exclusive. In combination they can be profoundly life affirming. To liken the anguished decisions and experiences of the Quinlans to the practices of the Nazis in World War II is a mistake. Clearer distinctions needed to be made, and they were coming soon.

For many years, physicians had routinely allowed patients to die, sometimes even playing an assisting role. These practices had evolved as doctors grew frustrated with how little they could do to ease the suffering of a prolonged life. By the mid-twentieth century doctors and their patients had access to new effective drugs and life-prolonging technologies that presented new, sometimes troubling, and frequently costly decisions. Guidance from the social, ethical, and legal climate lagged behind. In 1967, Dr. Walter Sackett, an experienced family practitioner, ran for office in his home state of Florida. At the age of 60, he was elected as a state representative. Chief among his aims was to bring about legal acceptance of what he knew to be widespread practices, including his own.

## Prolonged Death and the Public Good

Rep. Walter Sackett knew that a range of medical procedures, drugs, and technologies were keeping many patients alive when they didn't want to be. To Sackett, prolonging many of these lives made very little sense. It had resulted in what he called "the prolonged death syndrome."[25] As he saw it, advancing medical technology presented doctors with an "awesome choice: to make the process of dying mercifully brief or to drag it out at a high cost in discomfort and—I must add even if it does sound crass—in dollars." These were difficult choices that were suffused with uncertainty. It was important, he emphasized, "to make the wishes of patients or of those close to them paramount in determining that choice."

During his first term, Rep. Sackett impulsively entered his legislation as a state constitutional amendment. Many of his colleagues initially agreed with him, but after about an hour of discussion, support flagged. Disagreements emerged during an "enthusiastic debate" as reaction turned to shock from some aspects of what Rep. Sackett was proposing. In the end, the proposed amendment was defeated. Afterward, Sackett recalled, several dozen of his colleagues "came and knelt by my desk, or encountered me in the hallways, and urged me to return this bill in the next session." He did, and the second attempt also failed.

Sackett saw a clear application of his proposal to Florida's significant elderly population, many of whom were hopelessly ill and doomed to the life of a vegetable. He also saw applications for "severely retarded" people in that same situation. The State of Florida, Sackett noted, was caring for some 1,500 individuals "who will never go beyond the diaper stage and whom some would have difficulty in recognizing as human beings." They "can live until an age of between 50 and 60." This meant that the "care of these retarded can reach the sum of some 4 to 6 billion dollars." As an example, Sackett referred to "a Negro boy 25 years of age, staring up in the corner of the room, completely drawn up in a musculature contracture." To Rep. Sackett, prudence called for a remedy.

Advocates for the elderly supported the legislation, but Sackett's inclusion of the mentally handicapped met with strong opposition. In his framing rhetoric, echoes of Germany's treatment of "useless eaters" were too obvious to miss. He was told "to play down this aspect of the situation because everybody has a tremendous feeling for these [retarded] individuals." There was reluctance "to do anything that would interfere with their claim to existence." Undaunted by two successive failures, and attentive to the criticism, Sackett tempered his euthanasia-for-the-greater-good argument and concentrated instead on individual rights of the elderly to choose to die, introducing a revised bill in 1970.

Once again, his efforts failed—but they had not been in vain. His proposed legislation generated widespread national publicity. Sackett made appearances on syndicated daytime and night-time talk shows, as well as the popular news program *60 Minutes*.[26] The public's attention was beginning to turn to these matters.

By the mid-1970s, the competing points of view had been hashed out time and again, and advocates had sharpened their case with a clearer articulation of arguments. The right to privacy and autonomy of choice, newly solidified in the context of abortion, built a foundation for the right-to-die movement. Living wills were catching on among the general population. Euthanasia as a means to ration health care in support of the public good, however, was quite another matter. Very little, if any, serious support could be found.

## The Right-to-Die Movement Gains Momentum

And so the tide shifted toward replacing euthanasia, with its troubling links to Nazi "mercy killing" and genocide, with a framework that argued for the right to choose to die with dignity. In such a framework, abuses might occur but the decisions would remain in the hands of those most directly affected. By the early 1970s, "right-to-die" was generally accepted as the debate-framing phrase.[27] Members of the Euthanasia Society of America (ESA), which had been founded in 1938, were quick to respond. In 1974, the year following *Roe*, the ESA changed its name to become the Society for the Right to Die (SRD).

For more than a decade, the ESA had been a small, élite, and frequently splintered operation with a status approximating a pariah. Intellectuals from the membership sparred in professional journals and book-length treatises, but the appeal of their message remained narrow and, for many, off-putting.[28] Tainted by the lingering connotations of the term "euthanasia," the ESA was even having trouble buying advertising space to spread its message and thus increase membership and revenue.[29] By changing its name and reframing its message as a basic right to choose, the association aimed to join civil rights forces and become part of "an awesomely large revolution," and perhaps "ride the crest of a 'great wave' of youthful protest sweeping the nation."[30]

There was reason for this optimism: the rapidly expanding demand for living wills. In 1967, human rights attorney Luis Kutner gave a presentation at an ESA gathering. He was speaking from personal experience. Years earlier, Kutner had watched a friend die a slow, painful death from injuries suffered during a violent robbery. This experience prompted Kutner to suggest that people draft and sign a document he referred to variously as a "declaration determining the termination of life," "body trust," "declaration of bodily autonomy," and "living will." Whatever the label, the document's aim was to allow people to specify clearly their wishes regarding when life-sustaining medicine should be refused and life-support systems shut off. Kutner was quoted as saying,

> People do not want to accept the notion of death being final, and doctors, for differing reasons, have become obsessed with denying it. But where there is the possibility of continuing a life without value, when heroic measures will keep someone alive without any hope of restoring that life, it is barbaric, cruel, and costly to do so.[31]

In 1969—two years after his presentation to the ESA, and some seven years prior to when Karen Ann Quinlan's case was heard in New Jersey's courts—Kutner published his thoughts in a law journal article.[32] Within a few months of that publication, the Euthanasia Educational Fund (EEF), the educational arm of the ESA, drew up a template for a living will and printed 5,000 copies. The document began, "If the time comes when I can no longer take part in decisions for my own future, let this statement stand as the testament of my wishes." In the span of a few months, all 5,000 copies had been distributed.

Word spread, and demand grew. By the end of 1970, the EEF reported that it had distributed some 60,000 copies of the document. By the end of 1973, this number had quadrupled, as more than a quarter of a million living wills were in circulation. Living will articles appeared frequently in the public media. Perhaps the most significant mention in terms of boosting the profile of the ESA and expanding its membership was the publication of a letter from a reader with the pseudonym "Concerned" in a popular advice column, "Dear Abby," on April 1, 1973. "Concerned" had been moved to write because "they are trying to pass a law making it legal to let people die just by discontinuing treatment. . . . The thought of this is frightening. WHO will decide who is old enough and sick enough?"

"Dear Abby" used the increasingly contested term *euthanasia* in her response: "'Euthanasia' literally means 'the good death,' and I am all for it." She anchored her reasoning by quoting from the EEF's living will. In subsequent columns, readers were told how to secure a copy from the EEF and were also encouraged to support the cause by donating to the group (or at least sending a check to cover the costs of mailing). EEF records reveal that the "Dear Abby" column created a crisis of sorts. A decade earlier, the ESA's paid membership numbered just over 300. Largely as a result of the "Dear Abby" column, staff members suddenly found themselves sorting through thousands of letters, extracting money, and responding to the most urgent pleas. Money was pouring in so fast that staff members were making deposits several times a day.

For the first time the ESA was on sound financial footing, and membership swelled exponentially. What in the early 1960s was a small, élite, and narrowly drawn group with a few hundred members and an annual budget of about US$12,000 grew into an organization with some 70,000 members and a budget of more than US$400,000 by the mid-1970s. By 1978, an estimated three million living wills had been distributed.[33] "Dear Abby" had handed a great gift to activists seeking the right to determine when life had lost meaning, when suffering became unbearable, and when life was otherwise not worth living.

## Public Opinion and Legislative Action

Public opinion polls reflected this evolving moral landscape. In 1950, before the full effects of the biological revolution were yet known, the Gallup organization polled a set of respondents with the following question: "When a person has a disease that cannot be cured, do you think doctors should be allowed by law to end the patient's life by some painless means if the patient and his family request it?" Slightly over one-third (36 percent) of respondents agreed with the statement. In July 1973, Gallup pollsters asked the same question, and this time a majority

(53 percent) agreed. In 1977, the year following *Quinlan,* the National Opinion Research Center (NORC) released a poll again asking the same question. At that point in time, the percentage of those who agreed had risen to 62 percent. Over a period of twenty-five years, the proportion of supporters to those opposed had reversed.[34] As so often happens in receptive political climates, crystallizing events precipitate action. Joe and Julia Quinlan's widely publicized struggle to secure their daughter's right to die was just such an event, helping to precipitate legislative efforts in California in the early 1970s.

The author of the California legislation, freshman Sen. Barry Keene, like many reformers before him, drew motivation from personal experience. Both his neighbor's wife and then his own mother-in-law were subjected to unwanted life-prolonging treatments. When Keene, an attorney, was called on to provide legal assistance in his mother-in-law's case, he found that he had little to work with, despite the fact that she had signed a medical directive to limit treatment.

Keene's initial legislative efforts in 1974 were defeated, largely owing to opposition from three influential organizations: the California Pro-Life Council (CPLC), an arm of the National Right to Life Committee; the American Medical Association (AMA); and the California Catholic Conference. The CPLC was most adamantly against the law, drawing now-familiar comparisons to Nazi practices and warning of the slippery slope that led to the further degradation of life.

Keene sensed that the AMA had not understood the intent and specifics of his initial proposal, and he made plans to create a more thorough explanation and resubmit it for review. The California Medical Association (CMA) understood what he was attempting to accomplish and was actively advocating laws that would limit its personal legal liabilities. Keene was confident that such clarifications and protections could be crafted. Fortunately for Keene and his supporters, opposition from the Catholic Church had been softened by a fifteen-year-old declaration from Pope Pius XII that also gave him something to work with.[35]

Keene was aware that polling data indicated public support. This support was strengthened when the Quinlan case achieved widespread public exposure just as final negotiations regarding his revised bill's language were being worked out. The eventual compromises yielded a bill that was more restrictive than Sen. Keene had hoped for, but the final vote was decisive. When then-governor Jerry Brown signed the California Natural Death Act (NDA) into law in 1976, it became the first piece of legislation acknowledging that "modern medical technology has made possible artificial prolongation of human life beyond natural limits." It further established that:

> Adult persons have the fundamental right to control the decision relating to the rendering of their own medical care, including the decision to have life-sustaining procedures withheld or withdrawn in instances of a terminal condition.

While the California Natural Death Act marked an important turning point, its scope was limited. For example, it:

- contained exclusions and special provisions for certain people, including pregnant women and nursing home patients;
- only applied to situations where no cure was possible and death was imminent;
- was limited in application to those who were or at one time had been competent to make decisions.

Still, it was an important turning point. Seven related laws were enacted, mainly by neighboring states, in the following year. By 1990, this number had grown to forty-two. Most of these subsequent statutes were less restrictive than California's pioneering effort.

The path was further cleared in 1982 when the AMA endorsed, for the first time, the position that it was ethical for physicians to withdraw life support from hopelessly ill patients. Working in tandem with the AMA, a presidential commission initially convened in 1980 to develop a uniform definition of death became troubled by the Quinlan case and others like it. The Commission turned its attention to appropriate treatment of persons who are dying but not dead. The Commission's resulting set of recommendations, *Deciding to Forgo Life-Sustaining Treatment*, was released in March 1983. During this same period, 54 state court decisions were handed down that clarified a range of remaining issues defining the boundaries of protected life, the significance of senseless suffering, and patient autonomy regarding the right to die.

## Alleviating Suffering and Protecting Life: Who Decides?

The *Quinlan* decision, the wide dissemination of living wills, California's Natural Death Act, and laws that followed all assumed that the patients in question were at one point capable of making rational decisions; but who should decide if the capacity for rational decision-making was absent? In March 1976, related issues began winding their way through the courts of Massachusetts in the case of a severely retarded 67-year-old man named Joseph Saikewicz.

Since 1923, Saikewicz had lived in state institutions. Though severely limited mentally, he was not in a vegetative state. As described by the court, he was "physically strong and well built, nutritionally nourished, and ambulatory." Although his awareness and intellect were minimal, he had the ability to interact with those around him and to experience joy and discomfort. He did not, however, have the ability to communicate verbally. Instead, he communicated with grunts and gestures and had difficulty responding intelligibly to inquiries, such as to whether he was experiencing pain.

Saikewicz had been diagnosed with leukemia. If left untreated, the best prognosis was that he would live for perhaps several weeks or months and would die with relatively little pain. Treatment with chemotherapy would extend his life by perhaps a year and possibly longer, but would have many uncomfortable side-effects that would be difficult to explain to him and hard for him to understand. While most comprehending persons might choose to undergo this life-prolonging treatment, Saikewicz was different. He was not capable of granting informed consent or refusing treatment with full understanding of the implications.

Time was clearly a factor, as any delay diminished the likelihood of the chemotherapy's success. Family members were found, but they preferred not to become involved in the decision. A guardian was appointed to act in Saikewicz's best interests; the guardian recommended that he forgo the treatment. Those who saw value in protecting and prolonging Saikewicz's life went to court to contest the guardian's recommendation. Less than a month after the initial diagnosis, the judge in the case agreed with the guardian. The judge's decision was immediately appealed to Massachusetts' highest court. Responding to the now-urgent issues, the court affirmed the trial judge's decision and promised a detailed decision in the months ahead. On September 4, 1976, before that decision could be released, Joseph Saikewicz died—in relatively little pain—of pneumonia, a complication of his condition.

Was withholding Saikewicz's treatment an act of compassion to minimize his suffering, or an instance where the life of a man with severely diminished mental capacity was deemed less worthy of protecting and prolonging? How was this any different from the practices of Nazi doctors who decided that those less worthy should be allowed, or even assisted, to die? The Massachusetts court aimed to clarify in a detailed decision released in November 1977, some 14 months after Saikewicz died.[36]

Their grounding assumption was clearly stated. "The chance of a longer life carries the same weight for Saikewicz as for any other person, the value of life under the law having no relation to intelligence or social position." The difference, the court continued, came from the patient's inability to understand what was happening to him and the absence of hope, which would otherwise allow Saikewicz to understand treatment and tolerate suffering. Saikewicz's guardian had given voice to this "most troubling aspect" of the case in his trial testimony with this statement:

> If he is treated with toxic drugs he will be involuntarily immersed in a state of painful suffering, the reason for which he will never understand. . . . Patients who request treatment know the risks involved and can appreciate the painful side effects when they arrive. They know the reason for the pain and their hope makes it tolerable.

The appropriate question, the guardian continued, was not what would most persons do, but:

> whether a majority of people would choose chemotherapy if they were told merely that something outside of their previous experience was going to be done to them, that this something would cause them pain and discomfort, that they would be removed to strange surroundings and possibly restrained for extended periods of time, and that the advantages of this course of action were measured by concepts of time and mortality beyond their ability to comprehend.

Advocates for the disabled interpreted this perspective as an assertion that Saikewicz's life, even if it could be saved, would not be worth the effort expended.

The Massachusetts court was quick to firmly reject this conclusion. Rather than demeaning the value of the life of one who is mentally retarded, the Appeals Court asserted, "the decision to withhold treatment from Saikewicz was based on a regard for his actual interests and preferences and the facts supported this decision."

An uneasy balance was being achieved between intolerable suffering and the protective boundaries of life. In the years ahead, many related cases would follow.[37] One involved a New Jersey man who, like Saikewicz, was profoundly retarded and had spent all but the earliest years of his life in a state institution, the Newark Development Center. His widowed mother lived close by and visited him almost daily.

John Storar was 50, but he had an estimated mental age of 18 months. After blood was found in her son's urine, Storar's mother reluctantly consented to a series of tests. When the tests came back indicating cancer of the bladder, she agreed to a six-week regime of radiation treatment beginning in August, 1979.

The radiation treatment sent Storar's cancer into remission, but it reappeared a few months later, in March, 1980. This time, attempts to cauterize blood vessels to stop the associated bleeding were unsuccessful and his physicians concluded that the patient would die from the disease. By May of the same year, Storar needed blood transfusions to offset the bleeding. His mother did not initially consent to the transfusions, but a day later she withdrew her objection. For several weeks, Storar received the transfusions; they were clearly distressing to him, and he was given sedatives. After receiving the transfusions, however, Storar's energy picked up, and he was able to feed himself, shower, walk, run, and, on occasion engage in mischievous activities "such as stealing cigarette butts and attempting to eat them."[38] The transfusion treatments continued until June 19, when his mother decided to stop them.

The director of the center sought a court authorization to continue the transfusions to save his patient's life, but Storar's mother filed contending petitions. In the interim, the court ordered that the transfusions continue. At a subsequent hearing, it was noted that the cancer had spread to Storar's lungs and perhaps other organs. With the transfusions, his life would last for perhaps three to six months. Without them, he would die within weeks. Neither his mother, nor anyone else, was able to determine Storar's true wishes, but it was clear that he disliked the treatments and did his best to avoid them. Storar's mother wanted her son to be comfortable and for his suffering to end. After hearing arguments, the court agreed: Storar's mother was the best qualified person to make the decision, and the court denied the center's request to continue.

This would have ended the story, had the decision not been appealed and eventually heard by the Supreme Court of New York, where it was finally decided on December 15, 1981. The Court wrote, "Mentally John Storar was an infant"; this was "the only realistic way to assess his rights." Clearly, there were compelling state interests to protect the life of a child.

The need for a substituted judgment for John Storar was clear, and it was also clear that his best interests should guide this judgment. Unlike Karen Ann Quinlan, John Storar was not in a vegetative state. He was dying, but he had not lost all humanizing qualities. With transfusions, his life could continue—albeit for a short time—as it had before. Those last moments of life, the Court held, were worth protecting. We should not, the Court wrote, "allow an incompetent patient to bleed to death because someone, even someone as close as a parent or sibling, feels that this is best for one with an incurable disease." In this manner, it was decided that blood transfusions should have continued. The problem was that Storar had already died.

Those giving greatest weight to the protection of life and the worthiness of severely mentally retarded people praised the decision. Those who wanted decisions about these uncertain matters to be made by the loved ones most deeply affected considered the decision to be an unwarranted instance of governmental intrusion. The relief of suffering, the assessment of a life worth living, and the sanctity of life remained in tension.

## The Supreme Court Weighs In

Fifteen years after *Quinlan* and a host of frequently contradictory state court decisions, including those of Storar and Saikewicz, a related case made a seven-year journey to the U.S. Supreme Court. It involved a young woman, Nancy Cruzan, who had been rendered vegetative from severe injuries sustained in a Jasper County, Missouri, automobile accident in early January, 1983.

Three years after her injury, Cruzan's parents asked the hospital to terminate treatment and allow their daughter to die in peace. Cruzan's doctors, based on their understanding of a state law requiring "clear and convincing evidence" of the patient's wishes before withdrawing treatment, refused her parents' request. There was no living will or other formal declaratory document, but Cruzan's words lived on through the voices of others. Cruzan's co-worker, housemate, and sister all testified that Cruzan had stated that she would not wish to continue her life if she were sick or injured unless she could live at least "halfway normally." There was no doubt in their minds "that if we could call her up and ask, 'Nancy, what do you want?' She would say, 'Look, I realize it's hard on everyone else, but let me go. I've got other things to do, and I've got other places to go—so turn me loose.'"[39]

During the trial, Cruzan's father was asked, "Could you tell the court why you feel it is in Nancy's best interest that the feeding tube be discontinued?" He responded, "Primarily it's because we believe it is what Nancy's wish would be."

Cruzan's sister, Chris, and her mother were asked similar questions. Chris was unable to give specific, detailed expressions of what Nancy would have wished, but in an emotional testimony she responded, "Nancy would want to live where she could live to the fullest. Where she lives to the fullest is within us. It is not within that body that's being maintained at Mt. Vernon."

On July 27, 1988, the trial court found that the testimony constituted enough evidence to grant the Cruzans' request. After reading the decision to his family, Cruzan's father remarked, "So, if that's winning, we won."

The trial court's findings were immediately appealed to the State Supreme Court. In a split vote, the state appellate justices disagreed with the trial court. They found instead that the evidence of Cruzan's wishes was not clear and convincing, as demanded by Missouri law. They reversed the trial court decision. This reversal was, in turn, appealed to the U.S. Supreme Court.

In December 1989, the U.S. Supreme Court agreed to hear its first right-to-die case. On June 25, 1990, some seven and a half years after Cruzan's accident, *Cruzan v. Director, Missouri Department of Health*[40] was decided. The five-to-four decision, along with the appeals process leading up to it, was contentious, mirroring the well-developed national right-to-die debate. Chief Justice William Rehnquist wrote the Court's decision, which highlighted 54 reported decisions relevant to the case.[41] By then, it was well established that competent individuals had the right to refuse medical treatment. It was equally clear that there was a compelling state interest in protecting the sanctity of life. Cruzan's case was complicated by the fact that her wishes were unclear. The Missouri statute required "clear and convincing evidence" of a patient's wishes when determining the acceptability of a substituted judgment. The State Appellate Court found that the available evidence did not meet this standard. Rehnquist and four of his colleagues on the Court found no reason to question this finding.

Although the decision was not what the Cruzans had hoped for, it did create a small but important opening. In the main opinion, Rehnquist had written that a constitutional right existed for competent people to refuse medical treatment— the first time the Supreme Court had reached this conclusion. In a concurring opinion, Justice Sandra Day O'Connor noted that artificial feeding qualified as medical treatment—significant because it meant that it could be withdrawn if the patient's wishes were known. Embedded in the legal language of the opinion were eight important words that offered the Cruzans a glimmer of hope: "discovery of new evidence regarding the patient's intent." If new evidence of Cruzan's wishes surfaced that was clear and convincing, her parents' request would be honored.

The Cruzans' lawyer, Bill Colby, knew from previous conversations that additional evidence not presented at the original trial did in fact exist. He called Nancy Cruzan's father and read the opinion's language to him. Over the next few months, family and friends assembled additional evidence that Cruzan had expressed a wish to terminate treatment if her situation became hopeless. The evidence was entered in a new trial, and this time it was deemed to be clear and convincing. The medical treatment that had been keeping Cruzan alive could be discontinued. There were no further appeals.

Joe and Joyce Cruzan were both saddened and relieved. It had been a long and difficult journey, but Joe Cruzan could now follow through on an early commitment he had made to his daughter to "allow her to die with some dignity." In a statement, he wrote:

Because of Nancy, I suspect hundreds of thousands of people can rest free, knowing that when death beckons they can meet it face to face with dignity, free from the fear of unwanted medical treatment, unwanted and useless medical treatment. I think this is quite an accomplishment for a 25-year old kid and I'm damned proud of her. . . . Now we walk with her to the door of death so that she may at last pass through and be free.[42]

On December 15, 1990, the tube that provided Nancy Cruzan with nutrition was removed. She died eleven days later.

## The Gift of Death

During the final days of Nancy's life, protesters gathered outside the hospital. One regretted his inability to do anything: "If I could get up there . . . I would put the tube back in her myself."[43] Another voiced fear of the broader dehumanizing implications: "'Vegetable' is going to be just like 'fetus' was. That's the word they're going to use. It's not fully human and you can kill it. A vegetable isn't human." A third agreed, pointing to the emergent culture of death: "America has lost all sense of value for human life at all, you know, with abortion and now with this thing with Nancy."

At his daughter's burial, on December 28, 1990, Joe Cruzan turned the protesters' words back upon them:

> Today, as the protestor's sign says, we gave Nancy the gift of death. An unconditional gift of love that sets her free from this twisted body that no longer serves her. A gift I know she will treasure above all others, the gift of freedom. So run free Nan, we will catch up later. [44]

Nancy Cruzan's grave marker carries three dates:

> Born: July 20, 1957
> Departed: January 11, 1983
> At Peace: December 26, 1990

It had taken a decade and a half to reach this point. California's Natural Death Act was passed less than a year after Karen Ann Quinlan's case was decided. It led the way for the passage of related legislation in forty-two states. The *Cruzan* decision looked back on fifty-four related court cases.[45] Taken together, the boundaries of protected life and tolerable suffering, as well as the right to choose to leave life peacefully were clarified. The protection and support of life could, and frequently did, conflict with the alleviation of suffering. Tension-ridden choices were unavoidable. Justifications for a right to die were grounded in conclusions that some lives, and some moments in life, are more worthy of protection, support, and prolonging than others.

Following this defining *Quinlan*-to-*Cruzan* period, the core issue for the right-to-die movement became whether people who had the right to end their suffering or to leave life peacefully also had a right to receive assistance in doing so, even if they did not have an immediately terminal condition. On this point, substantial social, legal, medical, and religious disagreement remained.

The battle lines were drawn. One side was firmly committed to keeping uncertain, irrevocable, and life-ending decisions in the hands of those who were most intimately involved. They believed that in circumstances of intense suffering and terminal illness, people should have the right to choose their moment of death—and if they needed help, that help should be available to them. Assisted dying, not assisted suicide, should be the goal. On the other side were those who feared a slippery slope of diminished respect for life. They saw assisted dying as a threat to the sanctity of life. They believed that suffering can and should be endured. For many, God or vaguely defined natural forces should determine the moment of death.

## Uncertainty, a Duty to Die, and Rationed Health Care

There is substantial evidence that life-and-death decisions are governed in part by religious or spiritual beliefs,[46] but there are also other concerns. Health care is costly, and access is frequently limited. How should medical resources be distributed? How much care is too much? Is there a point at which the death of one might benefit the lives of others?

In 1958, a 27-year-old Minnesota Law School professor, Yale Kamisar, wrote of his "non-religious views"[47] and concerns for gravely ill persons. He took issue with liberalized euthanasia policies that had been developed in a recently published and much-discussed book, *The Sanctity of Life and the Criminal Law*, written by Glanville Williams, a jurist from the University of Cambridge.[48]

Surely, Kamisar wrote, the "freedom to choose a merciful death" was an important right. However, people who were in the throes of suffering and facing a painful road to the end of life were not in a good position to make life-ending decisions.[49] It would be foolish to assume otherwise. Even assuming that those who were considering suicide were fixed in resolve and rational in thought, Kamisar foresaw problems. He wondered: was this really the kind of choice

> that we want to offer a gravely ill person? Will we not sweep up in the process some who are not really tired of life, but think others are tired of them; some who do not really want to die, but who feel they should not live on, because to do so . . . would be a selfish or a cowardly act?
>
> Will not some feel an obligation to have themselves "eliminated" in order that funds allocated for their terminal care might be better used by their families or, financial worries aside, in order to relieve their families of the emotional strain involved?[50]

Kamisar's fears seemed to be confirmed in a speech given almost three decades later, on March 27, 1984. Then Colorado Governor Richard Lamm, a health care activist, was speaking to elderly constituents gathered in Denver to observe Senior Citizen Day. Lamm was concerned about the escalating costs of health care associated with the life-prolonging capabilities of new drugs, medical technology, and procedures. It was time, Lamm suggested, to consider setting limits. "We've got a duty to die and get out of the way with all of our machines and artificial hearts and everything else like that and let the other society, our kids, build a reasonable life."

The Governor's words were picked up in the press and created an immediate stir. Most reports and editorials focused on the phrase, "duty to die and get out of the way." Despite Lamm's immediate protests that his words had been mis-characterized and taken out of context, this phrase appeared repeatedly in subse-quent academic discussions, press accounts, and congressional hearings.[51] While a crassly stated duty-to-die message may not have been what Lamm intended to deliver, for many it was the message heard. Was this what patient autonomy had come to—a duty to die?

For Daniel Callahan, co-founder and director of the highly influential Hastings Center, a bioethics think-tank, Lamm's message deserved careful thought and even advocacy. Callahan had worried about the same problem for many years. He outlined his thoughts in the 1987 book *Setting Limits: Medical Goals in an Aging Society*. To Callahan, "the idea that the humane medical care and cure for the elderly sought in the 1960s and 1970s could turn out to be the occasion of a new social threat" might be hard to accept. Nevertheless, he was convinced that it was true, regardless of how "appalling and distasteful the idea may be."[52]

Though Callahan's argument was complex, he presented clear evidence that already limited resources were becoming increasingly strained. This trend was likely to continue into the foreseeable future. Just as was the case with the early allocation of dialysis machines,[53] priorities would have to be set, and life-protecting choices would have to be made. Unlike access to dialysis, however, building more machines or refining procedures could not solve the problem—we could not build our way out of this one. Refinement could only come via a new conception of what the waning years of life really meant.

Callahan clarified his message: He was not arguing that lives of the elderly were less valuable or less worthy of protection than those of the young. Nor was he an advocate for "rational" suicide or euthanasia then being proposed by such organizations as the Hemlock Society. He recognized that "a sanctioning of mercy killing and assisted suicide for the elderly would serve as a threatening symbol of devaluation of old age." Instead, Callahan asserted that life was finite and that each generation should give way to the next. Letting life go, in recognition of life's importance, was profoundly different than destroying life.

Near the end of *Setting Limits,* Callahan wrote in italics for emphasis:

*Cessation of life-extending treatment for the aged as a matter of social policy can be morally acceptable only within a context that accords meaning and significance to the lives of the individual aged and recognizes the positive virtues of the passing of the generations.*

At some point, given the high cost of medical treatments, Callahan believed that the dying simply needed to step out of the way and let nature take its course. Callahan wrote, "As part of my approach to health care for the aged, they would cease being eligible for government-supported life extension beyond a certain age."[54] Such a shift in thinking would take time. It was not an idea to be accepted casually or immediately without careful thought being given to its practical implications.[55]

After *Setting Limits* was published, the University of Illinois law school held a conference in October, 1989 to address Callahan's ideas.[56] One critic at the Illinois gathering warned, "Consider, then, the values that will flow from a societal decision that a compelling state interest in cutting costs justifies cutting off lives. That's not a slippery slope. That's an abyss."[57] Callahan's intended message was that restricting access by the elderly to finite medical resources was a move to protect the lives of others. He was not advocating ending the lives of the elderly. No matter how the argument was dissected, thinking of the elderly as Callahan had suggested meant that after some specified point, lives become less worthy of support and protection.

Around the same time that critics were gathering at the University of Illinois law school, physician and intellectual Leon Kass, a respected colleague frequently cited by Callahan, wrote a journal article about the unintended consequences of setting limits on who should be supported by health care resources. To Kass, it was not just a matter of economics. More importantly, such a shift would influence the nature of the doctor–patient relationship:

> Physicians get tired of treating patients who are hard to cure, who resist their best efforts, who are on their way down—"gorks," "gomers," and "vegetables" are only some of the less than affectionate names . . . Won't it be tempting to think that death is the best treatment for the little old lady "dumped" again on the emergency room by the nearby nursing home?[58]

The implications of such thinking—for many, not-so-subtle dehumanization— were far too clear to miss. They were not restricted to the elderly who Richard Lamm and Daniel Callahan had in mind. Advocates for the disabled were all too familiar with where such utilitarian logic, however refined it might be, could lead.

### Lives Less Worthy of Living?

There were few more articulate spokespersons than Harriet McBryde Johnson, self-described as a disabled, liberal, and atheist Democrat. Johnson opened a legal practice in Charleston, South Carolina, around the same time Lamm had given his Denver speech and Helga Kuhse and Peter Singer's controversial book *Should the Baby Live?* had been published. The statement Singer had written in a frequently quoted section from his *Practical Ethics* particularly incensed her: "The killing of a defective infant is not morally equivalent to the killing of a person; very often it is not morally wrong at all." [59] For Harriet, this characterization of the disabled was as offensive as it was dehumanizing.

Johnson and Singer first met when she challenged his position in a discussion session that followed a lecture he gave at the College of Charleston. A short time later, she was invited to debate Singer at Princeton University. She subsequently published her witty account of the debate in a cover story for the *New York Times Magazine*[60] and later in a book entitled *Too Late to Die Young*:

> He insists he doesn't want to kill me. He simply thinks it would have been better, all things considered, to have given my parents the option of killing the baby I once was, and to let other parents kill similar babies as they come along, and thereby avoid the suffering that comes with lives like mine and

satisfy the reasonable preferences of parents for a different kind of child. It has nothing to do with me. I should not feel threatened.[61]

Johnson and disability activists who agreed with her aimed to protect the lives and rights of infants born with a range of birth defects, as well as the rights of adults who lived lives with variously acquired and variously perceived disabilities. Their concerns were long-standing. They had been moved to more aggressive action by the pernicious (in their view) implications of Singer's, Callahan's, and Lamm's utilitarian arguments.

These activists knew that life-threatening consequences were at stake for those who might be perceived as a drain on public resources. They were also familiar with the widely debated case of Elizabeth Bouvia, a young woman who in 1983 sought assistance to die after a lifelong struggle with arthritis, severe cerebral palsy, and quadriplegia. Bouvia did not have a terminal illness, but given the severity of her disabilities she had decided that her life was no longer worth living. Aware of a number of successful right-to-die cases, she wanted to compel the Californian hospital in which she was staying to give her pain-relieving medication to ease the pain of self-starvation. The hospital refused, arguing that it had a responsibility to keep her alive. The hospital would force-feed her if necessary.

With the help of an American Civil Liberties Union (ACLU) attorney, Richard Scott, Elizabeth Bouvia filed a lawsuit, posing the question: How far should physicians go in assisting a rational, non-terminally ill, disabled person to end her life if she perceived it to be filled with intolerable suffering? No case law existed where a non-terminally ill, competent person had asked a hospital to provide pain-relieving drugs while she starved to death.

In a memorandum outlining Bouvia's argument, Scott, who was a staunch right-to-die advocate closely associated with the Hemlock Society and also a physician, pointed to the "pain, humiliation, and difficulty"[62] Bouvia's disabilities caused. Given her "incurable affliction" and "pitiful existence," her suffering had made life "intolerable."[63] Bouvia wanted to die, and she should be given assistance to ease her pain while doing so.

Disability activists were caught in a bind. On the one hand, they were working hard to establish respect for the independence and autonomy of persons with disabilities. Those efforts would soon result in the Americans with Disabilities Act of 1990. Elizabeth Bouvia needed assistance to exercise her rights, so why should such assistance be denied to her? For disability activists there was one major reason: the phrases and expressed wishes Scott used in his arguments were disturbing red flags. Scott's argument depicted the disabled person as helpless and miserable, living a life less worthy of protection and support.

Bouvia's pleas for an assisted suicide soon drew strong opposition from the very people who she might otherwise have seen as allies, including Paul Longmore and Harlan Hahn, disability activists who had recently launched the Program in Disability and Society at the University of Southern California. Bouvia was in a hospital in Riverside, California, some 60 miles away, and this proximity allowed Longmore and Hahn to pay close attention as the case moved through the courts.

As someone who worked tirelessly to establish respect for the autonomy and independent judgment of disabled people, Longmore was concerned about how Bouvia's life was being portrayed, not only by her lawyer, but in the media as well.[64] Her life was presented in the typical, prejudiced fashion the disabled frequently encountered in popular culture and media. Longmore used Woody Allen's 1977 comedy *Annie Hall* as an example. In one scene, disabled people were lumped together with the terminally ill. A character remarked, "I feel that life is divided up into the horrible and the miserable. . . . The horrible would be like, I don't know, the terminal cases, you know, and blind people, cripples. I don't know how they get through life."

To Longmore, this comment represented a serious distortion—essentially, the argument that a person was better off dead than disabled. The media's documentation of Bouvia's experience, both directly and indirectly, Longmore wrote, "epitomizes all of the devaluation and discrimination inflicted on disabled people by society."

What most worried Longmore and other like-minded activists was exactly why Bouvia believed her life was filled with intolerable suffering. Was it because of her obvious and difficult disabilities, or other, more recent events in her life that had clearly affected her sense of loss and lack of support? Her marriage had recently failed. She had miscarried a child. Her brother had recently died. Her mother had been diagnosed with cancer. The graduate school of social work at San Diego State University refused to allow her to conduct fieldwork in any area except with disabled people, provoking her to quit school and give up her hopes of being a social worker. These life events, in addition to her disabilities, were certainly enough to induce depression and a sense of hopelessness, both among the strongest indicators of suicidal impulses.

Was Bouvia simply in an early stage of unresolved loss and grief? Was she one of those people so worrisome to Yale Kamisar, those who were "not really tired of life, but think others are tired of them?" If so, ample evidence existed to show that her perspective might change. Life was too important to let lack of support and transient emotions determine its end.

A court decision was announced on December 16, 1983.[65] The judge found that Bouvia's requests were based on her physical disabilities and not on the transient emotions associated with troubling life events. She was judged to be rational and sincere in her requests. However, the judge also found that she could expect to live for another fifteen to twenty years; thus, she was not simply refusing life-saving medical treatment. She was asking the hospital's doctors and staff to help end her life prematurely as she starved herself to death.

The doctors, nurses, and administrators at the hospital did not want to participate in Bouvia's suicide. Such actions put them at legal risk and directly opposed their professional ethics and commitment to protect and prolong life. Assisting their patient as she starved herself to death would have, the judge concluded, "a profound effect on the medical staff, nurses and administrators," as well as a "devastating effect on other patients within Riverside Hospital and other physically handicapped persons who are similarly situated in this nation."

In short, the judge found that Bouvia's right to privacy and respect for her autonomy should be balanced with the effect that terminating her life would have on other members of society—some of whom were directly involved. Bouvia's request was denied. The judge wrote, "Established ethics of the medical profession clearly outweigh and overcome her own rights to self-determination."

The judge's ruling, however, did not resolve the issue. Four months after the decision, a prominent bioethicist, George Annas, published a critical assessment. He worried over where the public-good argument led. Annas reminded the judge, the public, and his colleagues that "the right to bodily integrity and control of one's fate are superior to institutional considerations." He was sympathetic to Bouvia's plight but argued for compromise. "If we simply accept her decision," he mused, "it is argued, we devalue all severely handicapped persons. But surely there is a middle ground between 'simply accepting' her decision, and violently force-feeding her."[66]

Those who argued in support of the judge's ruling found themselves turning the practical ethics of Daniel Callahan's *Setting Limits* on its head. Prolonging life was the prime value. The public good demanded the continued use of medical resources, even when a person found her life to be unworthy of the struggle involved. For these proponents, respect for individual autonomy was *not* the most important public policy principle. "Considerations of autonomy," they argued, "must give way to the broader notion of the public good, which gives primacy to the respect for life."[67]

Bouvia did not give up. After changing hospitals and moving to Mexico for a time, she returned to California. In 1986, her continuing requests found their way to California's Court of Appeals.[68] The appellate court struggled, as the trial judge had before, to balance the competing values, to place the hazy boundaries of protected life and intolerable suffering, and to set priorities to resolve the associated dilemmas.

The priorities established and the boundaries drawn by the Court of Appeals' 1986 decision were quite different from those set by the trial judge in 1983. The appellate judges ruled that the trial judge had "mistakenly attached undue importance to the amount of time [15 to 20 years] possibly available to the petitioner." The ruling continued:

> Who shall say what the minimum amount of available life must be? Does it matter if it be 15 to 20 years, 15 to 20 months, or 15 to 20 days, if such life has been physically destroyed and its quality, dignity and purpose gone? As in all matters lines must be drawn at some point, somewhere, but that decision must ultimately belong to the one whose life is in issue.

This was not a medical decision to be made by Bouvia's physicians, nor was it to be resolved by lawyers or judges or hospital committees. As Bouvia was a competent adult, it was her decision alone.

Force-feeding a patient against her will was troubling enough. If force-fed, Bouvia would face a painful, difficult existence made endurable only by the constant administration of morphine. She would have to be cleaned, turned, and toileted by others for the next fifteen to twenty years. "Her mind and spirit may be free to take great flights," the Court's opinion continued, "but she herself is imprisoned and must lie physically helpless subject to the ignominy, embarrassment, humiliation, and dehumanizing aspects created by her helplessness."

In Bouvia's view, such a dehumanized existence diminished her life "to the point of hopelessness, uselessness, unenjoyability and frustration." She was "lying helplessly in bed, unable to care for herself." She considered her existence "meaningless," a life not worth living. The Court found that in such circumstances, it was not:

> the policy of this state that all and every life must be preserved against the will of the sufferer. It is incongruous, if not monstrous, for medical practitioners to assert their right to preserve a life that someone else must live, or, more accurately, endure, for 15 to 20 years.

Bouvia was entitled, the Court concluded, "to the immediate removal of the nasogastric tube that has been involuntarily inserted into her body." The Court further held that the hospital "may not deny her relief from pain and suffering merely because she has chosen to exercise her fundamental right to protect what little privacy remains to her."

It was a troubling case—difficult to decide and aggressively argued. Again, there were implications beyond Elizabeth Bouvia herself. In the concluding paragraph of a separate concurring opinion, one of the justices expressed his hope that these implications would not be missed:

> Whatever choice Elizabeth Bouvia may ultimately make, I can only hope that her courage, persistence and example will cause our society to deal realistically with the plight of those unfortunate individuals to whom death beckons as a welcome respite from suffering. If there is ever a time when we ought to be able to get the "government off our backs" it is when we face death—either by choice or otherwise.

The decision's strongly worded and sometimes emotional arguments, opinions, and conclusions would be met with equally strong and emotional criticism from those seeking to affirm the intrinsic importance of all life—even of the severely disabled. Many disability activists, including Paul Longmore, saw the Court's rationale as a victory for bigotry against the disabled.[69] Advocates for assisted suicide, Longmore wrote, engaged in "Orwellian newspeak." They:

> assume a nonexistent autonomy. They offer an illusory self-determination ... Their arguments for euthanasia, aid-in-dying, assisted suicide, and medical cost-containment, simply rationalize the ultimate act of oppression. Their efforts are an assault on the rights and lives of people who are sick, old, or disabled.[70]

Bouvia's attorney saw things differently. In his closing statement, he noted:

> We do believe that this world will be a poorer place without that tortured but resilient and cheerful lady with so much potential, with so much to offer others. But Elizabeth Bouvia has no duty to make that offer nor does she have the obligation to endure what to her is unendurable.

Whether one agreed or disagreed with the Court's ruling, boundaries had been drawn, dilemmas had been resolved, and the decision had been issued: Elizabeth Bouvia was free to choose to die. The hospital that housed her was bound to comply and to provide relief from any pain or suffering that might result from her choice. Perhaps in confirmation of the uncertainty and competing considerations inherent in these troubling decisions, once granted her right to decide her own fate, Elizabeth ultimately chose not to terminate her life.

## Uncertainty

The uncertainty that must have suffused Elizabeth Bouvia's troubling decisions also permeated the broader community. One historian has noted:

> As the 1980s dawned, a new chapter was opening in the history of the euthanasia movement in twentieth-century America. More Americans than ever believed in a right to die, but agreement about what the right to die actually meant was increasingly difficult to reach.[71]

Uncertainty at a moment of public receptiveness was clearly evident in the early efforts of Americans against Human Suffering (AAHS), a group launched immediately after California's Supreme Court rendered its decision supporting Bouvia's request. Its organizers had followed closely the lower court battles, as well as two other recent cases in California.[72]

Their efforts began in California with a campaign to place the Humane and Dignified Death Initiative on the ballot in November 1988.[73] The immediate task was to secure some 450,000 signatures. There was reason for optimism, as virtually all public opinion polls indicated that somewhere between 60 to 70 percent of Californians supported the measure, and ample time remained to get the signatures. Or so it seemed.

Several well-funded and high-profile disability activist groups worked closely with the AMA, the California Medical Association (CMA), and the Catholic Church to oppose the proposed legislation. By the petition's deadline, only 130,000 signatures had been gathered—less than one-third of those needed. Citizens who answered pollsters and signed the petition seemed to be struggling with the same competing isssues that had made the judges so uneasy.

Prompted in part by the ongoing debate in California, on January 8, 1988, the editors of the *Journal of the American Medical Association (JAMA)* decided to publish a brief, firsthand account by an unnamed young gynecology resident who worked in a large, private hospital. The article was entitled "It's Over, Debbie."[74]

The resident had been called in the middle of the night to assist a 20-year-old ovarian cancer patient, "Debbie," who was having trouble getting to sleep. The young resident recalled that when he walked into the room, a friend of Debbie's was holding her hand. The patient's eyes were hollow; it had been two days since she had eaten or slept, and her weight had dropped to only 80 pounds. Chemotherapy had been ineffective, and she was being given supportive care only.

The resident wrote, "It was a gallows scene, a cruel mockery of her youth and unfulfilled potential. Her only words to me were, 'Let's get this over with.'" Leaving the room, the resident recalled thinking, "The patient was tired and needed rest. I could not give her health, but I could give her rest."

He asked the nurse to draw 20 milligrams of morphine sulfate into a syringe— in his words, "enough to do the job." He took the syringe into the room "and told the two women [he] was going to give Debbie something that would let her rest and to say goodbye." Debbie laid her head on the pillow "with her eyes open, watching what was left of the world." Seconds after the injection, her "breathing slowed to a normal rate, her eyes closed, and her features softened as she seemed restful at last."

As Debbie's companion stroked the hair of her dying friend, "with clocklike certainty, within four minutes the breathing rate slowed even more, then became irregular, then ceased." Debbie's friend "stood erect and seemed relieved." The resident's account closed with a simple remark: "It's over, Debbie."

"It's Over, Debbie" created an immediate stir. Over the next few weeks, *JAMA* received some 150 letters running four to one against the actions taken by the resident and three to one against the editors' decision to publish the piece. The most scathing review came from four leaders of the bioethics movement. One would go on to publish a more detailed critique a year later.[75]

"So-called active euthanasia practiced by physicians seems to be an idea whose time has come," one of the critics commented. "But, in my view, it is a bad idea whose time must not come—not now, not ever."[76]

Another letter read:

Is it morally irresponsible to promulgate challenges to our most fundamental moral principles without editorial rebuke or comment, "for the sake of discussion"? Decent folk do not deliberately stir discussion of outrageous practices, like slavery, incest, or killing those in our care. . . . The very soul of medicine is on trial.[77]

*JAMA*'s editors acknowledged competing ethical considerations, but remained firm in their position. "*JAMA* is the right place for issues in American medicine to be debated, and there is much debate." The response continued:

These are perilous times for our profession. The Hemlock Society and others are in the courts and legislatures trying to legalize killing by physicians at patient request. . . . Now is not the time for promoting neutral discussion . . . now is the time for the medical profession to rally in defense of its fundamental moral principles, to repudiate any and all acts of direct and intentional killing by physicians and their agents.[78]

### A Suicide Machine and a Cookbook of Death

The account of Debbie's assisted death was dramatic, but for the most part, the primary readers of the journal were physicians. By contrast, the assisted suicide of Janet Adkins on June 4, 1990 permeated the media. A *Newsweek* report on Adkins' assisted suicide[79] began with the sentence, "Sometimes, when ethical debates have run on interminably it takes a shocking incident to sear the old questions back into the public consciousness."

Adkins, a 64-year-old Oregon resident, suffered from Alzheimer's disease. Adkins had read a *Newsweek* article and seen an episode of the *Donahue* talk show featuring a Detroit pathologist, Jack Kevorkian, and his "Mercytron" suicide machine. With the support of her husband, she decided to look into the possibility of consulting Kevorkian. Over a period of months, Kevorkian talked not only with Adkins and her husband, but also with Adkins' doctor. Adkins, her husband, and a friend eventually flew to Michigan to meet with Kevorkian, ask his advice, and seek his assistance. After several conversations, they decided to proceed.[80]

In a deluge of subsequent nationwide coverage, the public learned much more about Kevorkian and Adkins. A *Newsweek* article chronicled the actual assisted suicide:

> While her husband waited at a nearby hotel, they [Adkins and Kevorkian] drove to a suburban campsite in Kevorkian's rusty Volkswagen van. He inserted a needle in her arm and started saline flowing. She pressed a button on his death machine that first sent a sedative, then deadly potassium chloride racing to her heart.[81]

With this action, the article continued, "Janet Adkins reignited debate over the right to die with dignity, the ethics of assisting such deaths and the alarming rate of suicide among the elderly."

The list of critics of Kevorkian and his Mercytron machine continued to grow.[82] Even some of the staunchest advocates for physician-aided dying believed that the Michigan doctor had gone too far. Derek Humphry, the founder of the Hemlock Society, noted that the jolting nature of Adkins' death further underscored the need for more rational, humane measures—in particular, the measures which he and the Hemlock Society advocated. Adkins was a Hemlock Society member, but this was not what the group had in mind: Traveling 2,000 miles from home to die in the back of a camper van was not a death with dignity.

With Janet Adkins' death, the saga of Jack Kevorkian was just beginning. In 1993, he appeared on the cover of *Time* billed as "Dr. Death," and a growing stream of feature stories about him appeared in newspapers across the country as well as in international publications such as *The Economist*.[83] Even late-night talk shows weighed in on Kevorkian with some gallows humor. One of David Letterman's top ten promotional slogans for Kevorkian's suicide machine was, "Just try it once, that's all we ask." Estimates varied, but Kevorkian himself acknowledged that he had assisted in about twenty suicides by the end of 1993.

Some articles drew parallels between Kevorkian and Humphry's activities with the Hemlock Society. This made Humphry uncomfortable. In *Final Exit*, Humphry revealed that around the time efforts to pass right-to-die legislation in California were finally starting to jell, Kevorkian approached the Hemlock Society with the idea of opening a suicide clinic in southern California, arguing "that not only was this necessary for humanity but, if he was prosecuted for assisting suicides, as seemed likely, the resulting publicity would benefit the euthanasia cause."

Humphry saw such strategies as counter-productive, and he rejected Kevorkian's idea. Yet ambivalence remained. On the one hand, Humphry praised Kevorkian for "breaking the medical taboo on euthanasia," suggesting, in June, 1993, "one could quibble about things with Dr. Kevorkian, but basically he's along the same lines as me."[84] Two months later, he underscored the connection. "It's a pincer movement. He's [Kevorkian] coming at it through the courts and we in the right-to-die movement are coming through the legislatures."[85] Later, however, Humphry wrote that the Michigan pathologist's sudden appearance on the right-to-die scene "transformed the issue from polite debate and courteous informal assistance [Hemlock's way] to in-your-face, controversial death-on-request."[86]

Others found little distinction between Kevorkian's actions and the Hemlock Society's goals. Adkins' involvement with both only accentuated this connection. Kevorkian and his suicide machine drew the loudest, most widespread opposition, but Derek Humphry and his arguments in *Final Exit* did not escape criticism. This small how-to volume was characterized as being "evil with a smile" in the normally reserved *Hastings Center Report*.[87] If not outright evil, it was an "ill-advised cookbook of death" which failed to address, let alone resolve, the profound moral, ethical, and personal uncertainties surrounding the meaning of euthanasia and assisted suicide.[88]

Opponents used extreme accounts of suicide vans and heightened fears of increased suicide rates to underscore the problems of assisted suicide—what they viewed as a dangerous, slippery slope. Humphry and Kevorkian were seen "at once a spur for the death with dignity movement and a lightning rod for criticism of its potential excesses."[89] In July 1991, a year after Adkins' death, a *Wall Street Journal* feature article picked up in numerous newspapers across the country pointed to the heated debate stirred by Humphry's book.[90] In August, the *New York Times* noted that *Final Exit* had topped its best-seller list—a rare accomplishment for a book from a small, obscure publisher.[91]

The small volume included specific dos and don'ts, along with a table of lethal dosages of various drugs, and what many considered to be its signature suggestion—the plastic bag method. To ensure the procedures it outlined were successful, *Final Exit* recommended that a plastic bag be placed over the patient's head and secured with a rubber band. In response, strongly worded personal accounts, such as Wesley Smith's article "The Whispers of Strangers," charged Humphry and the Hemlock Society with complicity in the deaths of their friends.[92]

Many began to ask whether *Final Exit* was responsible for a noticeable rise in the suicide rate among adolescents, the disabled, and the elderly.

In 1992, the *Journal of the American Medical Association*, the *American Journal of Psychiatry*, and the *New England Journal of Medicine* each published commentaries that explored this question.[93] In follow-up, a systematic study of suicides in New York City was reported in the *New England Journal of Medicine* in November 1993.[94] Suicides involving asphyxiation by plastic bag increased by more than 300 percent (from eight to thirty-three) during the period investigated, but other methods were less frequently used. There seemed to be a substitution effect—suicide rates were not, in fact, increasing overall but the methods by which people were committing suicide had shifted.

While these findings may have been reassuring, continuing concerns and widespread publicity surrounded Kevorkian. Efforts succeeded in early February 1991 to have his death machine declared illegal. Undaunted, Kevorkian responded by devising a new instrument and procedure which circumvented the recently passed law.

Some eight months later, in October 1991, he assisted the deaths of Sherry Miller, 43, and Marjorie Wantz, 58. Their assisted suicides came to light just days before voters in the State of Washington went to the polls to vote on a death-with-dignity measure, Initiative 119. Publicity surrounding the deaths of Sherry Miller and Marjorie Wantz was used to illustrate potential dangers. The initiative failed to pass by a margin of 54 percent to 46 percent. A year later, on November 3, 1992, a similar proposal finally found its way to the California voters, again supported and opposed by a now-familiar cast of activists and organizations. Californian voters also rejected the proposal by an identical margin to the residents of Washington—54 percent to 46 percent.

In February, 1993, after several failed attempts, Michigan's law banning assisted suicide finally went into effect. On August 4 of that year, Kevorkian provided assistance to Thomas Hyde, aged 30, who suffered from amyotrophic lateral sclerosis (ALS), commonly known as Lou Gehrig's disease. Following Hyde's death, charges were filed and Kevorkian was arrested. While jailed, he went on a hunger strike, and while out on bond he participated in several additional assisted suicides. Kevorkian believed that the existing laws were flawed and unjust, so he aimed to get them changed. Until they were changed, he would disobey them.

The trial involving Hyde's death was held in April 1994. As written, Michigan's recently passed statute applied to anyone who knew that another person planned to attempt suicide and knowingly provided the physical means or participated in a physical act by which the suicide was carried out. The law, of course, was clearly aimed specifically at Kevorkian. Bowing to a medical practice known to be widespread among physicians, however, it also contained an exception. "If the intent is to relieve pain and discomfort and not to cause death, even if the procedure may hasten or increase the risk of death," it was not assisted suicide.

In his opening statement, Kevorkian's attorney underscored this exception as he spoke to the jury:

> Humanity and compassion are on trial. You will be deciding one of the great issues in the struggle for human rights. . . . His intent is never to kill someone, but only to reduce suffering. . . . You will decide how much suffering all of us must endure before we go into that good night—some of us, not so gently.[95]

The trial became an examination of the hazy doctrine of double effect—Kevorkian's actions were acceptable because he intended good, knowing harm would follow.[96] Kevorkian's intention was not to kill, but instead to alleviate suffering in a life that had become, or was rapidly becoming, not worth living. A prominent Detroit internist called to testify on Kevorkian's behalf remarked, "I think the procedure was a heroic effort on Dr. Kevorkian's part to control pain and suffering which was otherwise out of control." In his own testimony, Kevorkian noted, "I had a fairly good idea that he would die, but my expectation was that his suffering would end."

A few days after this testimony was heard, a split jury acquitted Jack Kevorkian of all charges on May 2, 1994. It would not be the last time the doctor would stand trial, but for now the jury was convinced. A member of the jury—a nurse's assistant—reported that Kevorkian's testimony had turned the case in his favor. "He convinced us that he was not a murderer, that he was really trying to help people out, and I can't see anything wrong with it." Another juror, a computer repairman, agreed but had reservations. "I believe Dr. Kevorkian is doing the right thing, but he's not necessarily going about it in the right way. In the back of a van—I don't think that's the proper place for a medical procedure."[97]

Yale Kamisar, a legal scholar long involved in these matters, was disturbed by the finding. "The jury was obviously badly confused."[98] Kamisar pointed out that exceptions contained in the Michigan law were aimed at the administration of pain medication, not inhalation of carbon monoxide. To Kamisar, the jury's decision effectively negated Michigan's law.[99]

Wise or not, the verdict was in: Dr. Jack Kevorkian was free to continue his work. By the end of 1996 he had assisted nearly forty-five suicides; by March, 1999, the list had grown to more than 130. Other trials and other acquittals ensued, but Kevorkian was finally convicted of second-degree murder for his direct involvement in a videotaped death shown on the popular news program *60 Minutes*. In the video, he did not leave the final act to his patient—he performed it himself. Kevorkian was sentenced to prison.

Eight years later, in June 2007, the 79-year-old doctor was released. A spokesman for the archdiocese of Detroit issued a statement: "For 10 years, Jack Kevorkian's actions resembled those of a pathological serial killer. It will be truly regrettable if he's now treated as a celebrity parolee instead of the convicted murderer he is."

On the day of his release, however, a group of sign-carrying supporters waited outside the prison to greet the doctor. A friend and colleague reported that the doctor's views remained unchanged. According to the friend, Kevorkian continued to believe "this should be a matter that is handled as a fundamental human right that is between the patient, the doctor, his family and his God."[100] On June 3, 2011, his work ended for good; Jack Kevorkian died a reportedly peaceful death eight days after his eighty-third birthday.

## A Calmer Voice

As Jack Kevorkian's suicide machines and Derek Humphry's *Final Exit* gained notoriety, the calmer and more cautious voice of Dr. Timothy Quill joined the calls to legalize physician-assisted suicide. Quill aimed to bring widespread practices of physicians out into the open in his article "Death and Dignity: A Case of Individualized Decision Making" in the March 7, 1991 edition of *The New England Journal of Medicine*.[101] It was a brief, very personal account of how he had provided assistance to "Diane," a long-time patient and friend.

In "Death and Dignity," readers learned that though pain-controlling efforts had been beneficial for Diane, "bone pain, weakness, fatigue, and fevers" had begun to dominate her life. In the course of caring for his patient and friend, Quill wrote that Diane had taught him that he could "take small risks for people that I really know and care about." The need to act indirectly, however, meant that Diane ultimately had to die alone, with no one by her side in her final moments. Dr. Quill wondered how many severely ill or dying patients secretly took their lives, dying alone in despair. He wondered whether the image of Diane's final solitude would persist in the minds of her family, whether she struggled in that last hour, and whether the legal fiction of unintended consequences was in fact making matters worse.

In a follow-up article written two years later, Quill wrote, "physicians may retreat from aggressive palliative treatment out of fear of crossing the allegedly bright line between allowing patients to die and causing their death."[102] Quill had been accused by some of killing Diane; to him, killing implied "a desire to destroy a person's essence." Nothing could have been further from his intentions. Rather, "the possibility of death may have helped to preserve her integrity." Diane had taken her life "only when her personhood was being irretrievably lost."

In late July 1991, Quill's case was brought before a grand jury. Despite his admission of obvious illegal involvement in Diane's death, the grand jury failed to return an indictment. The state medical board also decided not to file disciplinary charges, reasoning that the drug Quill prescribed for Diane had a legitimate medical use. In a subsequent interview, Quill reported that he was tremendously relieved the ordeal was over, but remained clear in his belief that "the debate needs to go on and be broadened."[103]

With fellow advocates, Timothy Quill began to frame the right-to-aid-in-dying movement by writing a number of deeply informed, carefully argued articles made more compelling by the personal experiences they contained.[104] Legal reform was needed to achieve a better balance between the alleviation of suffering and the protection of life. We should look, Quill argued, for the middle ground, where we can maintain a reverence for life while acknowledging the possibility of intolerable suffering. He knew the idea was controversial, but it was a controversy worth engaging.[105]

## A Foothold Is Secured

The cause of physician-aid-in-dying received an unexpected boost from the Supreme Court in June, 1992. *Planned Parenthood v. Casey* dealt with restrictions on abortion, but it also provided a potential foundation for right-to-die arguments. The justices had written, "At the heart of liberty [is the] right to define one's own concept of existence, of meaning, of the universe, and of the mystery of human life." Such matters, the Court noted, should not be "formed under the compulsion of the State."[106] For those paying attention, the implications for assisted suicide were clear. The decision formed the bedrock on which the death-with-dignity cause would achieve future success.

Relying heavily on Quill's writings, right-to-die activists in Oregon aimed to protect life and acknowledge suffering with the reverence they both deserved. They took lessons from failed campaigns in California and Washington State. They distanced themselves from Kevorkian's methods. They also downplayed connections with Humphry's plastic-bag method, as well as his more recent controversial advocacy of suicide by lethal injection.[107] As voting day approached, adamant advocates lined up on both sides. The state-wide vote was close— 51 percent to 49 percent (a difference of some 32,000 votes)—but on November 8, 1994, the death-with-dignity forces won an historic victory. Oregon voters had approved Measure 16, the Oregon Death with Dignity Law, the first such law in the United States.

While victory had been secured, the fight was not over. Many religious leaders, disability activists, physicians, caregivers, and terminally ill patients opposing the law refused to give up, filing suit in the federal court later that November.[108] A temporary injunction was granted, and eight months later, in August 1995, a federal district judge issued a permanent injunction against the Act's enforcement.[109] This decision was appealed and subsequently overturned on procedural grounds.[110] On October 27, 1997, the injunction was finally lifted, making physician-assisted suicide an option for terminally ill patients in Oregon.

## Unanimous Ambivalence

While these legislative battles were being fought in Oregon, activists in other states filed court cases to challenge the constitutionality of existing laws prohibiting physician-assisted suicide. The litigated issues coalesced around whether assistance in this most assuredly private decision was not only acceptable, but also a constitutionally protected right. In 1994, two cases—one from Washington State and one from New York—began making their way to the Supreme Court.

The U.S. Supreme Court issued decisions in *Washington v. Glucksberg* and *Vacco v. Quill*[111] on June 26, 1997. The justices had a rich, frequently contradictory foundation on which to build. The list of friend-of-the-court briefs, which provides information and advice that proponents hope the court will find compelling, was long. The filers made up a "Who's Who" of the legal and ethical debates of the past two decades. They came from attorneys general from across the country; religious and social movement organizations both for and against assisted dying; people personally involved in right-to-die dilemmas; and ethicists, philosophers, and lawyers outlining their persuasive reasons to decide one way or another.

After considering these briefs and hearing the arguments, the frequently divided Supreme Court came to "ambivalent unanimity"[112] in five separate, concurring opinions. Though unanimous, these opinions were laced with ambivalent references to troubling and unresolved issues and suggestions that other cases might appropriately be brought to the Court in the future. With multiple voices, the justices unanimously found that access to assisted suicide was not a fundamental liberty interest. It also found that access to assisted suicide was not a matter of equity. The state had ample compelling interests to restrict its availability. Legitimate distinctions were drawn between letting a patient die and providing the drugs to hasten death.

Making reference to the permissive assisted suicide laws on the books in the Netherlands, along with the cases of Elizabeth Bouvia, Nancy Cruzan, and Jack Kevorkian (among others), the justices wrote that they found many reasons for governmental regulation. State regulation was justified when dealing with the serious public health problem of suicide, especially among the young, the elderly, and those suffering from untreated pain, depression, or other mental disorders. It was also justified as a means to protect the medical profession's integrity and ethics and to maintain physicians' role as healers. The state also had ample interest in protecting the poor, the elderly, disabled persons, the terminally ill, and persons in other vulnerable groups from indifference, prejudice, and psychological and financial pressure to end their lives. Finally, the justices argued that such prohibitive laws helped avoid a possible "slide towards voluntary and perhaps even involuntary euthanasia."

Ultimately, the Court's decision indicated that states could pass laws prohibiting assisted suicide, and that they also had the latitude to pass laws permitting the same. In his closing comments that reviewed the Washington case, Chief Justice William Rehnquist acknowledged the unresolved state of affairs.

> Throughout the Nation, Americans are engaged in an earnest and profound debate about the morality, legality, and practicality of physician assisted suicide. Our holding permits this debate to continue, as it should in a democratic society.

These were matters that voters in each of the states would have to decide.

## Voters Decide (Again) and Are Challenged (Again)

In 1994, voters had approved Oregon's Death with Dignity Act, but legal maneuvers had delayed its implementation until October 27, 1997. On November 4 of the same year, Oregonians voted—in a turnout reported to be the largest in three decades[113]—overwhelmingly in favor of rebuffing ongoing efforts to repeal their state's law allowing physician-assisted suicide. Oregon citizens had twice voted to allow "physician-assisted dying" under tightly controlled circumstances. However, unlike Rehnquist and his Supreme Court colleagues, some still believed that these deeply important matters transcended the will of the people.

This time, opposition came in the form of a letter from the director of the U.S. Drug Enforcement Agency (DEA), Thomas Constantine. It was written in response to a request he had received that July, a month following the Supreme Court's companion decisions, from two U.S. congressmen, Illinois Rep. Henry Hyde and Utah Sen. Orrin Hatch.

Hyde and Hatch had written to Constantine to get an agency opinion on whether:

> delivering, distributing, dispensing, prescribing, filling a prescription, or administering a controlled substance with the deliberate intent of assisting in a suicide [such as permitted by the Oregon statute] would violate the Controlled Substance(s) Act.

Referring to the recently passed Assisted Suicide Funding Restriction Act, their letter noted that there would be "serious concern [in Congress] were any federal agency to construe the intentional prescribing of legal drugs for suicide as a legitimate medical practice."

The DEA depended on Congress for funding, of course, so Constantine asked his staff to carefully review the matter. Some four months later, he and his staff were persuaded that delivering, dispensing, or prescribing a controlled substance with the intent of assisting a suicide did not meet the definition of a legitimate medical purpose. Such activities would be, in their opinion, a violation of the Controlled Substance Act—just the answer Hyde and Hatch had hoped for. Constantine's response was dated November 5, 1997—one day after Oregon voters had expressed their preferences for the second time.[114]

The congressmen then approached Attorney General Janet Reno to seek enforcement of the Act, but here they hit a brick wall. Reno's reply on June 5, 1998 did not agree with Constantine and his staff. Referring to Rehnquist's closing comment in *Washington v. Glucksberg*, she responded that she found no evidence that the DEA was assigned "the novel role of resolving the 'earnest and profound debate about the morality, legality, and practicality of physician-assisted suicide.'" The attorney general's response may have been anticipated, because on the same day Reno's letter was sent, Hyde introduced legislation that would clearly allow the DEA to discourage the prescription of life-ending drugs. A companion bill was filed in the Senate, and a month later hearings were held.

In remarks made on July 14, Hyde used now-familiar images to make his case. "Today," he stated, "we are forced to squarely face the reality of what has been called a culture of death." The slippery slope he had warned about

> back in 1973, when the Supreme Court sanctified abortion . . . now appears before us as a precipitous cliff, where the elderly, the infirm, the sick, the disabled are lined up at the top and invited to do the right thing and relieve their loved ones of their burdensome existence by plunging off this cliff under the care of a physician who will assist them in their suicidal journey.

Steadfastly opposed to this proposed legislation, Oregon's governor—himself a licensed physician—saw it as an inappropriate challenge to the will of Oregon's voters. A representative of the AMA, a powerful organization long opposed to physician-assisted suicide, agreed. Despite its previous opposition, the AMA weighed in against this particular legislation because the same drugs prescribed to alleviate pain could readily be used to end a life. Thus, the AMA feared, the real-world consequences of Hyde and Hatch's proposed legislation could have a chilling effect on the prescription of pain-relieving medication and appropriate palliative care.

In the end, the proposed federal legislation failed. With tenacity befitting a committed believer, however, Hyde immediately introduced yet another legislative proposal to ban the use of the drugs required in provisions of Oregon's law. This failed as well. A year later, George W. Bush was elected president and appointed as his attorney general John Ashcroft, a former Missouri governor and senator who was closely associated with Bush's evangelical right-to-life supporters. Ashcroft was well versed in the issues at hand, since in his home state of Missouri he had been involved in the Nancy Cruzan case. He took a very different view of federal oversight of the medical profession and physician-assisted suicide laws than his predecessor.

On November 9, 2001, Ashcroft sent a memorandum to the administrator of the DEA that referred specifically to his disagreement with Reno's assessment. The new attorney general believed that Constantine's original assessment had been correct. Assisting suicide was not a "legitimate medical purpose," and prescribing, dispensing, or administering controlled substances to assist a suicide violated the Controlled Substance Act. Given this assessment, Ashcroft directed the DEA, effective with the publication of his memorandum and "notwithstanding anything to the contrary," to enforce and apply the law based on his new assessment. This directive was not unexpected, but it was a stunning reversal.

At the time, however, few were paying attention. The nation's and the world's attention had turned elsewhere that year on September 11, when terrorists hijacked planes and flew them into the World Trade Center, the Pentagon, and a Pennsylvania field. Nearly 3,000 people had been killed, and the nation was under attack; physician-assisted suicide laws in Oregon were a minor distraction at best. Despite the fact that attention was turned elsewhere, Ashcroft's directive was appealed and eventually overturned by the U.S. Supreme Court on January 17, 2006. Oregon's law was finally fully implemented.

In March 2005, however, another high-profile right-to-die case drew substantial national attention.[115] Following prolonged, contentious, and highly politicized events involving the state legislature and courts as well as the U.S. Congress, the feeding tube of Terri Schiavo, a vegetative Florida woman, was removed. Schiavo died amidst protests and the frequent assertions that our civilization was moving rapidly toward a culture of death.

Back on the West Coast, laws that could provide easier access to assisted dying once again gained attention over the next two years. This time, Booth Gardner, a wealthy man who had served two terms as Governor of the State of Washington, was at the forefront. Gardner was suffering from Parkinson's disease and sought the right to die with dignity when he believed the time was right. Along with a coalition of state and national activists, Gardner aimed to change Washington's laws to allow him, and others who were suffering, to do just that.

"Under no circumstances," Gardner reasoned, "should my fate be put in the hands of a pinhead politician who can't pass ninth-grade biology."[116] In what he saw as his last campaign and the biggest fight of his career, the former governor saw his logic as impeccable. "[It is] my life, my death, my control."[117]

These arguments had been heard countless times before, but this time they were persuasive. On November 4, 2008, the voters in Washington went to the polls; by a wide margin (59 percent to 41 percent), Washington became the second state to pass a death-with-dignity law. With that, the pendulum swing of these perhaps ultimately unresolvable issues continued.

# 4

# Taking Life

## Lynching and Capital Punishment

We come now to the final topics: lynching and capital punishment. Turning a fully protected citizen into a dehumanized felon whose life can be taken is an uncertain business.[1] It has been so for a very long time. Historically, many actions have carried the death penalty, including disobeying one's parents, disregarding the Sabbath, blasphemy, shoddy construction, sodomy, adultery, abortion, robbery, rape, and murder. One thing has remained constant: those already on the margins of assessed social worth are those most vulnerable to receive death as a punishment. This conclusion has been widely noted and repeatedly illustrated across time, place, and life circumstances.[2] A clear example comes from the period when lynchings soiled the landscape of the United States.[3]

### Lynching and the Margins of Life

A 1905 study of this period began by telling readers:

> As will be made clear in the following pages, lynch-law has been resorted to in the United States in times of popular excitement and social disruption; it has been inflicted upon negroes, Indians, Italians, Mexicans; it has been inflicted upon disreputable characters.[4]

The same year this study was published, an editorial appeared in the *Times Clarion*, a Longview, Texas community newspaper. "Almost every day," the *Times Clarion* editorial began, "some negro brute assaults a white woman in this state, and often one to a half-dozen murders are committed in an effort to hide the crime. . . . If rape and murder by brutish negroes are to become common, the negro must expect extermination."[5] This Longview editorial did not stand alone. Similar articles and editorials, published mainly in the former Confederacy, joined the chorus in frequently frenzied animosity. More than anything else, lynchings illustrated the dehumanizing, suffering-inducing, and life-threatening consequences of an exclusionary society.

Such animosity was met with opposition. A year after the National Association for the Advancement of Colored People (NAACP) was founded in 1909, the organization began publishing *The Crisis: A Record of the Darker Races*. The journal's subject matter was wide ranging, but a special place was reserved for lynching. Anti-lynching efforts were soon organized into an aggressive campaign to oppose this egregious affront to common humanity.[6] These efforts began to yield fruit. A Republican congressman from Missouri named Leonidas Carstorphen Dyer, who represented a district that included areas of St. Louis with a high concentration of black citizens, worked closely with the NAACP to introduce anti-lynching legislation to the U.S. Congress in mid-April, 1918.[7] The Senate's majority whip, Kansas Sen. Charles Curtis, introduced related legislation to launch a congressional investigation into lynching.

While these legislative efforts ultimately foundered, the battle lines had been drawn. In late July, three months after Dyer's bill was introduced, U.S. President Woodrow Wilson responded to the mounting pressure from members of the NAACP and called on "the governors of all the states, the law officers of every community and, above all, the men and women of every community" to end the "disgraceful evil" of lynching.[8] Shortly thereafter, the NAACP published *Thirty Years of Lynching: 1889–1918*, a report that documented in careful detail the thousands of lynchings during this time period.

At the time, the nation was at war. Those most susceptible to lynching were being trained and deployed to take life and protect a way of life that was putting their own lives at risk. The armistice agreement ending World War I was signed on November 11, 1918. Six months later, W.E.B. Du Bois, on behalf of war-weary black veterans, published "Returning Soldiers" in the May, 1919 issue of *The Crisis*. Du Bois' words were forceful:

> This is the country to which we Soldiers of Democracy return. This is the fatherland for which we fought! . . . It was right for us to fight. . . . Under similar circumstances, we would fight again. But by the God of Heaven, we are cowards and jackasses if now that the war is over, we do not marshal every ounce of our brain and brawn to fight sterner, longer, more unbending battle against forces in our land.
> We return.
> We return from fighting.
> We return fighting.
> Make way for Democracy! We saved it in
> France, and by the Great Jehovah, we will
> Save it in the United States of America, or
> Know the reason why.

Du Bois' point was clear. He was not going to stand idly by while others justified the grotesque, dehumanizing practice of lynchings.

Immediately following the release of *Thirty Years of Lynching* and Du Bois' article depicting the intentions of returning soldiers, a dramatic upswing occurred in the frequency of lynchings and mob violence during what came to be known as the Red Summer of 1919. A May 10 race riot in Charleston, South Carolina marked the beginning of this five-month period of violence.[9] Throughout the summer, riots and lynchings occurred all across the country—north and south, east and west. The final burst of violence came in two neighboring rural communities in Arkansas.

## Crystallizing Events on the Road to Reform

Seemingly small and isolated events can sometimes illustrate issues with great clarity and thereby influence the road to reform. One such event occurred in late September, 1919, when a group of black farmers gathered in a small church in rural Phillips County, Arkansas. The men and women had gathered to discuss the festering disputes in the nearby communities of Hoop Spur, Helena, and Elaine over the price paid for cotton and the wages given to cotton pickers.[10]

While whites constituted a large majority (close to 75 percent) of the population state wide, in rural Arkansas they were a distinct minority. Some 80 percent of the roughly 35,000 residents in Phillips County were black. Plantation owners in these rural areas retained their traditional power through intimidation and legal privilege. Local black citizens had recently hired lawyers to help found the Progressive Farmers and Household Union of America, an organization focused on securing their rights and increasing their collective bargaining power.

Following the founding of the Union, organizing sharecroppers contacted a well-respected white lawyer named Ulysses Simpson Bratton, who along with his sons and associates was known for pursuing the interests of black tenant farmers with commitment and skill. The Brattons had a solid record of winning. Hiring Bratton, as a central figure in these events would eventually note,

> caused the landlords to take the new organization seriously because they knew Bratton would pull the cover from the unsavory system and, possibly, send some of them to federal prison for violation of the Thirteenth Amendment against slavery and the laws against peonage.[11]

The church where the local black farmers gathered was packed. The farmers carried guns for protection and posted guards outside the church. Rumors spread among whites in the area that the meeting was part of a sharecroppers' plot to launch an insurrection. To observe the meeting, three white citizens drove to the church and waited outside. Various versions of what followed and who fired the first shot have been recorded,[12] but according to one account, those attending the gathering were "thrown into panic as fusillade after fusillade of bullets poured into the crowded church, killing a number of women and men and wounding others."[13] Shots from the men who had been guarding the meeting killed one of the whites riding in the car and wounded another. It was as if a match had been dropped on a powder keg.

Word quickly spread of a "Negro insurrection." An estimated 600 to 1,000 whites from neighboring communities in Arkansas and from across the river in nearby Mississippi and Tennessee gathered for a "nigger hunt."[14] As the Supreme Court would later note in less racially loaded terms, "The report of the killing [outside the church] caused great excitement, and was followed by the hunting down and shooting of many negroes."[15]

The initial shootings had occurred on Tuesday evening. The next day the governor requested deployment of federal troops to help control the situation. The exact number of black men, women, and children who were killed was never firmly established, but most estimates settled on a total that exceeded 200 people, with a high estimate of 856.[16] In addition, more than 1,000 black men, women, and children were arrested and placed in a stockade.

Arkansas' governor convened a committee of seven prominent white citizens to investigate. They began their work on Saturday, October 4, and issued their report the following Monday. The U.S. Supreme Court would later summarize the committee's findings. The church gathering in Phillips County had been part of:

> a deliberately planned insurrection of the negroes against the whites, directed by an organization known as the "Progressive Farmers and Household Union of America" established for the purpose of banding negroes together for the killing of white people.[17]

The committee's conclusion, which mirrored accounts in the media across the nation, was immediately challenged by federal agents and eventually proved false beyond any doubt.[18] In the immediacy of the moment, however, these stories stirred emotions, precipitated action, and were used to justify the killings of black citizens.

Following the violence, more than 120 black citizens were indicted on a range of charges. In an atmosphere of violent intimidation, witnesses and defendants were tortured to confess and give testimony supportive of the prosecution.[19] One of the white participants in the interrogations later revealed:

> I saw a great many negroes whipped . . . to compel them to give evidence against themselves and others. . . . They were not only whipped but formaldehyde was put to their noses and they were stripped naked and put into an electric chair. . . . I not only personally saw a great many negroes whipped with a leather strap that would cut blood at every lick, but I whipped probably two dozen of them myself.[20]

The subsequent trials were perfunctory. Defendants had little or no contact with their lawyers and scant if any testimony or evidence presented in their defense.

The first trial was held on November 3, a month after the violence had broken out. It lasted less than an hour and a half. About fifteen seconds after the prosecution rested, the defense attorney cleared his throat and said in a loud voice: "The defense has no witnesses, Your Honor."[21] The all-white jury deliberated for eight minutes before reaching a guilty verdict.

The remaining trials were held in rapid-fire succession. For each, the time devoted to testimony and jury deliberation decreased. The last verdict took the jury two minutes, making it perhaps "some sort of national record for the fastest verdict ever in a capital case."[22] In only two weeks, twelve blacks had been sentenced to death and more than seventy others had been sentenced to prison terms ranging from one to twenty-one years. No whites were tried for the widespread killing that had followed the initial incident.

This was not what the framers of the Fourteenth Amendment to the Constitution and the Habeas Corpus Act of 1867 had in mind when writing, "nor shall any State deprive any person of life, liberty, or property, without due process of law; nor deny to any person within its jurisdiction the equal protection of the laws" shortly after the Civil War, as they aimed to protect former slaves from continuing enslavement. The problem was that intermittent Supreme Court decisions in the five decades between 1867 and 1919 had brought confusion over how the Amendment and Act should be applied when a conflict existed between state and federal jurisdictions.[23] Never before, no matter how egregious the violation, had a state criminal verdict been set aside by the U.S. Supreme Court—these were matters for local communities and the states to decide. Local officials seemed to be on a firm legal footing.

If the sentences of the organizing sharecroppers, who had now been convicted of murder, were to be challenged, their appeals would have to be carefully crafted. A small group of lawyers decided to take up the challenge. It was appropriate that the son of a former slave, Scipio Africanus Jones, born in 1863, stood most prominent among them. Judge Jones, as he was known locally (despite the fact that he was not a judge), bore most of the responsibility for crafting the appeals. As a young man, he had managed to secure a basic education and bachelor's degree. He then moved into the practice of law through an apprenticeship at a Little Rock law firm in the late 1880s. Over the years, Jones had developed a successful practice, and by 1919 he had argued before the Arkansas Supreme Court seventeen times, winning eight of the cases. Judge Jones was well versed in how the Fourteenth Amendment and the wider ranging Habeas Corpus Act might be used effectively to protect his clients.

Jones and his colleagues approached the national office of the NAACP for support. For reasons that remain unclear, the NAACP was not immediately responsive.[24] Eventually, however, a visit from Ulysses Bratton, who had traveled north to vouch for Jones, secured some action. After Bratton's visit, the NAACP began mobilizing resources, and various appeals took various paths. The cases of six of the defendants who had been sentenced to death included brothers Ed and Frank Hicks and fellow Progressive Farmers and Household Union of America organizers J.C. Knox, Ed Coleman, Paul Hall, and Frank Moore.

It took legal skill, diplomatic tenacity, and three and a half years, but in the end, these cases found their way to the U.S. Supreme Court in *Moore et al. v. Dempsey*.[25] The NAACP would eventually refer to this appeal as the "most important case of its kind in the history of America." Looking back decades later, an account would conclude, "Out of the ashes of the Phillips County massacre came a legal victory that set the country on a new course."[26]

Justice Oliver Wendell Holmes wrote the decision for the six-to-two majority of the Court (one seat on the Court was vacant). It was released in mid-February 1923, some three and a half years after violence had exploded in Phillips County. Summarizing the Court's findings, Justice Holmes was clear and to the point: "A trial for murder in a state court in which the accused are hurried to conviction under mob domination without regard for their rights is without due process of law and absolutely void." With this language, *Moore et al. v. Dempsey* marked a turning point for how free citizens could be transformed into convicted felons.

## Evolving Protections for Those on the Margins

The decision did not bring lynchings and sparse procedures in sham trials to a halt, but change could be detected. Between 1891 and 1893, approximately 189 lynchings occurred each year—about one every other day.[27] Thirty years later, between 1920 and 1922, the three-year average was sixty-one. Starting with 1923, the year of the *Moore* decision, the yearly numbers dropped dramatically over the following three years: thirty-three, sixteen, and seventeen, respectively. A slight uptick occurred in 1926, but the overall downward trend continued until the early 1930s, when the effects of the Great Depression were being felt. From 1933 to 1935, there were twenty-six, fifteen, and twenty lynchings, respectively, and thereafter, the decline continued. From 1939 to 1941, reported lynchings had decreased to three, five, and four, respectively, per year.

As the frequency of lynchings diminished, the number of formal trials and state-sanctioned executions rose. A substitution of sorts seemed to be taking place.[28] Once again, isolated local events played a crystallizing role. This was dramatically illustrated by the response to the gruesome burnings and hangings of nine black citizens accused of a range of crimes in a small Texas community about seventy miles east of Waco in May, 1922.[29] A local citizen, J.W. Thomas, became deeply disturbed by these events and ran for the state senate with the single-minded intent of passing a law that would remove hangings from the frequently frenzied emotional environment in local communities and transfer them to the prison in Huntsville. Thomas was ultimately successful.

With the passage of the Thomas legislation, Texas joined a growing number of states that prohibited local hangings and chose electrocution as a more humane method of execution.[30] Shortly after midnight on February 8, 1924, in Huntsville, Texas, the first application of the new law resulted in what one newspaper called a "Harvest of Death."[31] Starting at 12:09 a.m., four executions were carried out in the space of an hour and a half. A fifth man, after a brief, last-minute stay of execution, was electrocuted and pronounced dead around 2:00 a.m. All five men were black. All had been convicted of murder.

Progress was being made, but for those on the margins of life, protective boundaries were still all too readily breached. Many of these cases involved crimes grounded in what came to be called a "peculiar kind of chivalry." One such event occurred in 1930 in Sherman, Texas, a town sixty-five miles north of Dallas. The case involved a black man who had recently arrived in the community as a farm laborer; he was later characterized as "ignorant and feeble-minded." He was charged with the rape of his employer's wife, a white woman. At the time, little more than six years had passed since the Texas electrocution statute had yielded the initial harvest of death.

On May 9, as the alleged victim arrived on a stretcher immediately prior to the scheduled trial, an enraged crowd set fire to the courthouse. The only person left in the building was the defendant, who was locked up on the second floor. His body was later removed and, according to one account, the corpse was dragged "to a cottonwood tree in the Negro business section. There it was burned; afterward the crowd looted and destroyed most of the black-owned property in town."[32] As the melee went on, the police directed traffic.

The repulsive nature of this event, combined with concern over a surge in lynchings in the early 1930s, precipitated further reform efforts on two fronts. On one, a group of concerned writers and academics centered primarily at the University of North Carolina began compiling reports and publishing articles, pamphlets, and books on lynchings and related subjects. Their objective was to better understand and inform the public of the nature of racial violence. Among this group were legal scholars and social scientists, including James Chadbourn, who published *Lynching and the Law* in 1933. A companion book, *The Tragedy of Lynching*, by Arthur Raper, was published that same year. Both works would frame much of the academic discussion in the decades ahead. These scholars, along with colleagues at the historically black schools Tuskegee University, Atlanta University, and Fisk University, were thorough and persistent. They were also exclusively males.

Jessie Daniel Ames was among the women left on the sidelines. She was intensely invested in the issues at hand. Ames had grown up as a white woman in east Texas in the small community of Palestine, which lies south of Dallas and east of Waco. She had long been concerned by the negative consequences of a "peculiar chivalry" she saw all around her that placed white women on a pedestal—separated from full participation in community affairs and considered to be in need of protection. Ames was convinced that this ill-conceived chivalry was a cornerstone in the argument used to justify lynchings when a black man was charged with the rape of a white woman.[33]

Through a series of religious and social networks, Ames was well connected with women throughout the South. About six months following the burning of the Sherman courthouse, she became convinced that something had to be done. Excluded from the work of the male scholars in North Carolina, Ames decided that women could and should organize reform efforts of their own. "The men were out making studies," she once remarked, "and so the women had to get busy and do what they could to stop lynchings!"[34]

Ames invited twenty-six women from six southeastern states to join her in Atlanta on November 1, 1930. Together, they founded the Association of Southern Women for the Prevention of Lynching (ASWPL). Over the next decade, they mobilized church communities and local action groups by giving speeches and distributing pamphlets. The ASWPL's message was focused. In an interview given eight months after the organization was established, Ames stated,

> Public opinion has accepted too easily the claim of lynchers and mobsters that they were acting *solely in the defense of womanhood.* . . . Women dare no longer to permit the claim to pass unchallenged nor allow themselves to be the cloak behind which those bent upon personal revenge and savagery commit acts of violence and lawlessness.[35]

Galvanized by the egregious inhumanity of lynchings, the ASWPL would not suspend its campaign until 1942, when lynchings had all but disappeared from the nation's landscape.

## Another Crystallizing Event

These early efforts were further energized by yet another charge of rape in 1931. This incident occurred on a March day on a freight train traveling from Chattanooga, Tennessee, through Alabama on its way to Memphis. Some two dozen young black and white men, mostly teenagers, caught a ride on the freight train. The men were looking for work as the Great Depression moved through its darkest days. There were also two young white women—17 and 21 years of age—riding in one of the cars; both were returning home to Huntsville, Alabama, after a failed search for work in Tennessee.

As the train wound its way through northern Alabama, words were exchanged between two of the young men—one black, one white. A fight broke out, and the young black men prevailed. With one exception, the white teens left the train. Once off the train, they spread word of the fight, and when the train made a scheduled stop in Paint Rock, Alabama, nineteen miles west of the county seat in Scottsboro, the remaining travelers were told to get off. A short time later, one of the young women who had been on the train approached the sheriff and accused the nine black men of gang-raping her and her companion after the whites had left the train.[36]

The accused men were arrested and taken to the county jail in Scottsboro. A black man raping a white woman was seen as a particularly egregious offense, and the fact that *nine* men had allegedly been involved escalated the emotion to fever pitch. On Monday, April 6, not quite two weeks after the incident and six days after the defendants had been indicted, the trials of the nine defendants, ranging from ages 19 down to 13, began. In three days, all nine defendants were convicted. Eight were sentenced to death and one of the youngest, aged 13, was given a life sentence.

The abbreviated nature of the legal proceedings drew national attention. The offices of the NAACP and the International Labor Defense (ILD), an arm of the Communist Party of the United States, soon became involved. (The ILD eventually took charge of the legal matters in the appellate process.) The Alabama Supreme Court rejected all appeals on March 24, 1932, almost a year to the day after the initial incident, but the U.S. Supreme Court agreed to hear the case. On November 7, *Powell v. Alabama*,[37] a seven-to-two decision consolidating the nine cases, was released.

Justice George Sutherland, writing for the court, reviewed the facts:

> [On] April 6, six days after indictment the trials began. When the first case was called, the court inquired whether the parties were ready for trial. The state's attorney replied that he was ready to proceed. No one answered for the defendants or appeared to represent or defend them.

After some discussion ensued in the courtroom, a single attorney indicated that he was willing to represent the defendants, and the trial proceeded. This meant, Justice Sutherland's opinion continued, that:

until the very morning of the trial, no lawyer had been named or definitely designated to represent the defendants. . . . The defendants, young, ignorant, illiterate, surrounded by hostile sentiment, hauled back and forth under guard of soldiers, charged with an atrocious crime regarded with especial horror in the community where they were to be tried, were thus put in peril of their lives within a few moments after counsel for the first time charged with any degree of responsibility began to represent them.

For seven of the Supreme Court justices, the evidence was clear and the outcome unacceptable. The state could not sentence persons to death in such a cavalier manner. When it did, there was precious little difference between a trial and a lynch mob. Sutherland continued:

A defendant, charged with a serious crime, must not be stripped of his right to have sufficient time to advise with counsel and prepare his defense. To do that is not to proceed promptly in the calm spirit of regulated justice, but to go forward with the haste of the mob.

Following the *Powell* decision, the nine young men, now known as the "Scottsboro Boys," who had been riding a train looking for work in Depression-era Alabama and instead found themselves charged with raping two women, would be retried, re-retried, and then retried again.[38] What began in 1931 with the arrest and conviction of nine young men finally ended in 1976, when the sitting governor of Alabama, George Wallace, pardoned the last of the Scottsboro Boys. Wallace's pardon noted that the conviction of all nine had been a tragic mistake. It had taken four and a half decades to right this wrong.

The two Supreme Court decisions, *Moore v. Dempsey* and *Powell v. Alabama*, became important decisions going straight to the heart of a deep sense of injustice stemming from an exclusionary and dehumanizing society. Resistance, however, remained.

### Stark Inhumanity Further Energizes a Movement

Emmett Till (known as "Bo" to his family and friends) was 14 years old in the summer of 1955 when his mother's uncle, Moses Wright, came to Chicago in August to attend the funeral of a family member. Mamie Till, Emmett's mother, had migrated north from Mississippi with her parents in 1924 at the age of 2. Her family moved to a small community just outside Chicago, but their contact with family members who decided to stay in Mississippi remained strong.

Mamie and Emmett Till, along with the rest of their Illinois family, were delighted to see Wright, who they called "Papa Mose." Papa told great stories and loved to entertain the family with tales of the simple pleasures of fishing and long summer nights in the Mississippi Delta. For the young Chicago-raised boys in the family who listened to these stories, the Delta became the land of adventure. "For a free-spirited boy who lived to be outdoors," Mamie Till would later write, "there was so much possibility, so much adventure in the Mississippi his great-uncle described."[39]

When Emmett found out that two of his cousins were planning to visit Papa Mose a few weeks later, he began working on his mother and grandmother to let him join the fun. At first, both refused, but Emmett persisted. Eventually, like "two hens coming to fuss over this one little chick," his mother and grandmother drove to the nearby home of Papa Mose's daughter, where he was staying. To the amusement of all, both mother and grandmother came seeking promises of care and reassurances of safety. Once given, the trip was planned.

First, however, Mamie Till knew she had to talk to her son about the ways of the American South. "It was the talk every black parent had with every child sent down South back then," Mamie later recalled. "We went through the drill." It was important that Emmett should know that Chicago and Mississippi were very different places. For example, he should not start conversations with white people, and he should always put a polite handle on his answers: "Yes, ma'am"; "No, ma'am"; "Yes, sir"; "No, sir." If a white woman approached him on the street, he should not look her in the eye; instead, he should step off the sidewalk and lower his head. He should make every effort to humble himself.

To a free-spirited young teenager who knew only of life in Chicago, this all seemed quite incredible. "Oh, Mama," Emmett replied. "It can't be that bad." Mamie Till knew that only a few months earlier, on separate occasions, black men who were attempting to vote had been shot and killed in full view of others not far from where her son was going to visit. She replied, "Bo, it is worse than that." As the talk continued, Mamie took pains to re-emphasize various points. Emmett listened and finally said, "Mama, I know how to act. You taught me how to act."

On Saturday morning, August 20, 1955, Papa Mose, Emmett, and one of Emmett's cousins, Wheeler Parker, boarded the *City of New Orleans* and headed south. Another cousin, Curtis Jones, would join them later. Knowing that they would not be able to use the dining car on the train because of their color, Emmett's mother packed food for her son in a shoebox. Mamie would later recall that it was a bit like sending Emmett to summer camp. A few days after he left, missing her son, she decided to call to see how he was doing and if he wanted to come home early. Instead, Emmett asked if she could send him some more money.

"More money?" His mother wondered. He had left home with plenty as far as she was concerned. Well, Emmett replied, he had been buying sweets for some of his new friends, so he could use a bit more. He also asked if she would make sure his motorbike was fixed before he returned home. On August 27, Mamie received a short letter from her traveling son, who wrote in closing, "I am going to see Uncle Crosby Saturday. Everybody here is fine and having a good time. Tell Aunt Alma hello (out of money). Your son, Bobo."

Emmett's mother had her answer: her son was doing fine and having a grand time—"too good a time to even think about returning sooner."

Early the next morning, on Sunday, August 28, her phone rang. Willie Mae Wright, Moses Wright's daughter, was on the phone. Her son, Curtis, had called Willie Mae to tell her the news. "I don't know how to tell you. Bo . . ."

"Bo, what?" Mamie remembered asking as she sat up with a jerk. "Willie Mae, what about Bo?"

"Some men came and got him last night." That was all Willie Mae knew: Curtis had reported that some men had come to Wright's home at around 2:30 a.m. on Sunday morning and had taken Emmett. Emmett's mother, now deeply concerned, needed more information, but despite several attempts, the women could not reach Papa Mose. They finally reached another uncle, who told them that the other boys were fine and that he and Wright were going to the sheriff to report the incident.

On Monday, the next day, two men—Roy Bryant, owner of the small grocery store in Money, and his half-brother J.W. Milam, who managed local cotton pickers—were arrested. They admitted to forcibly taking the boy from Wright's house but said they had let him go. When asked why, they responded that Emmett had insulted Bryant's wife on the previous Wednesday.

Emmett and his cousin, Wheeler Parker, had arrived in Mississippi on Sunday, August 21. Each day, they were required to do various chores around the house and help pick cotton during the day with several adults and other teenagers. On Wednesday, after working in the fields all day, Emmett joined six other boys and a girl on a trip to Bryant's Grocery and Meat Market to relax and buy some candy.

Accounts of what came next vary, but all agree that Emmett went into the store to buy some bubble gum and, prodded by his friends, apparently forgot some of the details his mother had warned him about. After buying the bubble gum, he spoke directly to Carolyn Bryant, Bryant's 21-year-old wife, and placed the money in her hand instead of on the counter as local custom dictated. Some reported that a short time later, Emmett had whistled at Mrs. Bryant when she came out of the store. Offense was taken, and the peculiar chivalry that had long bothered Jessie Daniel Ames was about to be enraged.

Mrs. Bryant was taking care of the store that day with Juanita Milam, J.W. Milam's wife, as her husband Bryant was in Texas delivering some shrimp. At first, the two women decided not to tell their husbands, but the story began to circulate around town. After Bryant returned from Texas on the Friday, his wife recounted what had happened. Bryant finished up some work on Saturday and then called his brother Milam. In the early hours of that Sunday morning, August 28, the two brothers headed for Moses Wright's house in their pickup truck.

What followed was cruel, gruesome, and well documented.[40] The perpetrators themselves admitted to taking Emmett from Wright's home, but not to driving him to numerous locations, beating him, mutilating his body, shooting him in the head, and throwing his body into a nearby river with a large cotton-gin fan attached to his neck with barbed wire to make sure it did not surface. Three days later, on August 31, Emmett Till's decomposing body was discovered and sent back to Chicago so that his mother could bury her son. After an abbreviated trial, Roy Bryant and J.W. Milam were acquitted less than a month after Till's murder.

Following the trial, *Look Magazine* paid Bryant and Milam US$4,000 for their account of what had happened. The story ran on January 24, 1956.[41] In the article, both men admitted to kidnapping, torturing, and killing Emmett Till. J.W. Milam was satisfied with *Look*'s portrayal. Talking with a reporter after the article appeared, Milam smiled and said, "I'll say one thing for the article, it was written from a Mississippi viewpoint. I've gotten a lot of letters from people commending me for what *Look* did."[42]

Mamie Till's decision to let the world see what had happened to her son in an open-casket funeral meant that photographs of his maimed and disfigured corpse were widely published. Those images, in conjunction with widespread media coverage of the killing, the subsequent perfunctory trial and acquittal of clearly guilty, admitted killers, and the callous response of those killers, struck a deep chord of revulsion across the country.

A clearer example of the exclusionary, dehumanizing consequences of deeming some lives less worthy of support and protection could hardly be found. Events such as these were, sadly, accumulating. In jarring detail, Emmett Till's death clarified issues and deepened a sense of injustice. The profound injustices so readily evident in the lynchings of the early twentieth century, the perfunctory trials and convictions of the Scottsboro Boys, and the unpunished torture and murder of young Emmett Till did not go unnoticed. These and similar events formed a motivating backdrop for questioning the legitimacy of capital punishment and for launching a campaign for its abolition.

## A Sense of Injustice and Questioned Legitimacy

On August 28, 1963, Martin Luther King's "I Have a Dream" speech on the steps of the Lincoln Memorial inspired the country. King told the crowd of some 200,000 people:

> Now is the time to rise from the dark and desolate valley of segregation to the sunlit path of racial justice. Now is the time to lift our nation from the quick sands of racial injustice to the solid rock of brotherhood. Now is the time to make justice a reality for all of God's children.

While urging non-violent, patient, and tenacious commitment, King also wanted all to remember the

> fierce urgency of now. . . . There will be neither rest nor tranquility in America until the Negro is granted his citizenship rights. The whirlwinds of revolt will continue to shake the foundations of our nation until the bright day of justice emerges.

It was a powerful speech. It moved a nation. On July 2, U.S. President Lyndon B. Johnson signed the Civil Rights Act of 1964 into law. It struck directly at the heart of the dehumanizing and exclusionary policies, practices, and laws that plagued the nation and marked important progress toward a more inclusive society. There remained, however, the glaring and dehumanizing legacy of lynchings that continued in a disturbing pattern of state-sanctioned executions.

Anthony (Tony) Amsterdam is the attorney most frequently identified as the architect of the campaign to challenge and eventually abolish capital punishment. He recalled:

I think that in the minds of everyone [involved in the NAACP's Legal Defense Fund (LDF) efforts to abolish capital punishment] the Scottsboro Boys trial stood as a constant background symbol of "Judge Lynch"—the constant danger of perversion of the criminal justice system into an instrument of oppression and subordination of African Americans.

Lou Pollak was an adviser to LDF in a lot of its projects; his father, Walter, had been one of the Scottsboro Boys' lawyers; Lou's presence was something of a reminder of those cases. It was because the Scottsboro Boys cases had demonstrated the need to go to the defense of African Americans charged with capital crimes against whites that LDF was still sending lawyers into that breach in the early '60s; that tradition led us into the cases that, in turn, turned into the campaign against the death penalty.[43]

In the midst of the deeply troubling, yet hope-inspiring events of 1963 and the passage of the 1964 Civil Rights Act, a small group of lawyers and social scientists began to plot a course to eliminate capital punishment in the United States. They were convinced, as a member of the legal team would later recall, that "capital punishment in the United States was in good measure arbitrarily applied, infrequently employed, and of questionable utility."[44] For Jack Greenberg, the director-counsel of the NAACP Legal Defense Fund, this assessment had been a long time coming. Greenberg later recalled:

One of the first cases I became involved in (end of 1949, beginning 1950 and onwards), was known as "Groveland,"[45] named after a community in which an alleged crime occurred. Four young blacks were charged with rape of a white woman. One was killed while hunted by police, one killed by the sheriff en route to trial, one sentenced to life imprisonment, one sentenced to death but after a lengthy effort his sentence was commuted. . . .

Another early case was that of a black man executed for rape of which I'm confident he was innocent. He happened to have been circumcised shortly before the alleged crime. It would have been physically impossible (or nearly so) for him to have committed the crime. 90 percent plus of those executed for rape were blacks accused of having raped whites. I vowed that if I could, I would end that some day.[46]

By 1963, that day had come. Greenberg and his colleagues viewed these as injustices, a view that was widely shared, but the LDF's resources were limited. What Jessie Daniel Ames and the women she mobilized had labeled "a peculiar chivalry," the justification of taking a life in cases involving a black defendant charged with the raping of a white woman, particularly disturbed them. Department of Justice statistics revealed that there had been 455 executions for rape over the years, and 405 of them (90 percent) had involved black defendants. In addition, of the ninety-eight persons executed in the United States for crimes involving an attempted rape, but no murder, all but three were black defendants.[47]

Capital cases involving rape—with particular attention paid to black defendants charged with raping a white woman—became the first priority for LDF lawyers, but as their work progressed, they decided to broaden their strategy and defend murderers as well as rapists, whites as well as blacks, all across the country. As Tony Amsterdam later put it, "We said, 'What the hell! Are we going to let these guys die?' It was like somebody was bleeding in the gutter when you've got a tourniquet." At that point, Amsterdam added, "We were in the execution-stopping business."[48]

### A Campaign Is Launched

There was reason to believe that success was within reach, as executions in the United States had been on the decline for years. The five-year average with the highest frequency occurred from 1935 to 1939, with 178. By the period of 1945 to 1949, the yearly average was 128. By the period of 1955 to 1959, it had fallen to sixty-one. In 1963, when the LDF lawyers launched their initial efforts, the number had fallen to twenty-one.[49]

In October, 1963, the lawyers received "what could only be called an invitation to start attacking capital punishment"[50] from Supreme Court Justice Arthur Goldberg, who disagreed with his colleagues' refusal to review a case involving the conviction of a black man sentenced to death in Alabama for rape.[51] Goldberg thought the case should be reviewed because it involved "a convicted rapist who [had] neither taken nor endangered human life."

Was the taking of human life in such circumstances, Goldberg wondered, "consistent with the constitutional proscription against punishments which by their excessive severity are greatly disproportioned to the offenses charged?" Were these practices, Goldberg wondered, consistent with "evolving standards of decency that mark the progress of our maturing society?" Could legitimate aims of punishment be achieved "as effectively by punishing rape less severely than by death?" If so, did a death sentence in such cases constitute "unnecessary cruelty?" Goldberg argued, with support from two other justices, that given evolving standards of decency, the time had come to call into question the constitutional acceptability of removing the protective boundaries of life in instances where the criminal in question had not taken a life.

Jack Greenberg, Anthony Amsterdam, and their colleagues did not miss the import of Goldberg's words. Here was a justice of the Supreme Court outlining a road-map for a possible attack on capital punishment. Writing years later, Greenberg recalled:

> [Goldberg's] opinion signaled that the time to launch the effort had arrived. Shortly afterward, I announced to the board that we would launch a full-scale attack on capital punishment for rape. By mid-decade, we had seventeen cases.[52]

One of Amsterdam's social science colleagues at the University of Pennsylvania, Marvin Wolfgang, seemed like a perfect ally. Wolfgang recognized the importance of carefully collected and analyzed data. He was well versed in the nuances of the capital punishment debate, having just published an article on differential death sentencing patterns the previous year.[53] In addition, he was sympathetic to the LDF's reform efforts.

Greenberg, Amsterdam, and Wolfgang were joined by a contingent of lawyers that eventually grew into an informally organized nationwide network. The first task was to systematically collect data on executions for rape in the former Confederacy. For this, they needed help. In the spring of 1965, they approached the Law Students Civil Rights Research Council (LSCRRC) for assistance. The multiracial group of law students had been founded two years earlier with the explicit purpose of supporting the Civil Rights Movement.[54]

In June of the same year, students interested in summer internships were brought to the University of Pennsylvania in Philadelphia for orientation and training. At the end of the training, each student received a geographic assignment along with a list of friendly local contacts they could reach out to, should they need assistance. Given his assignment, one student remarked, "I feel as if we're parachuting behind enemy lines."[55] The seven-year journey leading up to the landmark case, *Furman v. Georgia*,[56] had begun.

Over the summer of 1965, rape-case data were collected. In the fall, Wolfgang enlisted a group of graduate students to begin the analysis. The time pressures were real, since defendants continued to be convicted and sentenced to death as the students worked. One early case involved William L. ("Willie Lee") Maxwell, a black man from Arkansas in his early twenties. Maxwell had been convicted in Hot Springs, Arkansas, for the rape of a 35-year-old white woman in 1961. His case had moved forward through several appeals, including an unsuccessful trip to the U.S. Supreme Court in 1965, just as the LSCRRC students began collecting data.[57]

Maxwell was scheduled to die on September 2, 1966. In early August of that year, LDF lawyers convinced a judge to review the data they had collected. Perhaps overwhelmed by the sheer volume of the information the LDF had gathered, the other side put forth no objection.[58] The appellate hearing began on August 22. Wolfgang had been rehearsing with his colleagues how to best present the sometimes complex and frequently mind-numbing statistics. When called on to testify, he reported that even after statistically adjusting for a multitude of contending explanations, the data remained compelling. The discriminatory nature of punishment of blacks in Arkansas for the crime of rape was clear, and it was very unlikely that these findings were due to random chance. Put in lay terms, if race was not systematically related to receiving a death sentence for rape in Arkansas, the results observed would have occurred by chance in only two or fewer similar time frames since the birth of Christ.[59]

The judge was listening, but he was not completely sympathetic. Despite the fact that he was impressed by Wolfgang's findings, he still had questions. The alternative explanations Wolfgang had explored were numerous, but not exhaustive. Racial discrimination was a subtle process. Statistical patterns did not define actions taken in this particular case. In a statement that must have made Wolfgang cringe, the judge concluded, "Statistics are elusive things at best, and it is a truism that almost anything can be proven by them."[60] On Friday, August 26, 1966, the judge dismissed the petition and declined to stay Maxwell's execution. It would proceed as planned the following week.

Amsterdam and his colleagues persisted, petitioning the Eighth Circuit Court. There, they hit a brick wall. Maxwell's execution would not be postponed while further appeals were pursued. Time was running very short, as the execution was scheduled for the coming Friday. Three LDF attorneys flew to Washington D.C. to file a request for a stay of execution with the U.S. Supreme Court, where they finally met with success. Just days before Maxwell was to be executed, the Eighth Circuit was told by the Supreme Court that issues raised by the LDF attorneys regarding sentencing guidelines being provided to juries, trial structure, and exclusion of jurors who expressed reservations about the imposition of capital punishment were important. The nation's highest court recommended a stay of execution while these issues were resolved.

LDF lawyers knew of many similar cases across the country. With a decision from the nation's highest court in hand, they now had criteria on which their appeals could proceed. They acted quickly to get the word out to their colleagues. Their aim was to secure a stay on all executions in the country. Amsterdam worked with a newly hired graduate of Harvard Law School, Jack Himmelstein, to create what came to be known as the "Last Aid Kit." As Amsterdam later remarked,

> We needed form documents to (1) ship out to lawyers all across the U.S. who were handling cases which were approaching an execution date and (2) enable us to move into new cases quickly ourselves if there were no other lawyers capable of handling the case.[61]

Despite the flurry of activity surrounding Maxwell's case, it took until June 11, 1968—almost two years—to secure a decision from the Eighth Circuit. Circuit Judge Harry Blackmun wrote the opinion, which first concentrated on the most prominent assertion of injustice—that death sentences for rape were racially biased. Having studied mathematics as an undergraduate, Blackmun was comfortable with statistical arguments. While impressed with Wolfgang's data, he rejected the associated legal claims. Statistics dealt with averages and patterns of behavior, but they did not go directly to the question of whether this particular defendant had been discriminated against.

It should be noted, Blackmun wrote,

> whatever suspicion [statistical evidence] may arouse with respect to Southern interracial rape trials as a group over a long period of time, and whatever it may disclose with respect to other localities, we feel that the statistical argument does nothing to destroy the integrity of Maxwell's trial. . . .
>
> Improper state practice of the past does not automatically invalidate a procedure of the present. . . . We are not yet ready to condemn and upset the result reached in every case of a Negro rape defendant in the State of Arkansas on the basis of broad theories of social and statistical injustice.[62]

Blackmun closed his written opinion with an unusual personal note that was not signed by his Eighth Circuit colleagues. Executing convicted offenders, he said, was personally "excruciating," as he was not convinced of the rightness of capital punishment. Capital punishment was, however, "a policy matter ordinarily to be resolved by the legislature or through executive clemency and not by the judiciary."[63] This would not be the last time Blackmun and Amsterdam would engage one another about when, by whom, and through what procedures capital punishment should be carried out—nor would it be the last time Blackmun would be bothered by his own decisions.

The Eighth Circuit's decision was appealed to the Supreme Court, and there Amsterdam presented his final argument for Maxwell on May 4, 1970. If blatantly discriminatory outcomes would not move the Court, Amsterdam began, perhaps arguments based on flawed procedures would. There were three problems.

In the first instance, it seemed self-evident that when removing the protective boundaries of life, juries should be given appropriate guidelines. There were none. Without standards, Amsterdam argued, there was no rule of law. It was more like rolling dice, with the outcome dependent on the whims and biases of the moment.

In the second instance, Amsterdam continued, the decision to execute a person should be reached only after securing full information about the circumstances surrounding the offense, as well as the defendant's background and character. The structure of capital punishment trials in the vast majority of states precluded this from happening. If the defendant's character and background were introduced during the guilt-or-innocence phase of the trial, it would likely be seen as an admission of guilt. Some separate procedure should be established, Amsterdam argued, that did not "whipsaw [a] capital defendant between his privilege against self-incrimination and his right to provide the jury with adequate information to make an informed sentencing choice."[64]

Last, there was the matter of jury selection. In states all across the nation, potential jurors expressing any reservations about imposing capital punishment were routinely removed from jury pools. This meant that jurors who were being empaneled were biased in favor of a sentence of death. In 1968, the Supreme Court had released a decision declaring this winnowing of jurors unconstitutional.[65] Amsterdam reminded the Court of its *Witherspoon v. Illinois* decision, noting that such exclusion of jurors remained widespread despite the decision, and had occurred in the Maxwell trial.

After listening for almost two and a half hours to arguments on both sides and considering the voluminous amount of supporting material, the Supreme Court, reiterating its earlier *Witherspoon* decision, held:

> A sentence of death cannot be carried out if the jury that imposed or recommended it was chosen by excluding [potential jurors] simply because they voiced general objections to the death penalty or expressed conscientious or religious scruples against its infliction.[66]

The Court was silent on Amsterdam's remaining two issues. Still, Maxwell would receive another trial as reformers moved gradually toward their goal.

## Efforts Intensify

Six months later, on December 22, 1970, another positive development occurred. Arkansas Governor Winthrop Rockefeller, who was in many ways sympathetic with the abolitionists' arguments, hosted a group of LDF lawyers, prison officials, and personal aides in Hot Springs to discuss the wisdom of commuting death sentences in Arkansas. As he spoke to Amsterdam, who had been speaking as the meeting drew to a close, the Governor was admiring and appreciative. "Thank you very much," Rockefeller said. "I had made up my mind, but what you were saying was so interesting that I did not want to interrupt you. . . . I have decided to commute them all."[67] A week later, on December 29, 1970, Rockefeller formally announced the commutation of fifteen Arkansas death sentences to life in prison, and urged other governors to follow his lead. Maxwell was among the inmates whose lives were spared by Rockefeller's act.

For those seeking the abolition of capital punishment, it was a moment to celebrate—but only a moment. A little more than four months later, on May 3, 1971, another Supreme Court decision was released involving two cases, one from California and one from Ohio.[68] Both cases raised once again the questions of whether guidelines were needed when juries sentenced a defendant to death and whether capital punishment trials should be split into guilt-or-innocence and punishment phases. Both questions had been left unresolved in the Court's *Maxwell* decision.

In a six-to-three opinion, the Court decided in the first instance that while guidelines for removing the protective boundaries of life might be helpful, they were not mandatory. As the Court put it,

In light of history, experience, and the present limitations of human knowledge, we find it quite impossible to say that committing to the untrammeled discretion of the jury the power to pronounce life or death in capital cases is offensive to anything in the Constitution.

Likewise, the Court ruled, constitutional standards were not violated by trial procedures combining consideration of guilt and punishment, even if defendants were, as Amsterdam had put it, "whipsawed" between self-incrimination and the right to provide adequate information for an informed sentencing choice.

Following these two decisions, Greenberg believed that the LDF's "capital punishment effort looked hopeless."[69] The Court had specifically rejected the two remaining mainstays of the LDF's strategy. Those seeking to abolish capital punishment were now involved in a last-ditch effort. Their strategy needed to be adjusted and clarified.

## The Core Question for a Last-Ditch Effort

The major focus of the LDF strategy had been procedural, but what about the core question? Was the taking of life for a crime committed ever appropriate, no matter the procedures? The Supreme Court had never directly ruled on this question, but the prospects were not good. In the opinion he wrote in the Ohio and California cases, Justice Hugo Black had noted that it was inconceivable that the framers of the Constitution would consider executions unacceptable. Executions for crimes committed had been imposed since the birth of the nation, and long before that. On what rationale was capital punishment unconstitutional? He could think of none.

For others, however, the issue was not so clear. In a dissenting opinion written in 1963, Justice Arthur Goldberg had argued just the opposite. Moral systems evolved, and many punishments once thought to be acceptable were no longer allowed. Jack Greenberg had seen Goldberg's dissent as an invitation to launch the LDF's anti-death penalty crusade. Tony Amsterdam would later note with a poetic touch:

> The Goldberg dissent was an important item on the legal horizon that bounded the playing field on which we made our decisions and plans. It was one peak in a mountain chain whose tops were visible over the horizon.[70]

After leaving the Court, Goldberg and his former law clerk Alan Dershowitz had elaborated on Goldberg's argument for death penalty abolition in the article "Declaring the Death Penalty Unconstitutional."[71] "We are in the midst of a great national debate over capital punishment," Goldberg and Dershowitz began. "The debate is being carried on in the legislative, executive and judicial chambers of our state and national governments." At issue was whether the nation should take, as Albert Camus had called it, the "great civilizing step" of abolishing the death penalty.

LDF lawyers experienced an increased sense of urgency. They had intended to hold a planning conference in February, 1972. It would now take place on May 15 and 16, 1971, some eight months earlier than originally planned. Amsterdam would provide the keynote address. Among the materials distributed to those attending was a revised Last Aid Kit, which had first been put together in 1968.[72] A month later, on June 28, the Supreme Court agreed to consider the remaining core question: Did the imposition and carrying out of the death penalty constitute cruel and unusual punishment? It was the moment LDF lawyers had been working toward.

Four cases were being reviewed: one from California, two from Georgia, and one from Texas. The California State Supreme Court was simultaneously hearing the California case, which involved a particularly gruesome set of facts and a defendant twice convicted of rape and murder. Given the heinous offense involved and the defendant's background, if the California case were combined with the other three cases, the argument before the U.S. Supreme Court would be difficult. The LDF attorneys were relieved when California's Supreme Court accepted Amsterdam's argument that capital punishment was degrading, dehumanizing, incompatible with the dignity of man, unnecessary to any legitimate goal, and therefore in violation of the state's constitution.[73]

The California case was separated from the other three, where the charges were much less severe. One of the Georgia cases involved a burglar who had tripped while fleeing after being discovered by the home owner. The gun he was carrying went off and killed a member of the household, apparently by accident. The other Georgia case and the Texas case involved death sentences for rape.

## Arbitrary and Capricious Procedures

It was hard to argue that the Constitution forbade executions. Clearly, they had been allowed for centuries for a wide range of offenses. However, in years gone by, whippings, brandings, and the amputation of ears had also been allowed—all practices that had been abandoned in modern times as being barbaric. After all, there was once a time when boiling in oil and disembowelment were also seen as effective deterrents or acceptable retribution. These punishments were now viewed as repulsive offenses to the dignity of all humanity—no matter the crime, and no matter the impact on future offenses.

The question was: Had the U.S.A. evolved to a point where killing people as punishment was no longer acceptable? Arguing his case before the Supreme Court on January 17, 1972, Amsterdam underscored this question and drew parallels with the dramatic decline in executions over the past several decades. While not determinative, this trend was important, since it suggested that moral standards had shifted toward the total abolition of capital punishment.

Even if moral standards justifying capital punishment remained in place, Amsterdam continued, another important matter remained: the ample evidence that existing procedures were not even-handed. He introduced an updated version of the Wolfgang study documenting the inequality of punishment, showing that capital punishment had been and continued to be unpredictably and unevenly applied. While the Constitution might not prohibit the death penalty per se, it most certainly did not tolerate such inequality.

As the arguments drew to a close, optimism among LDF lawyers was waning. Michael Meltsner, a leading attorney on the team, wrote about the period, "It was not overstating the matter to say that a victory for abolition would rank among the greatest surprises in American legal history."[74] Five and a half months later, on June 29, 1972, that surprise arrived as the Court released its ruling on *Furman v. Georgia*[75]—a contentious five-to-four decision.

There was little agreement among the justices in *Furman*, even among those who reached the same conclusion. The majority, however, concluded in this landmark decision that while capital punishment was not categorically unconstitutional, the current practice of it was. Among those working for reform, "Fantasy had become reality. Against every expectation, by the slimmest of margins, the future of the death penalty in America had been irrevocably altered."[76]

By a narrow margin, and for kaleidoscopic reasons, capital punishment as it was currently practiced in the United States had been declared arbitrary and capricious. If states could come up with remedies for the various procedural problems noted, however, capital punishment could once again be justified. The states did not take long to respond.

## Procedures for Taking Life Are Clarified

Every state that had a capital punishment statute prior to *Furman* passed new death penalty statutes. The new laws were responsive to the procedural and substantive concerns raised in *Furman*. Using these statutes, trials were held and convictions secured. By the end of 1975, three years after *Furman* had emptied death rows across the nation, 400 new inmates were awaiting execution. Attorneys working with the LDF were representing about a hundred of these cases.[77]

On January 22, 1976, the Supreme Court agreed to review five death sentences that had emerged from the revised statutes, as each were representative of the new laws that had been passed. All five came from Southern states: Florida, Georgia, Louisiana, North Carolina, and Texas.[78] In 1977, and then again in 1978, two additional cases—one from Georgia and one from Ohio—would be decided.[79] Together, these seven cases mapped new roads along which death sentencing procedures could travel. Additional refinements would come, but by the end of 1978 legal justifications were once again in place for justifying the taking of a life in exchange for acts committed.

As Amsterdam noted, the revised statutes were designed to provide "the road to death with avenues of discretionary mercy shooting off from the beginning of the process to the end."[80] As the Court's various affirmations and rejections had been written and released, they clarified the revised path for removing the protective boundaries of life and imposing death. Bifurcated trials that separated the finding of guilt from the assessment of punishment were a good idea, but were not required. Guidelines for judges and juries, which were aimed at balancing mitigating and aggravating circumstances of the defendant's character and the nature of the offense, were mandatory. Mandatory sentences or sentences grossly disproportionate to the crime committed were prohibited.

While some fog had been lifted, a great deal remained. What constituted a grossly disproportionate sentence? What were the important dimensions of a defendant's background and character? A pattern of past violent behavior was relevant, but did the offender's age matter? If so, what was the appropriate threshold? Did mental retardation mitigate the level of punishment a particular crime demanded? If so, what level of retardation was required? Did a defendant's chronological or mental age shift his or her culpability? Was it possible to prohibit mandatory sentences and demand consideration of a defendant's character and circumstances of the crime without introducing personal bias and associated inequalities?

As lawyers and appellate justices grappled with these questions, frustration and mixed messages frequently emerged. The uncertain complexity of conflicting imperatives led some key players to change their minds.

The first post-*Furman* execution in the United States occurred on January 17, 1977.[81] It had been almost a decade since the last execution had taken place in June, 1967. There were no executions in 1978, and a total of five between 1979 and 1982. In 1983 and 1984, several remaining details of the post-*Furman* statutes were clarified.[82] In 1983 there were five executions. Then, in 1984, there were twenty-one. The post-*Furman* era of executions had begun. Yearly fluctuations characterized the second half of the 1980s, with a high of twenty-five (1987) and a low of eleven (1988). In the 1990s, executions turned sharply upward, more than quadrupling from twenty-three to ninety-eight between 1990 and 1999. While death sentences were being imposed across the country, it was in the former Confederacy that the disproportionate number, hovering around 90 percent, of executions was taking place. It had been almost fifty years since the annual national total had reached this level. Public support for capital punishment was firmly in place, with approval ratings fluctuating at around 80 percent.

## The Pendulum Swings

By 1994, however, Justice Harry Blackmun, who had been elevated to the Supreme Court, was thoroughly disenchanted. In February of that year, he wrote,

> From this day forward, I no longer shall tinker with the machinery of death. For more than 20 years I have endeavored—indeed, I have struggled—along with a majority of this Court to develop procedural and substantive rules that would lend more than the mere appearance of fairness to the death penalty endeavor. Rather than continue to coddle the Court's delusion that the desired level of fairness has been achieved and the need for regulation eviscerated, I feel morally and intellectually obligated simply to concede that the death penalty experiment has failed.[83]

Blackmun had specific reasons for his disenchantment. There was continuing evidence of inequitable punishment. There was also growing concern about the possible innocence of some who had been sentenced to death. While such concerns were long-standing,[84] recent events had underscored the possible pervasiveness of the problem.

To Blackmun, it was time to admit failure and call a halt to all death penalty proceedings. Referring to a 1987 case from Georgia,[85] he chided his colleagues for having turned their backs on "staggering evidence" that racial prejudice continued to infect Georgia's capital sentencing scheme.[86] Since that decision, broad-ranging evidence of this prejudice had continued to mount,[87] and eventually, Blackmun had come to question whether the problem was at all resolvable. Was there truth in the suggestion, he wondered, "that discrimination and arbitrariness could not be purged from the administration of capital punishment without sacrificing the equally essential component of fairness—individualized sentencing?"[88]

Inequitable sentencing was only part of the story. In the same year that the staggering evidence of continuing racial bias had been presented, and in Blackmun's mind ignored, the *Stanford Law Review* published a detailed examination of some 350 cases involving convictions of individuals who were later found to be innocent. The conclusions of this widely cited article were again unequivocal. If the evidence presented failed "to convince the reader of the fallibility of human judgment," the authors wrote, "then nothing will."[89] Five years later, the study was updated.[90] The conclusions remained the same.

## Science, Technology, and Innocence

The Human Genome Project was launched in 1990, and the emerging techniques of DNA profiling it yielded were increasingly used over the ensuing years. The forensic significance of these techniques was quickly recognized. In 1992, two lawyers who had been litigating cases founded an organization called The Innocence Project, which was dedicated to proving the innocence of wrongfully convicted people through DNA testing.[91] Kirk Bloodsworth, who had been sentenced to death in 1984, left a Maryland prison in 1993 as the first man ever to be exonerated on the basis of DNA evidence.[92] Bloodsworth had been sentenced to death and held in prison for nine years for a crime he did not commit. In 1995, two additional DNA-related exonerations were uncovered in Illinois. More would follow.[93]

Concerns over executing an innocent defendant were magnified when—in the same year Kirk Bloodsworth left prison and a year prior to Blackmun's decision to no longer "tinker with the machinery of death"—the Supreme Court refused Leonel Herrera's request for a stay of execution. Evidence had come to light that suggested his innocence. The evidence was not based on DNA, but instead on new testimony from people associated with the crime.

On appeal, the Supreme Court concluded that Herrera's case had not passed the extraordinarily high threshold for mandating further review of evidence presented at trial. If the Court granted this request, six justices concluded, a flood of cases would surely follow, and the system would collapse under its weight. With barely restrained anger, Blackmun wrote,

> Of one thing I am certain, just as an execution without adequate safeguards is unacceptable, so too is an execution when the condemned prisoner can prove that he is innocent. The execution of a person who can show that he is innocent comes perilously close to simple murder.[94]

On May 12, 1993, Leonel Herrera was executed. He had been on death row for more than eleven years. His last words were,

> I am innocent, innocent, innocent. Make no mistake about this; I owe society nothing. Continue the struggle for human rights, helping those who are innocent, especially Mr. Graham. I am an innocent man, and something very wrong is taking place tonight. May God bless you all. I am ready.[95]

Gary Graham, the inmate Herrera had mentioned in his statement, was executed some seven years later.[96]

For Blackmun, the proper course in the face of what he now viewed as a deeply flawed system, namely inequitably executing individuals and refusing to respond to possible innocence, was clear. Focusing on the contradictory demands of two earlier decisions,[97] the remedy was not, Blackmun wrote, "to ignore one or the other, nor to pretend that the dilemma does not exist, but to admit the futility of the effort to harmonize them. This means accepting the fact that the death penalty cannot be administered in accord with our Constitution."[98] Progress had been made, but important and perhaps irremediable problems remained.[99]

Blackmun's change of heart was not shared by the majority of his colleagues on the Supreme Court, but Justice Lewis Powell was an exception. Like Blackmun, Powell had repeatedly voted in favor of the constitutional standing of executions. Speaking with his biographer in 1991, some four years after his retirement from the Court, Powell was asked whether he would change his vote in any case. He replied, "I would vote the other way in any capital case . . . I have come to think that capital punishment should be abolished." The convoluted procedures that had emerged in the post-*Furman* years had led Powell, like Blackmun, to believe that the seemingly endless litigation in capital cases brought "discredit on the whole legal system."[100]

The disenchantment Blackmun expressed in 1994, coupled with Powell's equally negative assessment, did not go unnoticed. The pioneering Innocence Project was soon joined by some eighty similar efforts involving a number of law schools, journalism programs, and public defender offices across the nation. Together, they formed the core of what came to be called "The Innocence Network."[101] Numerous articles about their work began appearing in academic journals and the popular press. For example, two law professors writing in the *Harvard Law Review* in 1995 published a lengthy account of how the Court had created a body of law that was "at once so messy and so meaningless."[102]

## A Messy and Meaningless System

Exonerations of the wrongfully convicted continued to grow in number. In mid-November, 1998, the National Conference on Wrongful Convictions and the Death Penalty was held just outside Chicago at the Northwestern University School of Law. The conference was spurred by recent findings of innocence, most immediately in Illinois. Among the meeting's attendees were twenty-eight people who had been sentenced to death for crimes they had not committed and had subsequently been exonerated. About 1,200 academics, lawyers, and activists involved in the now-growing Innocence Network also attended. The conference served as the launching pad for the Northwestern University Law School Center on Wrongful Convictions.[103]

As the strength of Innocence Network mounted, concern deepened. In February and April, 2000, U.S. Senator Patrick Leahy of Vermont, U.S. Representatives Bill Delahunt of Massachusetts and Ray LaHood of Illinois, and eighty-one other co-sponsors introduced versions of an Innocence Protection Act in both houses of Congress. Six months later, on June 12, 2000, three colleagues working at Columbia University Law School and New York University's Sociology Department published a research paper entitled *A Broken System: Error Rates in Capital Cases, 1973–1995*.[104] The executive summary of this lengthy report was clear and direct: the concerns voiced by Blackmun and Powell were well founded. Serious, documented, and reversible errors had been found in 68 percent of the 4,578 cases since capital punishment had been reinstated.

In the introduction section, the authors of *A Broken System* wrote, "There is a growing bipartisan consensus that flaws in America's death-penalty system have reached crisis proportions." Many feared that a substantial number of persons on death row did not belong there. As the first statistical study ever undertaken of modern American capital appeals, this research paper suggested that both claims were correct. "Our 23 years' worth of results," the authors concluded, "reveal a death penalty system collapsing under the weight of its own mistakes."

On July 3, 2001, a year after *A Broken System* was released, Supreme Court Justice Sandra Day O'Connor, who, like Powell and Blackmun, had upheld capital punishment in rulings on numerous occasions, gave a widely reported speech to the Minnesota Women Lawyers Association. "If statistics are any indication," she reported, "the system may well be allowing some innocent defendants to be executed." On April 8, 2002, Ray Krone became the hundredth former death row inmate freed because of innocence in the post-*Furman* years, and the twelfth who was freed on the basis of DNA evidence. He had spent ten years in Arizona's prison system for a crime he had not committed. In the coming years, inmates like Krone became more common.[105]

Around this same time, an unexpected trend began to emerge. After rising throughout the 1990s, the number of yearly executions began to decline. Executions had quadrupled in frequency, from twenty-three in 1990 to a total of ninety-eight in 1999. In 2000, there were eighty-five executions. By 2005, the total was sixty. By the end of the decade, they had dropped to roughly half the rate in 2000.[106] Statistics published by the Bureau of Justice reflected a parallel decline in the number of death sentences imposed. In the mid- to late 1990s, around 300 per year were given. By 2010, the number was closer to a hundred. This reduction in death sentences signaled a further decline in executions in the years ahead.

## A Watershed Moratorium

Building on the growing chorus for reform, on January 31, 2000, less than two weeks prior to the introduction of the Innocence Protection Act in Congress, Illinois Governor George Ryan declared a moratorium on executions in his state. Ryan believed that the specter of killing possibly innocent persons had become too great. Ryan's actions crystallized thought and precipitated dramatic action for reform across the country.

A series of precipitating events preceded Ryan's moratorium:

- The Conference on Wrongful Convictions, which had been held at Illinois' Northwestern University a little more than a year earlier, had drawn the Governor's attention. At the conference, four cases of wrongful convictions in Illinois were spotlighted.
- There was evidence that while twelve people had been executed in Illinois since *Furman,* thirteen people had been sentenced to death and later found to be innocent.
- The *Chicago Tribune* published a series of articles on a range of death penalty issues. The week prior to Ryan's announcement, one *Tribune* headline read,

"Half of State's Death-Penalty Cases Reversed,"[107] The accompanying story included the "amazing figure" that among death penalty cases in Illinois, exactly half (130) had been reversed for a new trial or sentencing hearing—a fact that underscored the findings reported in *A Broken System*.

Like justices Blackmun and Powell, Governor Ryan was convinced that the system of capital punishment was flawed beyond repair.

During the Illinois moratorium, the governor established a commission to investigate the state's apparently flawed system of justice. On January 11, 2003, after the commission reported its findings, the Governor spoke to an overflow crowd at the Center on Wrongful Convictions. He told his audience,

> Our capital [punishment] system is haunted by the demon of error, error in determining guilt and error in determining who among the guilty deserves to die. What effect was race having? What effect was poverty having? Because of all these reasons, today I am commuting the sentences of all death row inmates.[108]

Ryan granted outright pardons to four inmates. The death sentences of approximately 170 (estimates varied slightly) other convicted offenders were commuted to life in prison without parole. Echoing Blackmun, Ryan reviewed his decision while talking with inmates on death row. "Because the Illinois death penalty system is arbitrary and capricious—and therefore immoral," he told them, "I no longer shall tinker with the machinery of death."

Some, however, did not view the Governor's decision as a mark of progress. Family members of victims like Ollie Dodds, whose daughter had been killed in a fire allegedly started by one of the pardoned men, was among them. She saw Ryan's action as a mockery. The man she held responsible for her daughter's death had been convicted and sentenced to death. With the stroke of a pen, the Governor now said he could live, and then went even further, releasing him from prison altogether. The still-grieving mother simply did not understand "how he could do that."[109]

As the first decade of the twenty-first century unfolded, those opposing capital punishment had successfully shifted the framing argument away from an emphasis on inequity and toward the question of innocence.[110] A new battleground had been forged. The efforts of those who wished to abolish or drastically revise the death penalty system began to be felt. On October 30, 2004, almost five years after Ryan's death penalty moratorium in Illinois, a revised version of the Innocence Protection Act was signed into law by President George W. Bush.[111] Given the numerous documented convictions of innocent people and the high probability of further mistakes, willingness to use the death penalty seemed to be on the wane. "A social cascade, starting with legal clinics and innocence projects," the authors of a 2008 study reported, "has snowballed into a national phenomenon that may spell the end of the death penalty in America."[112]

In the post-*Furman* era, thirty-seven states enacted revised capital punishment statutes. In December, 2007, twenty-five years after its new death penalty statute had been enacted in 1982, New Jersey became the first post-*Furman* state to abolish capital punishment and replace it with life in prison without the possibility of parole.[113] New Mexico followed in March, 2009. When signing his state's bill, New Mexico Governor Bill Richardson, who had been a proponent of capital punishment, pointed to the dehumanizing impact of a flawed system. "The potential for . . . execution of an innocent person," Richardson announced, "stands as anathema to our very sensibilities as human beings."[114]

Innocence was not the only issue. Whether, and the extent to which, people were culpable for their actions depended as well on their age and state of mind.

### Mental Retardation and Age

On June 26, 1989, the Supreme Court released a five-to-four decision in a case from Texas involving a convict by the name of Johnny Paul Penry.[115] The opinion did not express a belief that Penry was innocent. Before the victim died, she had described her assailant, and Penry fit the description. Penry had twice confessed to the brutal rape, beating, and stabbing, which had taken place in Livingston, Texas, in October, 1979. The problem was that Johnny Penry was 22 years old with the mental age of a 6-year-old, and the social maturity of a 9- or 10-year-old. His IQ was assessed as being in the severely retarded range, somewhere close to 55.

At issue in the Supreme Court appeal was whether the Constitution categorically prohibited Penry's execution because he was mentally retarded. In divergent opinions that reflected the hazy boundaries and the dilemmas involved, the justices had expressed both support for and opposition to this assertion. In the end, Justice O'Connor, writing for the five-to-four majority, found no "sufficient objective evidence today of a national consensus against executing mentally retarded capital murderers."

Most of the justices were aware that public opinion might someday turn against executing the mentally retarded, but, they noted, the "petitioner has cited only one state statute that explicitly bans that practice, and has offered no evidence of the general behavior of juries in this regard." O'Connor's written decision expressed skepticism: "Opinion surveys indicating strong public opposition to such executions do not establish a societal consensus, absent some legislative reflection of the sentiment expressed therein."

This was in June, 1989.[116] Thirteen years later, on June 20, 2002—half a year before Ryan commuted the sentences of death row inmates in Illinois—in a six-to-three decision involving a case from Virginia, the Court found that "much has changed since *Penry's* conclusion."[117]

This time, the conviction being appealed involved a robbery and murder committed by two men in 1996. One of the men, Daryl Atkins, was judged to be mentally retarded. During the thirteen years that had passed since the *Penry* decision, eighteen of the thirty-seven states with post-*Furman* death penalty statutes had passed laws limiting execution of the mentally retarded. The Court noted,

> Given that anticrime legislation is far more popular than legislation pro-
> tecting violent criminals, the large number of States prohibiting the execution

of mentally retarded persons (and the complete absence of legislation reinstating such executions) provides powerful evidence that today society views mentally retarded offenders as categorically less culpable than the average criminal.

To the majority of the Court, arguments for retribution and deterrence applied to the mentally retarded were not persuasive. When it came to retribution, the Court noted, "The severity of the appropriate punishment necessarily depends on the offender's culpability."

Because those who lacked substantial mental capacity were now considered less culpable, death sentences could not be justified. The same could be said about deterrence. By this time, the vast majority of studies and the opinions of professionals directly involved in law enforcement suggested that capital punishment had very little, if any, deterrent effect. Among the mentally retarded, the Court found, the threat of the death penalty would have even less of an effect. Justice John Paul Stevens wrote for the majority:

> The same cognitive and behavioral impairments that make the mentally retarded defendants less morally culpable also make it less likely that they can process the information of the possibility of execution as a punishment and, as a result, control their conduct based upon that information.

Finally, the Court found that executing a mentally retarded offender increased the likelihood of taking a life from someone who was wrongfully convicted. "They [the retarded] will unwittingly confess to crimes they did not commit." They have a lessened ability to "give their counsel meaningful assistance." Their general demeanor "may create an unwarranted impression of lack of remorse for their crimes." Thus, for reasons of evolving standards of decency, reduced justification based on deterrence and retribution, and heightened likelihood of killing the innocent, the Court ruled in 2002 that executing mentally retarded offenders violated the Constitution's prohibition against cruel and unusual punishments.

Writing in harsh dissent, Justice Antonin Scalia and two of his colleagues suggested that the majority's attempt to "fabricate" evidence for a shifting moral consensus was feeble at best. As for culpability, Scalia noted that:

> only the *severely* or *profoundly* mentally retarded, commonly known as "idiots," enjoyed any special status under the law. . . . Mentally retarded offenders with less severe impairments—those who were not "idiots"—suffered criminal prosecution and punishment, including capital punishment.

Conflating mental retardation with mental illness and insanity, Justice Scalia and his dissenting colleagues went on to note, "It is very difficult to define the indivisible line that divides perfect and partial insanity." "This newest invention," Scalia continued, "promises to be more effective than any of the others in turning the process of capital trial into a game."

Scalia's views were already well known. Years earlier, in the same session during which Johnny Penry's case was decided, Justice Scalia had elaborated on his views.[118] Two cases—one from Kentucky and one from Missouri, both of which involved brutal murders—had been consolidated in 1989. Instead of mental retardation, the issue before the Court in these cases was chronological age. One case involved a 20-year-old woman named Barbel Poore, who had been raped, sodomized, and then shot point-blank in the face and back of the head during the course of a robbery in Jefferson County, Kentucky. The robbery had netted 300 cartons of cigarettes, two gallons of fuel, and a small amount of cash. The offender, Kevin Stanford, was only eight months shy of his eighteenth birthday at the time of the offense, which had taken place on January 7, 1981.

Kentucky law allowed Kevin Stanford to be tried as an adult. He was convicted and sentenced to death. Stanford's behavior belied the idea of the deterrent effect of capital punishment—in fact, it suggested that the threat of execution had actually encouraged the murder. A correctional officer testified about a conversation he had had with Stanford in which the accused explained his behavior.

> I had to shoot her, [she] lived next door to me and she would recognize me. . . . I guess we could have tied her up or something or beat [her up] . . . and tell her if she tells, we would kill her. . . . Then after he said that, he started laughing.

The second case was from Missouri, where the law permitted teenagers between the ages of 14 and 17 to be tried as adults. The offender, Heath Wilkins, was approximately 16 years old when the crime occurred on July 27, 1985. Wilkins and an accomplice had planned to rob a store in Avondale, Missouri. Before the robbery, they agreed to kill whoever was behind the counter because "a dead person can't talk." The victim, Nancy Allen, was a 26-year-old mother of two. She had been repeatedly stabbed in the heart and neck and left to die after Wilkins and his accomplice left the store with liquor, cigarettes, rolling papers, and approximately US$450 in cash and checks.

After reviewing the two cases, Scalia and four of his colleagues on the Court found nothing in the Constitution that would prohibit executing people like Wilkins and Stanford. Regardless of their age, these men had done things that negated their right to live. Writing for the majority, Scalia concluded,

> We discern neither a historical nor a modern societal consensus forbidding the imposition of capital punishment on any person who murders at 16 or 17 years of age. Accordingly, we conclude that such punishment does not offend the Eighth Amendment's prohibition against cruel and unusual punishment.

This was in 1989. By 2005, things had changed.[119] The case of *Roper v. Simmons* involved two offenders. Only 17 years old, high school junior Christopher Simmons and a 15-year-old accomplice set out at 2:00 a.m. with the intention of robbing and killing someone. They picked the home of Shirley Crook, who had been involved in a car accident with Simmons. They entered Crook's home, woke her, bound her, and drove her to a nearby park. There, they further secured her hands with electrical wire, wrapped her face in duct tape, and threw her off a bridge; Crook drowned in the water below.

Simmons had told his accomplice they could get away with the crime because they were minors. The day after the murder, Simmons was heard bragging to others about how he had killed the victim "because the bitch seen my face." There was no question that Simmons had committed the crimes he was charged with—robbery, kidnapping, and murder.

The convictions of both Simmons and his accomplice were appealed. The appeal asked the Supreme Court to reverse its 1989 decision based on an extension of the same reasoning used to prohibit the execution of the mentally retarded. Was there evidence that standards of decency had evolved to the point where executing convicted offenders under a certain age was no longer acceptable? Did the Court believe, due to reduced culpability, that the death penalty was a disproportionate punishment for juveniles?

In 1989, when the cases involving Kevin Stanford and Heath Wilkins had been decided, twenty-five states prohibited the death penalty for juveniles. In the intervening years, five additional states had abandoned the practice of sentencing juveniles to death, and no state had lowered the minimum age for capital punishment. Even in states that permitted the execution of juvenile offenders, the practice was rarely carried out. Even in Kentucky—despite the outrage of the victim's family—the state's governor had ended up commuting Stanford's sentence to life.

In its 2005 ruling, the majority of the court agreed that enough evidence existed to suggest that moral standards had changed. As it had found in the case of mental retardation, the Court now found "the susceptibility of juveniles to immature and irresponsible behavior" meant that their wrongful conduct was "not as morally reprehensible as that of an adult." Juveniles also had "a greater claim than adults to be forgiven for failing to escape negative influences." Finally, given their still-malleable identities, it was "less supportable to conclude that even a heinous crime committed by a juvenile is evidence of an irretrievably depraved character." Justices voting with the majority recognized that drawing a line at 18 years of age was subject "to the objection always raised against categorical rules." But a line had to be drawn somewhere.

Five of the justices involved in the 2005 decision believed that the Court's 1989 decision was no longer binding. In his announcement of the verdict, Justice Anthony Kennedy remarked, "Today our society views juveniles as categorically less culpable than the average criminal . . . the death penalty may not be imposed on offenders who were under 18 when they committed the crime."[120]

Justice Antonin Scalia, joined by Chief Justice William Rehnquist and Justice Clarence Thomas, again gave strong voice to those who stood in opposition; they found little reason to grant mercy. The crime was as calculated as it was chilling. The offenders knew precisely what they were doing. They should be held accountable. Scalia found it implausible that moral standards for capital punishment could have evolved that dramatically in so short a time—that "a national consensus that could not be perceived in our people's laws barely 15 years ago now solidly exists." Simmons' act was a horrendous crime that easily crossed the threshold of acts deserving of death. The three dissenting justices took offense at the majority's ruling and viewed with disdain the idea that the Court would proclaim itself "sole arbiter of our nation's moral standards." This role was better left to legislators and juries.

They disagreed also with the majority's assessment of culpability. Hadn't the American Psychological Association (APA) asserted, on the basis of "a rich body of research," just the opposite in a case occurring only a few years earlier? (That case involved questions about securing an abortion without parental consent.[121]) Hadn't the APA concluded that by age 14 or 15 a person's ability to make moral judgments was well in place? Hadn't it stated that juveniles had developed "abilities similar to adults in reasoning about moral dilemmas, understanding social rules and laws and reasoning about interpersonal relationships and interpersonal problems?" Which took greater maturity, Scalia wondered: "Deciding whether to have an abortion or deciding what the 17-year-old defendant in this case had to decide, whether to throw a live and conscious woman to her death over a bridge?"[122] Such contradictory conclusions by the APA were scientifically disturbing, and when used by the Court to justify their decisions they were a travesty.

## Shifting Standards

As these cases suggest, the threshold for legitimized execution has shifted dramatically over time. It is increasingly evident when you compare current practices with those proposed in the kingdom of Hammurabi, the chosen people of Israel, or the followers of Prophet Muhammad. If you visit the Louvre museum in Paris, you will find on display a large, fine-grained, polished volcanic stele that stands about two and a half meters high. It dates from the eighteenth century BC, when it stood on public display in Babylonia. Later, after being pillaged, it was displayed in what is now southwestern Iran. Etched on the surface of the stele is the Code of Hammurabi. The preface to the Code reveals that Hammurabi was chosen by the gods to bring law and justice to his people. The laws Hammurabi transcribed were numerous (around 282, depending on the translation), specific, and harsh.[123]

In Hammurabi's day, the penalty could be death for burglary, robbery, and looting (with special protections for slave owners and the property of gods and kings). Aspects of family life, a range of sexual relations, and women bearing children also received special protections through the imposition of death. Shoddy workmanship could result in the deaths of the craftsman and his offspring. With a wide array of capital offenses in place, accurate accusations were critical. People were discouraged from bringing false charges or charges without convincing evidence—the penalty for which was also death. Such was the Code of Hammurabi.

Laws rooted in this Code were still enforced centuries later. Early in the Book of Genesis, the devastating floodwaters that had drowned the world receded when God spoke to Noah. As he outlined the conditions of his Covenant, God told Noah,

"I will demand an accounting for the life of another human being. Whoever sheds human blood, by human beings shall their blood be shed; for in the image of God has God made humankind." To believers, these are powerful words with long-lasting impact. Like the Code of Hammurabi, the Jewish Torah justifies capital punishment for anyone who threatens the fabric of communal life. The taking of a life was an appropriate punishment for crimes that threatened to destabilize commerce, endangered the family, involved deviant sexual behavior, and offended God.

Reflecting the continuity of the Abrahamic faiths, similar passages that refer to Moses and the People of Israel are found in Allah's Final Revelation to Muhammad in the Holy Qur'an. These passages reaffirmed the harsh punishment that awaited anyone who dared threaten God, his community, and his messenger. Like the laws of Hammurabi and those found in the Torah, the Qur'an demanded the execution of anyone who threatened the stability of communal and family life. As one translation puts it, death awaits those who "spread mischief in the land."[124]

While no records exist of the patterns of punishments—who, by what means, and for what offenses—that befell the citizens in these ancient civilizations, it is likely that those already near the margins of assessed social worth were those most likely to receive death as their punishment. This conclusion has been widely noted and repeatedly illustrated across time, place, and life circumstances.[125]

We come, then, to the end. The paradox of protecting life by taking life remains troubling. The thresholds and procedures for removing the protective boundaries of life remain in question. We have seen these questions raised in each of the preceding chapters. Given the uncertain and shifting boundaries of assessed social worth, and the inherent moral dilemmas which by definition cannot be satisfactorily resolved, the related questions of who should live, who should die, and who should decide are unlikely to disappear anytime soon.

# Epilogue
## Six Lessons Learned

This book has focused on a single defining question: How do communities go about justifying the violation of deeply important moral imperatives, while holding firmly to their importance? The answer we have repeatedly found is that boundaries are drawn and dilemmas resolved. Two of these moral imperatives absorbed our attention:

- Life is sacred (intrinsically important) and should be protected.
- Suffering, once detected, should be alleviated.

Six general lessons may be drawn from the events chronicled here.

**Lesson One: The Power of Assessed Social Worth.** Justification of the violation of imperatives calling for the protection of life and the alleviation of suffering are grounded in socially defined, historically variable definitions of social worth. The protective boundaries of life are rearranged accordingly. Through logic and empathy, mentally handicapped people become "parasites," fetuses become "non-persons," "monstrosities at birth" become "imperiled infants," lives become "vegetative," and convicted felons become demonized animals.

**Lesson Two: Change Comes Along a Jagged and Contentious Path.** Moral systems evolve along a jagged and contentious path. One source of discontinuity is science and associated technologies. With unexpected breakthroughs, new questions emerge. Current moral and legal systems are simply not up to the task. We have seen many examples of the ensuing "cultural lag."

Newly refined kidney machines, respirators, and organ transplant procedures brought hope to people previously facing certain death. On what basis should limited life-prolonging resources be distributed: first-come, first-served; random assignment; ability to pay; or assessment of social worth? New medical treatments have provided the ability to prolong the lives of young infants. Should these treatments be used, even if they mean the child's short life will be filled with suffering and resource-draining medical care? Medical technology now allows a life to be maintained, even when the person in question has lost all cognitive and emotional capacity. In other situations, these technologies can be used to keep someone alive, only to face a life filled with suffering. Is life in a vegetative state, or a life filled with suffering, a life worth prolonging and protecting?

The debates over these questions have been contentious and long running. Major shifts have occurred at points where crystallizing events clarified the implications of one action or another. Again, supporting evidence is abundant. *Buck v. Bell,* the thalidomide scare, the *Quinlan* case, the radiation, Willowbrook, and Tuskegee experiments, the trials of the Scottsboro Boys, and the torture and killing of Emmett Till all clarified issues and precipitated otherwise elusive reforms. The Civil Rights Movement proceeded with increased force, and the first-ever piece of legislation calling for the development of a national moral framework was passed into law. A set of bioethical principles aimed at enhancing and clarifying the moral significance of individual autonomy, justice, and beneficence became the law of the land.

**Lesson Three: The Importance of Analogies, Metaphors, Images, and Stories.** Adjustments in the assessment of social worth and resolution of deeply important moral dilemmas are achieved when analogies are drawn, metaphors identified, empathy-generating images fashioned, and stories told. Supreme Court justices have grounded their logic in analogies found in the penumbras of the Constitution. Theologians and religious zealots look to the similarly shadowed niches of sacred scriptures to find their guidelines. Pro-life films are produced and graphic posters carried to generate empathy for the human qualities of a fetus. "Partial-birth abortion" becomes a phrase of political art.

From such analogies, metaphors, images, and stories, the protective boundaries of life and tolerable suffering are redefined. In the process, the legitimacy of existing understandings and practices is reassessed. Yet uncertainty and disagreements remain.

**Lesson Four: Who Decides?** Many social movements are designed to rectify perceived injustices and establish legitimate authority for decision makers. These movements—often likened to moral crusades—succeed or fail according to their ability to coalesce networks, mobilize resources, and frame issues. These purpose-driven reform efforts are evidenced in the eugenics movement of the late nineteenth and early twentieth centuries, which eventually led to the *Buck v. Bell* decision. They are manifest in the pro-life movement's protests, clinic blockades, and violence against abortion providers. They are found in debates over the individual's right to die. They are no less evident in the reform movements aimed at redefining the legitimacy of capital punishment practices. In each case, perceived injustice, assessed legitimacy, and the intensity of efforts to reform are bound together as forces shaping the nature of power and political struggles over who should decide these uncertain and contentious issues.

**Lesson Five: Dilemmas Lead to Cyclical Change.** From these widely varied arenas, a general proposition emerges: Dilemmas involving competing and deeply important moral principles produce cyclical social change. In the early twentieth century, a loose network of individuals and organizations used the findings and theories of Charles Darwin as a cornerstone to organize their efforts, mobilize resources, and frame issues. Ultimately, their efforts produced a Supreme Court decision that legitimized the mandatory sterilization of those judged to be less worthy of support and protection. This eugenics movement, framed as a route to enhancing and protecting lives in society as a whole, went about this mission by actively eliminating those judged to be "parasites" and "useless eaters."

Emerging from the revulsion toward the atrocities of World War II, a more inclusive sense of social worth took shape. This rethinking was joined by a scientific and technological revolution that raised moral and ethical questions not previously encountered. Without careful and more inclusive restructuring of our sense of social worth, we stood in danger of becoming scientific giants but ethical infants.

The major testing grounds for the emerging moral adjustments were abortion, neonatal care, and assisted dying, with capital punishment entering the discourse from time to time. The political arena separated into camps: pro-life and pro-choice. Those claiming the pro-life position accused their opponents of devaluing life and promoting a culture of death. The pro-choice movement countered by saying that none of its proponents was anti-life or in favor of a culture of death, dismissing such claims as nonsense. Rather, the pro-choice mindset gave reverence to the autonomy of individuals, the quality of life, and the elimination or reduction of suffering. Highly contentious life-and-death decisions, shrouded as they were in uncertainty and ambiguity, should be kept firmly in the hands of those most immediately involved.

Many pro-choice proponents also noted that most of those who chose the pro-life position were also in favor of imposing death on convicted felons. How could this be? What was the threshold of offense? Clearly, this had shifted over time. Death penalty supporters responded to these critics by evoking the suffering. They believed that a criminal's life should be taken to alleviate the suffering inflicted on those left behind.

**Lesson Six: Tension Remains.** When the desire to identify the protective boundaries of life competes with the desire to alleviate suffering, unavoidable dilemmas, infused with uncertainty, emerge. Such dilemmas, by definition, are not resolvable without residual tension. In an important sense, both sides are right. If so, tension will always remain. Perhaps this is the final lesson learned.

# Notes

## 1 A Moral System Evolves

1   For eugenics as a global social movement see: Deborah Barrett and Charles Kurzman, "Globalizing Social Movement Theory: The Case of Eugenics," *Theory and Society* 33 (2004): 487–527. For detailed accounts see: Daniel Kevles, *In the Name of Eugenics* (New York: Knopf, 1985); Stefan Kühl, *The Nazi Connection: Eugenics, American Racism, and German National Socialism* (New York: Oxford University Press, 1994); Edwin Black, *War Against the Weak: Eugenics and America's Campaign to Create a Master Race* (New York: Four Walls Eight Windows, 2003); Alexandra Minna Stern, *Eugenic Nation: Faults & Frontiers of Better Breeding in Modern America* (Berkeley: University of California Press, 2005).

2   Francis Galton, "Eugenics: Its Definition, Scope, and Aims," *The American Journal of Sociology* 10 (1904): 1–27.

3   Francis Galton, *Memories of My Life* (London: Methuen, 1908), 323.

4   Francis Galton, *Hereditary Genius* (New York: Macmillan and Company, 1869), 11.

5   Francis Galton, *Hereditary Genius*, 11.

6   Francis Galton, *Hereditary Genius*, 11.

7   For a thorough summary of this movement see: Julie Beicken's *Eugenics: An Elite Social Movement* (2010), Masters Thesis, University of Texas, Austin.

8   Mark Granovetter, "The Strength of Weak Ties: A Network Theory Revisited," *Sociological Theory* 1 (1983): 201–233; David. A. Snow, Louis, A. Zurcher and Sheldon Ekland-Olson, "Social Networks and Social Movements: A Micro-Structural Approach to Differential Recruitment," *American Sociological Review* 45 (1980): 789.

9   Garland E. Allen, "The Eugenics Record Office at Cold Spring Harbor, 1910–1940: An Essay in Institutional History," *Osiris* 2 (1986) 225–264: 234.

10  Allen, "The Eugenics Record Office," 226.

11  Barbara A. Kimmelman, "The American Breeders' Association: Genetics and Eugenics in an Agricultural Context, 1903–13," *Social Studies of Science* 13 (1983): 163–204.

12  See: Archival material collected by Julie Beicken, "Eugenics," 512–515.

13  Genevieve C. Weeks, *Oscar Carleton McCulloch 1843–1891: Teacher and Practitioner of Applied Christianity* (Indianapolis: Indianapolis Historical Society, 1976), 130–156.

14  These and subsequent quotes are taken from McCulloch's *Tribe of Ishmael: A Study of Social Degradation* (National Conference of Charities at Buffalo, July 5–11, 1888).

15  Book of Matthew 25: 34–45.

16  Weeks, *Oscar Carleton McCulloch, 1843–1891*.

17  David Starr Jordan, *The Human Harvest: A Study of the Decay of Races Through the Survival of the Unfit* (Cambridge: American Unitarian Association, 1907).

18  David Starr Jordan, *The Days of a Man, Volume 1 1851–1899* (Yonkers-on-Hudson: World Book Co., 1922), 314.

19  Peter J. Bowler, *Evolution: The History of an Idea* (Berkeley: University of California Press, 2003).

20  Charles B. Davenport, Eugenics Record Office Bulletin No. 6, *The Trait Book* (Cold Spring Harbor, 1912).

21  Henry Herbert Goddard, *The Kallikak Family: A Study in the Heredity of Feeble-Mindedness* (New York: The Macmillian Co., 1912).

22    Arthur H. Estabrook, *The Jukes in 1915* (Washington, DC: Carnegie Institute of Washington, 1916).

23    Eugenics Record Office, Bulletin No. 10A: *Report to the Committee to Study and to Report on the Best Practical Means of Cutting Off the Defective Germ Plasm in the American Population: The Scope of the Committee's Work* (n.p., 1914); Eugenics Record Office, Bulletin No. 10B: *Report to the Committee to Study and to Report on the Best Practical Means of Cutting Off the Defective Germ Plasm in the American Population: The Legal, Legislative and Administrative Aspects of Sterilization* (1914).

24    *Buck v. Bell* 274 U.S. 200 (1927).

25    Stern, "'We Cannot Make a Silk Purse Out of a Sow's Ear,'" 12.

26    Legislation repealing the law was precipitated by a class action suit, *Madrigal v. Quilligan,* involving coerced post-partum tubal ligations of predominantly working-class women of Mexican origin. See Stern, *Eugenic Nation,* 200.

27    *Smith v. Board of Examiners of Feeble-Minded* 88 A. 963, decided November 18, 1913. Among other reasons, this case is interesting since later in his life Harry Laughlin would find that he, too, was epileptic. Many critical commentators would note the irony of Laughlin's diagnosis in later years.

28    *Haynes v. Lapeer* Cir. Judge, 201 Mich. 138, 144–145, 166 N.W.938, 940–941 (1918); *Osborne v. Thomson,* 103, Misc. 23, 33–36, 169 N.Y.S. 638,643–645, aff'd; 185 App. Div. 902, 171 N.Y.S. 1094 (1918).

29    Paul A. Lombardo, "Three Generations, No Imbeciles: New Light on *Buck v. Bell,*" *New York University Law Review* 60 (1985): 30–62. *Buck v. Bell* 274 U.S. 200 (1927). The following summary is based on Lombardo's account.

30    See Lombardo's review in "Three Generations, No Imbeciles," 50–55.

31    Cited by Lombardo, "Three Generations, No Imbeciles," 56.

32    *Buck v. Bell* 274 U.S. 200 (1927).

33    See Albert W. Alschuler, *Law Without Values: The Life, Work, and Legacy of Justice Holmes* (Chicago, IL: University of Chicago Press, 2000), 27–30.

34    Joseph Fletcher, *Morals and Medicine* (Princeton, NJ: Princeton University Press, 1954), 168.

35    Philip R. Reilly, "Involuntary Sterilization in the United States: A Surgical Solution," *The Quarterly Review of Biology* 62 (1987): 162.

36    Alschuler, *Law Without Values,* 27–30.

37    "Eugenical Sterilization in Germany," *Eugenical News* 18 (1933): 89–94.

38    Leo Alexander, "Medical Science under Dictatorship," *New England Journal of Medicine* 241(2) (1949): 39–47.

39    http://www.jewishvirtuallibrary.org/jsource/Holocaust/Nuremberg_Code.html

40    William Ogburn, *On Culture and Social Change,* ed. Otis Dudley Duncan (Chicago, IL: The University of Chicago Press, 1964), 86–95.

41    See: Albert Jonsen, *The New Medicine & The Old Ethics* (Cambridge, MA.: Harvard University Press, 1990); David J. Rothman, *Strangers at the Bedside: A History of How Law and Bioethics Transformed Medical Decision Making* (New York: Basic Books, 1991).

42    Belding H. Scribner, "Ethical Problems of Using Artificial Organs to Sustain Human Life," *Transactions—American Society for Artificial Internal Organs* 10 (1964): 209—212.

43    C.R. Blagg, "Development of Ethical Concepts in Dialysis: Seattle in the 1960s," *Nephrology* 4 (1998): 236.

44    Shana Alexander, "They Decide Who Lives, Who Dies: Medical Miracle And A Moral Burden of a Small Committee," *Life,* November 9, 1962: 103–128. The following quotes come from this article.

45    Albert R. Jonsen, "The Birth of Bioethics," *Special Supplement, Hastings Center Report* 23 (6) (1993): S1.

46    This account of Seattle's first dialysis center is gleaned largely from Alexander, "They Decide Who Lives, Who Dies," *Life,* November 9, 1962: 106–123.

47    J.E. Murray et al., "Kidney Transplantation in Modified Recipients," *Annals of Surgery* 156 (1962): 337–355; T.E. Starzl, T.L. Marchioro and W.R. Waddell, "The Reversal of Rejection in Human Renal Homografts with Subsequent Development of Homograft Tolerance," *Surgery, Gynecology, and Obstetrics* 117 (1963): 385–395; D.M. Hume et al., "Renal Homotransplantation in Man in

Modified Recipients," *Annals of Surgery* 158 (1963): 608–644; M.F. Woodruff et al., "Homotransplantation of Kidney in Patients Treated by Preoperative Local Radiation and Postoperative Administration of an Antimetabolite," *Lancet* 2 (1963): 675–682; J.E. Murray et al., "Prolonged Survival of Human Kidney Homografts by Immunosuppressive Drug Therapy," *New England Journal of Medicine* 268 (1963): 1315–1323.

48   Figures cited by David Sanders and Jesse Dukeminier, Jr., "Medical Advance and Legal Lag: Hemodialysis and Kidney Transplantation," *UCLA Law Review* 15 (1968): 366.

49   Sanders and Dukeminier, 357–413.

50   So labeled by Albert R. Jonsen, in *The Birth of Bioethics* (New York/Oxford: Oxford University Press, 1998), 13. Jonsen's book remains the most comprehensive account of the emergent bioethics movement.

51   From the dust-jacket of *Life or Death: Ethics and Options* (Seattle: University of Washington Press, 1966), a publication of edited papers presented at a symposium entitled "The Sanctity of Life" held at Reed College, March 11–12, 1966.

52   For one listing of many of the prominent players focusing on medical aspects of these issues see: Albert R. Jonsen, ed., "The Birth of Bioethics," *Special Supplement, Hastings Center Report* 23 (6) (1993): S16.

53   H.K. Beecher. "Medical Research and the Individual," in *Life or Death: Ethics and Options* (Seattle: University of Washington Press, 1968), 116.

54   "Experimentation in Man," *Journal of the American Medical Association* 169 (1959): 461–478.

55   "Ethics and Clinical Research," June, 1966; 274: 1354–1360.

56   There was some short-lived controversy in apartheid South Africa because Darvall was white and the recipient of her kidneys, 10-year-old Jonathan van Wyk, was "colored."

57   See: http://www.time.com/time/magazine/article/0,9171,837606,00.html and later Donald McRae, *Every Second Counts: The Race to Transplant the First Human Heart* (New York: Putnam, 2006), 192.

58   Cited in David J. Rothman, *Strangers at the Bedside* (New York: Basic Books, 1991), 160–161.

59   Special Communication, "A Definition of Irreversible Coma, Report of the Ad Hoc Committee of the Harvard Medical School to Examine the Definition of Brain Death," *Journal of the American Medical Association* 205 (1968): 337–340.

60   In Houston, Texas, Denton Cooley performed a second human heart transplant in June of the same year.

61   Quoted in Rothman, *Strangers at the Bedside*, 172–173.

62   Margaret Farley, foreword to *The Patient as Person: Explorations in Medical Ethics*, 2nd edn, ed. Paul Ramsey (New Haven, CT: Yale University Press, 2002).

63   Albert R. Jonsen, "The Structure of an Ethical Revolution: Paul Ramsey, the Beecher Lectures, and the Birth of Bioethics," in *The Patient as Person: Explorations in Medical Ethics*, 2nd edn, ed. Paul Ramsey (New Haven, CT: Yale University Press, 2002), xvi–xxvii.

64   Dianne N. Irving, "What Is Bioethics?" Presented at the American Bioethics Advisory Commission, Washington, DC, 2000: 1–66.

65   See: Eileen Welsome, *The Plutonium Files: America's Secret Medical Experiments in the Cold War* (New York: The Dial Press, 1999). For an account of the Cincinnati Radiation research, see Martha Stephens, *The Treatment: The Story of Those Who Died in the Cincinnati Radiation Tests* (Durham, NC: Duke University Press, 2002). For more contemporary accounts, see: Jerome Stephens, "Political, Social, and Scientific Aspects of Medical Research on Humans," *Politics and Society* 3 (1973): 409–427 and Richard N. Little, Jr., "Experimentation with Human Subjects: Legal and Moral Considerations Regarding Radiation Treatment of Cancer at the University of Cincinnati College of Medicine," *Atomic Energy Law Journal* 13 (1972): 305–330.

66   The following quotes are taken from Martha Stephens, *The Treatment: The Story of Those Who Died in the Cincinnati Radiation Tests.*

67   David J. Rothman and Sheila M. Rothman, *The Willowbrook Wars* (New York: Harper & Row, 1984), 16.

68   Stuart Warmflasher, *Unforgotten: Twenty-Five Years After Willowbrook,* Jack Fisher, Director (City Lights Pictures).

69   Rothman and Rothman, *The Willowbrook Wars,* 16.

70    James H. Jones, *Bad Blood: The Tuskegee Syphilis Experiment* (New York: The Free Press, 1981), 206–207.

71    Science Policy Division, Congressional Research Service, Library of Congress, "Genetic Engineering, Evolution of a Technological Issue," Report to the Subcommittee on Science, Research and Development, House Committee on Science and Astronautics, November 8, 1972, 40.

72    Jones, *Bad Blood*, 214.

73    Jonsen, *The Birth of Bioethics*, 94.

74    Jonsen, *The Birth of Bioethics*, 98.

75    Albert R. Jonsen, "On the Origins and Future of the Belmont Report," in *Belmont Revisited: Ethical Principles for Research with Human Subjects*, ed. James F. Childress, Eric M. Meslin and Harold T. Shapiro (Washington, DC: Georgetown University Press, 2005), 3–11.

76    Tom L. Beauchamp and James F. Childress. *Principles of Biomedical Ethics*, 6th edn (Oxford: Oxford University Press, 2009).

77    See Tom L. Beauchamp, "The Origins and Evolution of the *Belmont Report*," in *Belmont Revisited: Ethical Principles for Research with Human Subjects*, ed. James F. Childress, Eric M. Meslin and Harold T. Shapiro (Washington, DC: Georgetown University Press, 2005), 12–25; Tom L. Beauchamp, "The Origins, Goals, and Core Commitments of *The Belmont Report and Principles of Biomedical Ethics*," in *The Story of Bioethics: From Seminal Works to Contemporary Explorations*, ed. Jennifer K. Walter and Eran P. Klein (Washington, DC: Georgetown University Press, 2003), 17–46.

78    John H. Evans, "A Sociological Account of the Growth of Principlism," *Hastings Center Report* 3 (2000): 31–38.

79    K. Danner Clouser and Bernard Gert, "A Critique of Principlism," *The Journal of Medicine and Philosophy* 15 (1990): 219–236.

80    See Edwin R. Dubose, Ronald P. Hamel and Laurence J. O'Connell, eds, *A Matter of Principles? Ferment in U.S. Bioethics* (Valley Forge, PA: The Trinity Press International, 1994).

81    See Albert R. Jonsen, Mark Siegler and William Winslade, *Clinical Ethics*, 4th edn (New York: McGraw Hill, 1998).

## 2  The Early Moments and Months of Life: Should the Baby Live?

1    Pope Paul VI, "On the Regulation of Birth," *Humanae Vitae Encyclical*, July 25, 1968.

2    See Howard Becker, *Outsiders: Studies in the Sociology of Deviance* (Glencoe, IL: The Free Press of Glencoe, 1963), 147–163.

3    Esther Katz, Cathy Moran Hajo and Peter C. Engelman, eds, *The Selected Papers of Margaret Sanger* (Urbana and Chicago: University of Illinois Press, 2003).

4    *Griswold v. Connecticut*, 381 U.S. 479 (1965).

5    *Eisenstadt v. Baird*, 405 U.S. 438 (1972).

6    See Kristin Luker's interviews as reported in *Abortion and the Politics of Motherhood* (Berkeley: University of California Press, 1984), 62–65.

7    James Risen and Judy L. Thomas, *Wrath of Angels: The American Abortion War* (New York: Basic Books, 1998), 14

8    R. Sauer, "Attitudes to Abortion in America, 1800–1973," *Population Studies* 28 (1974): 53–67.

9    Statement by Virginia Apgar, M.D., Vice President for Medical Affairs of the National Foundation—March of Dimes to Subcommittee on Health, Senate Committee on Labor and Public Welfare, June 30, 1969.

10    C.E. Joffe, T.A. Weitz and C.L. Stacey, "Uneasy Allies: Pro-Choice Physicians, Feminist Health Activists, and the Struggle for Abortion Rights," *Sociology of Health and Illness* 26 (2004): 775–796.

11    *Honoring San Francisco's Abortion Pioneers—A Celebration of Past and Present Medical Public Health Leadership* (San Francisco, CA: Center for Reproductive Health Research & Policy, 1953).

12    Leslie J. Reagan, *When Abortion was a Crime: Women, Medicine, and Law in the United States, 1867–1973* (Berkeley: University of California Press, 1997), 14.

13  Ronald Reagan, "Abortion and the Conscience of the Nation," *The Human Life Review*, 1983.

14  *People v. Belous,* 71 Cal.2d 954, 458 P.2d 194, 80 Cal.Rptr. 354 (1969).

15  Luker, Interviews, 1984, 97.

16  Edward Duffy, *The Effects of Changes in the State Abortion Laws* (Washington, DC: U.S. Department of Health, Education, and Welfare, Public Health Service, 1971).

17  Luker, Interviews, 1984, 137.

18  Linda Greenhouse, *Becoming Justice Blackmun: Harry Blackmun's Supreme Court Journey* (New York: Times Books, Henry Holt and Company, 2005), 80.

19  *Eisenstadt v. Baird,* 405 U.S. 438 (1972).

20  Greenhouse, *Becoming Justice Blackmun*, 100.

21  John Hart Ely, "The Wages of Crying Wolf: A Comment on *Roe v. Wade,*" *Yale Law Journal* 82 (1973): 920–949.

22  Ely, "The Wages of Crying Wolf," 926.

23  James Davison Hunter, *Cultural Wars: The Struggle to Define America* (New York: Basic Books, Harper Collins, 1991). See also Morris P. Fiorina with Samuel J. Abrams and Jeremy C. Pope, *Culture War? The Myth of a Polarized America* (New York: Pearson Longman, 2006).

24  Symposium: The End of Democracy? *Judicial Usurpation of Politics*, November, 1996.

25  Symposium: The End of Democracy?

26  Symposium: The End of Democracy?

27  One prominent contributor, Robert H. Bork, stood by his critical analysis and wished the editors had not made their suggestions. In a follow-up letter to the editors, he wrote, "The necessity for reform, even drastic reform, does not call the legitimacy of the entire American 'regime' into question." In another letter to the editors, a member of the *First Things* editorial board resigned, suggesting that the editors had "raised so grave and, in my opinion, irresponsible an issue, and given it such prominence, that I cannot, in good conscience, continue to serve."

28  See, for example, Teresa Iglesias, "*In Vitro* Fertilisation: The Major Issues," *Journal of Medical Ethics* 10 (1984): 36; Peter Singer, *Practical Ethics* (Cambridge: Cambridge University Press, 1993); Massimo Reichlin, "The Argument from Potential: A Reappraisal," *Bioethics* 11 (1997): 1–23.

29  Bernard Nathanson, *The Hand of God: A Journey From Death to Life by the Abortion Doctor who Changed His Mind* (Washington, DC: Regnery Publishing, 1996), 140.

30  See "The Facts Speak Louder than 'The Silent Scream,'" Planned Parenthood, http://www.planned parenthood.org/news-articles-press/politics-policy-issues/abortion-access/anti-abortion-video-6136.htm.

31  Francis Schaeffer, *A Christian Manifesto* (Westchester, IL: Crossway Books, 1981), 120.

32  Dallas A. Blanchard, *The Anti-Abortion Movement and the Rise of the Religious Right* (New York: Twayne Publishers, 1994).

33  Dallas A. Blanchard and T.J. Prewitt, *Religious Violence and Abortion: The Gideon Project* (Gainesville: University Press of Florida, 1993).

34  Risen and Thomas, *Wrath of Angels*, 94.

35  Risen and Thomas, *Wrath of Angels*, 263.

36  http://forerunner.com/forerunner/X0471_Randall_Terry_Interv.html.

37  The Ku Klux Act of 1871.

38  See http://www.dr-tiller.com/mercy.htm.

39  Jayne Bray et al., *Petitioners v. Alexandria Women's Health Clinic et al.*

40  Larry Rohter, "Towering Over the Abortion Foe's Trial: His Leader," *New York Times*, March 5, 1994.

41  Shelley Shannon's papers collected at trial.

42  Freedom of Access to Clinics Entrances (FACE) Act—Statute 18 U.S.C. § 248.

43  HBO's 2000 "America Under Cover" documentary, *Soldiers in the Army of God*, featured Horsley, along with Paul Hill, Bob Lokey, and Michael Bray.

44  This piece was later revised and posted on his website, www.christiangallery.com. In his introduction to the revised article, Horsley writes: "I originally wrote this article in the immediate aftermath of a Birmingham abortion clinic bombing in 1997 when someone—Eric Rudolph?—

sent a note saying the Army of God had planted the bomb. Post 9/11/2001, the only thing I add to what I wrote before is to point out that Muslim terrorists call themselves the Army of God just as this abortion clinic bomber did. It is most remarkable that President George W. Bush has finally acknowledged and admitted and declared the war that had gone undeclared in this nation ever since 1973 when the government of the USA in *Roe v. Wade* effectively declared war against the children of God. If you want to understand the Army of God in the USA, read the article entitled 'Exploding the Myth of the Army of God.'"

45  See http://www.armyofgod.com/EricRudolphHomepage.html.

46  http://www.armyofgod.com/PHillbookIntro.html. Among other topics, Hill's manuscript sets out a point-by-point rebuttal of the Southern Baptist Convention's denunciation of the use of violence by anti-abortionists.

47  Office of the Clark County Prosecuting Attorney, http://www.clarkprosecutor.org/html/death/ US/hill873.htm.

48  In addition to Drs John Britton and David Gunn, in 1994 two clinic receptionists were killed in Massachusetts and Virginia. In 1998, a security guard at a clinic was killed in Alabama. In that same year, Dr. Barnett Slepian was shot to death in his home in New York. In addition, as reported by the National Abortion Federation, there were numerous attempted murders and assaults during this same period.

49  Sandy Veritas, "George Tiller was a Mass-Murderer, says Randall Terry—We Grieve That He Did Not Have Time to Properly Prepare His Soul to Face God," http://www.christiannewswire.com/ news/8967610531.html.

50  http://www.armyofgod.com/GeorgeTillerBabyKillerIndex.html.

51  Jayne Bray et al., *Petitioners v. Alexandria Women's Health Clinic et al.*

52  The Partial-Birth Abortion Ban Act (Pub. L. 108–105, HR 760, S 3, 18 U.S. Code 1531).

53  Martin Haskell, "Dilation and Extraction for Late Second Trimester Abortion," Presented at the National Abortion Federation Risk Management Seminar, September 13, 1992.

54  "Second Trimester Abortion: An Interview with W. Martin Haskell, MD," *Cincinnati Medicine*, Fall 1993, 18.

55  "Second Trimester Abortion," 18.

56  "Second Trimester Abortion," 18.

57  "Second Trimester Abortion," 18.

58  "Second Trimester Abortion," 18.

59  "Second Trimester Abortion," 18.

60  Testimony of Brenda Pratt Shafer, Subcommittee on the Constitution, U.S. House of Representatives, March 21, 1996.

61  See: Cynthia Gorney, "Gambling with Abortion: Why Both Sides Think They Have Everything to Lose," *Harper's Magazine*, November 2004, cover story.

62  http://mikeaustin.org/AAA/Partial%20Birth%20Abortion/PartialBirthAbortion.jpg.

63  Cited in Gorney, "Gambling with Abortion."

64  Cited in Gorney, "Gambling with Abortion."

65  House of Representatives: 288–139; Senate: 54–44.

66  Congressional Record, September 19, 1996.

67  Congressional Record, September 19, 1996.

68  House of Representatives: 295–136; Senate: 64–36.

69  The Gallup Poll: Public Opinion 2002, 206–207.

70  530 U.S. 914 (2000).

71  Estimates varied, depending on how wording was interpreted.

72  In the Senate, the initial vote was 64–33–3. The House of Representatives passed its version without objection, but there were differences in the Senate. These were worked out and on October 2, 2003, a vote of 281–142–12 was recorded. The Senate then voted in support 64–34–2.

73  "My Late-Term Abortion," *Boston Globe*, January 25, 2004.

74  Carey Goldberg, "Shots Assist in Aborting Fetuses Lethal Injections Offer Legal Shield," *Boston Globe*, August 10, 2007.

75  Mary Spaulding Balch quoted in Eric Eckholm's "Several States Forbid Abortion After 20 Weeks," *New York Times*, June 26, 2011.

76  See, for example, Wesley J. Smith, *Culture of Death: The Assault on Medical Ethics in America* (San Francisco, CA: Encounter Books, 2000).

77  "Children from the Laboratory," *American Medical Association Prism*, May, 1973, 13.

78  This and following quotes come from: Jeffrey H. Reiman, *Abortion and the Ways We Value Human Life* (New York: Rowman & Littlefield, 1999), 108.

79  See: Joseph Fletcher, *Morals and Medicine* (Princeton, NJ: Princeton University Press, 1954); Michael Tooley, "Abortion and Infanticide," *Philosophy & Public Affairs* 2 (1972): 37–65; Paul Ramsey, *Ethics at the Edges of Life* (New Haven, CT: Yale University Press, 1978); H. Tristram Engelhardt, Jr., *The Foundations of Bioethics*, 2nd edn (New York: Oxford University Press, 1996), esp. ch. 4.

80  George F. Will, "The Killing Will Not Stop," *Washington Post*, April 22, 1982: A29.

81  Cited in Kuhse and Singer, *Should the Baby Live* (New York: Oxford Univeersity Press, 1985), 16.

82  Cited in Kuhse and Singer, *Should the Baby Live*, 16.

83  The genesis of President Reagan's several orders are somewhat unclear. See: Lawrence D. Brown, "Civil Rights and Regulatory Wrongs: The Reagan Administration and the Medical Treatment of Handicapped Infants," *Journal of Health Politics, Policy and Law* 11(1986): 234.

84  Joseph Fletcher, *Morals and Medicine* (Princeton, NJ: Princeton University Press, 1954), 207; Glanville Williams, *The Sanctity of Life and the Criminal Law* (New York: Alfred A. Knopf, 1957), 20–24.

85  Cited in Kuhse and Singer, *Should the Baby Live*, 43, gleaned from several illustrative statements of concern in materials submitted to the Court by the American Academy of Pediatrics.

86  These exceptions were: (1) the infant is chronically and irreversibly comatose; (2) the provision of such treatment would merely prolong dying, not be effective in ameliorating or correcting all of the infant's life-threatening conditions, or otherwise be futile in terms of the survival of the infant; or (3) the provision of such treatment would be virtually futile in terms of the survival of the infant, and the treatment itself under such circumstances would be inhumane.

87  George. J. Annas, "The Case of Baby Jane Doe: Child Abuse or Unlawful Federal Intervention?" *American Journal of Public Health* 74 (1984): 727–729.

88  Marcia Chambers, "Initiator of 'Baby Doe' Case Unshaken," *New York Times*, November 13, 1983.

89  *Bowen v American Hosp. Ass'n*, 476 U. S. 610 (1986): 621, 632.

90  See George J. Annas, "Asking the Courts to Set the Standard of Emergency Care—The Case of Baby K.," *New England Journal of Medicine* 330 (1994): 1542–1545.

91  Quoted in Ronald M. Perkin, "Stress and Distress in Pediatric Nurses: The Hidden Tragedy of Baby K.," 1996, http://www.llu.edu/llu/bioethics/update12_2.htm.

92  *In the Matter of Baby K*, 832 F. Supp. 1022 (E.D. Va. 1993). *In the Matter of Baby K*, 16 F.3d 590 (4th Cir. 1994).

93  This case received a great deal of local and national attention. See "Dying Boy's Case Likely to Reverberate in Law, Religion," *Austin American Statesman*, April 15, 2007: A01; "Case Puts Texas Futile-Treatment Law Under a Microscope," *Washington Post*, April 11, 2007: A03; Gudrun Schultz, May 22, 2007, "Toddler Emilio Gonzales Dies Naturally from Terminal Illness," http://www.life sitenews.com/news/archive/ldn/2007/may/07052201.

94  The *Advance Directives Act* (1999), ch. 166 of the Texas Health & Safety Code, esp. Section 166.046, Subsection (e).

95  Guidelines for Resolving Futility Cases under the Texas Advance Directives Act, 1999.

96  "Medical Futility in End-of-Life Care: Report of the Council on Ethical and Judicial Affairs," *Journal of the American Medical Association* 281 (1999): 937–941.

97  Quoted in "Case Puts Texas Futile-Treatment Law Under a Microscope," *Washington Post*, April 11, 2007: A03.

98  House Bill 3325.

99  L.J. Schneiderman, N.S. Jecker and A.R. Jonsen, "Medical Futility: Its Meaning and Ethical Implications," *Annals of Internal Medicine* 112 (1990): 949–954.

100  For argument from potential in other bioethical settings, see: Peter Singer and Karen Dawson, "Technology and the Argument from Potential," *Philosophy and Public Affairs* 17 (1988): 87–104; Massimo Reichlin, "The Argument from Potential: A Reappraisal," *Bioethics* 11 (1997): 1–23.

101  H. Tristram Engelhardt, Jr., *The Foundations of Bioethics,* 2nd edn (New York: Oxford University Press, 1996), 139.

## 3 The Boundaries of Tolerable Suffering

1  Quotes below are from: C. Everett Koop, "The Challenge of Definition," Presented at the International Conference on Euthanasia and the Future of Medicine, Clark University, Worcester, Massachusetts, October 24, 1988.

2  In 1920, two distinguished German scholars, law professor Karl Binding and medical doctor Alfred Hoche, wrote a widely disseminated pamphlet, "The Permission to Destroy Life Unworthy of Life" (*Die Freigabe der Vernichtung lebensunwerten Lebens*). Leo Alexander, "Medical Science Under Dictatorship," *The New England Journal of Medicine,* July 14, 1949, 39–47.

3  See *Time Magazine,* "Mother May's Holiday," March 11, "The Right to Kill," November 18, "The Right to Kill (Cont'd)," November 25, and "The Right to Kill (Cont'd)," December 2, 1935.

4  This and subsequent quotes from: Joseph Lelyveld, "1936 Secret is Out: Doctor Sped George V's Death," *New York Times,* November 28, 1986.

5  Max Schur, *Freud: Living and Dying* (New York: International University Press, 1972), 528–529.

6  See, for example, Ian Dowbiggin, *A Merciful End: The Euthanasia Movement in Modern America* (New York: Oxford University Press, 2003), 32–62.

7  Quoted in Robert Jay Lifton, *The Nazi Doctors: Medical Killing and the Psychology of Genocide* (New York: Basic Books, 1986), 63.

8  The original English title was *From Death Camp to Existentialism.* Eventually, multiple millions of copies were sold. Some indication of the book's impact comes from a survey done by the Library of Congress Book of the Month Club, asking readers to name a "book that made a difference in your life." By this standard, *Man's Search for Meaning* was among the ten most influential books in America. The following quotes come from this book.

9  Margaret S. Stroebe et al., eds, *Handbook of Bereavement Research: Consequences, Coping, and Care* (Washington, DC: American Psychological Association, 2001); Margaret S. Stroebe et al., eds, *Handbook of Bereavement Research: Advances in Theory and Intervention* (Washington, DC: American Psychological Association, 2008).

10  The following quotes are taken from: Robert B. White, *Please Let Me Die* (Galveston, TX: University of Texas Medical Branch, 1974).

11  James F. Childress and Courtney C. Campbell, "'Who Is a Doctor to Decide Whether a Person Lives or Dies?' Reflections on Dax's Case," in *Dax's Case: Essays in Medical Ethics and Human Meaning,* ed. Lonnie D. Kliever (Dallas, TX: Southern Methodist University Press, 1989), 25. See more generally: James F. Childress, *Who Should Decide* (New York: Oxford University Press, 1982).

12  See: H. Tristram Engelhardt, Jr., Edmund L. Erde and John Moskop, "Euthanasia in Texas: A Little Known Experiment," *Hospital Physician* 9 (1976): 30–31.

13  This and following quotes from: Keith Burton, *Dax's Case* (Unicorn Media, Inc., 1985).

14  Leon R. Kass, "'I Will Give No Deadly Drug': Why Doctors Must Not Kill," in *The Case Against Assisted Suicide,* ed. Kathleen Foley and Herbert Hendin (Baltimore, MD: Johns Hopkins University Press, 2002), 32, 36.

15  Interview in "Dax's Case."

16  Interview in "Dax's Case."

17  Burton, *Dax's Case.*

18  Quotes from "A Happy Life Afterward Doesn't Make up for Torture," *Washington Post,* June 26, 1983: D3.

19  Burton, *Dax's Case.*

20  Julia Duane Quinlan, *My Joy, My Sorrow: Karen Ann's Mother Remembers* (Cincinnati: St. Anthony Messenger Press, 2005), 37.

21  Bryan Jennett and Fred Plum, "Persistent Vegetative State after Brain Damage," *The Lancet*, April 1, 1972: 734–737.

22  *In Re Quinlan*, 70 N.J. 10, 355 A.2d 647 (1976).

23  This and following quotes are from: Julia Duane Quinlan, *My Joy, My Sorrow*, 53–54.

24  Quinlan, *My Joy, My Sorrow*, 105–106.

25  This quote and those that follow are taken from his later recollections: Walter Sackett, "Death With Dignity," *Southern Medical Journal* 64 (1971): 330–332; Walter Sackett, "I've Let Hundreds of Patients Die. Shouldn't You?," *Medical Economics*, April 2, 1973, 92–97.

26  For a more complete account of Walter Sackett's endeavors see: Henry R. Glick, *The Right to Die: Policy Innovation and Its Consequences* (New York: Columbia University Press, 1992), 104–120.

27  Numerous detailed accounts have been provided of this period. See: Glick, *The Right to Die*; Peter G. Filene, *In the Arms of Others: A Cultural History of the Right-to-Die* (Chicago, IL: Ivan R. Dee, 1998); Ian Dowbiggin, *A Merciful End: The Euthanasia Movement in Modern America* (New York: Oxford University Press, 2003).

28  See: Joseph Fletcher, *Morals and Medicine* (Princeton, NJ: Princeton University Press, 1954); Glanville Williams, *The Sanctity of Life and the Criminal Law* (New York: Alfred A. Knopf, 1957); and Yale Kamisar, "Some Non-Religious Views Against Proposed 'Mercy Killing' Legislation," *Minnesota Law Review* (1958): 969–1042.

29  Notably in *Harper's* and *Atlantic Monthly*. See Ian Dowbiggin, *A Merciful End: The Euthanasia Movement in Modern America* (New York: Oxford University Press, 2003), 107, 205, fn 33.

30  Quotes from personal correspondence and annual presidential reports cited in Dowbiggin, *A Merciful End*, 119.

31  "The 'Living Will' Gains Acceptance," *New York Times*, September 20, 1984; "Luis Kutner, Lawyer Who Fought for Human Rights, Is Dead at 84," *New York Times*, March 4, 1993.

32  "Due Process of Euthanasia: The Living Will, a Proposal," *Indiana Law Journal* 44 (1969): 539–554.

33  Dowbiggin, *A Merciful End,* 121 and 211, fn 99.

34  See John Ostheimer, "The Polls: Changing Attitudes Toward Euthanasia," *Public Opinion Quarterly* 44 (1980): 123–128.

35  Pope Pius XII, "The Prolongation of Life," *The Pope Speaks* 4 (1958).

36  *Superintendent of Belchertown State School et al. v. Joseph Saikewicz*, Mass., 370 N.E.2d 417, 1977. Quotes that follow come from this decision.

37  See: Ezekiel J. Manuel, "A Review of the Ethical and Legal Aspects of Terminating Medical Care," *The American Journal of Medicine* 84 (1998): 291–301.

38  *In re Storar* 52 N.Y.2d 363; 420 N.E.2d 64 (1981).

39  These and following quotes are taken from William H. Colby, *Long Goodbye: The Deaths of Nancy Cruzan* (Carlsbad, CA: Hay House, Inc., 2002), 41, 170, 178, 233, 320.

40  *Cruzan v. Director, MDH*, 497 U.S. 261 (1990).

41  For specifics see: Manuel, "A Review of the Ethical and Legal Aspects of Terminating Medical Care," 291–301.

42  PBS Frontline, March 24, 1992.

43  This and subsequent quotes come from PBS Frontline, March 24, 1992.

44  Cited in Colby, *Long Goodbye,* 391.

45  Federal legislation called the Patient Self-Determination Act, prompted by the Cruzan family's struggles and introduced by Missouri's U.S. Sen. John Danforth, became law. See Lawrence P. Ulrich, *The Patient Self-Determination Act: Meeting the Challenges in Patient Care* (Washington, DC: Georgetown University Press, 1999).

46  For the details see: Sheldon Ekland-Olson, *Who Lives, Who Dies, Who Decides?* (New York: Routledge).

47  Yale Kamisar, "Some Non-Religious Views Against Proposed 'Mercy Killing' Legislation," *Minnesota Law Review* (1958): 969–1042.

48  Glanville Williams, *The Sanctity of Life and the Criminal Law* (New York: Alfred A. Knopf, 1957).

49  Kamisar saw, with less psychological and interpersonal precision, what Elisabeth Kübler-Ross, drawing from her conversations with the terminally ill, would give empirical substance to a decade later in *On Death and Dying*.

50  Kamisar, "Some Non-Religious Views," 990.
51  See "Gov. Lamm Asserts Elderly, If Very Ill, Have 'Duty To Die," *New York Times*, http://query. nytimes.com/gst/fullpage.html?res=9E01E5D91E39F93AA15750C0A962948260&sec=health&spo n=&pagewanted=1.
52  Daniel Callahan, *Setting Limits: Medical Goals in an Aging Society* (Washington, D.C.: Georgetown University Press), 20–21.
53  Shana Alexander, "They Decide Who Lives, Who Dies: Medical Miracle and a Moral Burden of a Small Committee," *Life*, November 9, 1962, 103–128.
54  Daniel Callahan, *Setting Limits*, 186.
55  Daniel Callahan, *Setting Limits*, 198.
56  Robert L. Barry and Gerard V. Bradley, eds, *Set No Limits: A Rebuttal to Daniel Callahan's Proposal to Limit Health Care for the Elderly* (Champaign: University of Illinois Press, 1991).
57  Barry and Bradley, eds, *Set No Limits*, xvi.
58  Leon R. Kass, "Neither for Love nor Money: Why Doctors Must Not Kill," *Public Interest* 94 (1989): 25–46.
59  Peter Singer, *Practical Ethics*, 2nd edn (Cambridge: Cambridge University Press, 1993), 184.
60  "Unspeakable Conversations," *New York Times*, February 16, 2003.
61  Harriet McBryde Johnson, *Too Late to Die Young* (New York: Picador, 2006), 201.
62  Quoted in Adrienne Asch, "Disability, Bioethics and Human Rights," in *Handbook of Disabilities Studies*, ed. Gary L. Albrecht, Katherine D. Seelman and Michael Bury (New York: Sage, 2001), 297–326, 311.
63  Quoted in Asch, "Disability, Bioethics and Human Rights," 297–326, 311.
64  The following quotes are taken from: Paul K. Longmore, "Elizabeth Bouvia, Assisted Suicide and Social Prejudice," *Issues in Law & Medicine* 3 (2) (1987): 146–147, 152.
65  *Bouvia v. Co. of Riverside*, No. 159780, Sup. Ct., Riverside Co., CA, December 16, 1983, Tr. 1238–1250.
66  George J. Annas, "Law and the Life Sciences: When Suicide Prevention Becomes Brutality: The Case of Elizabeth Bouvia," *The Hastings Center Report* 14 (1984): 20–46.
67  Francis I. Kane, "Keeping Elizabeth Bouvia Alive for the Public Good," *The Hastings Center Report* 15 (1985): 5–8.
68  *Bouvia v. Superior Court (Glenchur)* (1986) 179 Cal.App.3d 1127, 225 Cal.Rptr. 297.
69  "Urging the Handicapped to Die: Bouvia Decision is Victory for Bigotry, Not Self- Determination," *Los Angeles Times*, April 25, 1986.
70  Longmore, "Elizabeth Bouvia," 168.
71  Ian Dowbiggin, *A Merciful End: The Euthanasia Movement in Modern America* (New York: Oxford University Press, 2003), 135. More generally, see ch. 5.
72  *Barber v. Superior Court*. California Court of Appeals, Second District, 1983. 147 Cal.App.3d 1006, 195 Cal.Rptr. 484; *Bartling v. Superior Court* (1984), 163 Cal.App.3d 186 [209 Cal. Rptr. 220].
73  See: Robert L. Risley, *A Humane and Dignified Death: A New Law Permitting Physician Aid-In-Dying* (Americans Against Human Suffering, 1987).
74  The following quotes come from: "It's Over, Debbie," *Journal of the American Medical Association* 259 (1988): 272.
75  W. Gaylin et al., "Doctors Must Not Kill," *Journal of the American Medical Association* 259 (1988): 2139–2140; K.L. Vaux, "Debbie's Dying: Mercy Killing and the Good Death," *Journal of the American Medical Association* 259 (1988): 2140–2141; G.D. Lundberg, "'It's Over, Debbie' and the Euthanasia Debate," *Journal of the American Medical Association* 259 (1988): 2142–2143; Leon Kass, "Neither for Love nor Money: Why Doctors Must Not Kill," *Public Interest* 94 (1989): 25–46.
76  Kass, "Neither for Love Nor Money," 26.
77  Gaylin et al., "Doctors Must Not Kill."
78  Gaylin et al., "Doctors Must Not Kill."
79  "The Doctor's Suicide Van," June 18, 1990.
80  For an account of these early dealings, see Neal Nicol and Harry Wylie, *Between Dying and the Dead* (Madison: The University of Wisconsin Press, 2006), 147–150.
81  "The Doctor's Suicide Van," June 18, 1990.

82  See, for example, http://topics.nytimes.com/top/reference/timestopics/people/k/jack_kevorkian/index.html?offset=15&s=oldest.

83  "Death's Dissident," *The Economist*, November 13, 1993, 34.

84  "Founder Defends Euthanasia Action," *The Lima News*, October 16, 1993, B1; Paul Verschuur, "Euthanasia Advocates Say Death Machine Raises Few New Issues," Associated Press wire service, June 7, 1990.

85  Quoted in: "Dr. Death's Trial Intrigues Legal Experts," *The Beacon Journal*, August 19, 1993, A6.

86  Derek Humphry and Mary Clement, *Freedom to Die: People Politics and the Right-to-Die Movement* (New York: St. Martin's Griffin, 2000), 132.

87  Leon Kass, "Suicide Made Easy, The Evil of 'Rational' Humaneness," *Hastings Center Review* (1991): 19–24.

88  See Sherwin Nuland, *How We Die: Reflections on Life's Final Chapter* (New York: Random House, 1993), 156–157.

89  Daniel Hillyard and John Dombrink, *Dying Right: The Death With Dignity Movement* (New York: Routledge, 2001), 245.

90  M. Cox, "Suicide Manual for Terminally Ill Stirs Heated Debate," *Wall Street Journal*, July 12, 1991, B1, B8.

91  L.K. Altman, "How-to Book on Suicide Is Atop Best-Seller List," *New York Times*, August 9, 1991, A10.

92  Wesley J. Smith, "The Whispers of Strangers," *Newsweek*, June 28, 1993; *Forced Exit: The Slippery Slope from Assisted Suicide to Legalized Murder*. This 1997 publication was followed by *Culture of Death: The Assault on Medical Ethics in America*.

93  Phillip B. Chappel, Robert A. King and Michael Enson, "Final Exit and the Risk of Suicide," *Journal of the American Medical Association* 267 (1992): 3027; M.H. Sacks and I. Kemperman, "Final Exit as a Manual for Suicide in Depressed Patients," *American Journal of Psychiatry* 149 (1992): 842–842; M.R. Lavin and Martin A. Roy, "Rational Suicide and Psychiatric Disorders," *New England Journal of Medicine* 326 (1992): 890–893.

94  "Increase in Suicide by Asphyxiation in New York City after the Publication of Final Exit," *New England Journal of Medicine* 329 (November 11, 1993): 1508–1510.

95  Geoffrey Fieger in his opening statement in the 1994 trial of Jack Kevorkian; cited in Neal Nicol and Harry Wylie, *Between Dying and the Dead* (Madison: The University of Wisconsin Press, 2006), 189.

96  See: http://plato.stanford.edu/entries/double-effect/.

97  Quotes taken from "Kevorkian Takes Stand in Own Defense," *New York Times*, April 28, 1994.

98  Cited in: David Margolick, "Jury Acquits Dr. Kevorkian of Illegally Aiding a Suicide," *New York Times*, May 3, 1994.

99  Cited in: Margolick, "Jury Acquits Dr. Kevorkian of Illegally Aiding a Suicide."

100 Kathy Barks Hoffman, "Kevorkian Leaves Prison After 8 Years," The Associated Press, June 1, 2007.

101 Quotes below come from this article.

102 "The Ambiguity of Clinical Intentions," *New England Journal of Medicine* 329 (1993): 1039–1040.

103 Lawrence K. Altman, "Jury Declines to Indict a Doctor Who Said He Aided in a Suicide," *New York Times*, July 27, 1991.

104 Timothy E. Quill, *Death and Dignity: Making Choices and Taking Charge* (New York: W.W. Norton, 1993). See also: Franklin G. Miller, Timothy E. Quill, Howard Brody, John C. Fletcher and Lawrence O. Gostin, "Regulating Physician-Assisted Death," *New England Journal of Medicine* 331 (1994): 119–123; Timothy E. Quill, Christine K. Cassel and Diane E. Meier, "Care of the Hopelessly Ill: Proposed Clinical Criteria for Physician Assisted Suicide," *New England Journal of Medicine* 327 (1992): 1380–1381; Timothy Quill, "The Rule of Double Effect—A Critique of Its Role in End-of-Life Decision Making," *New England Journal of Medicine* 337 (1997): 1768–1771; Timothy Quill, *Caring for Patients at the End of Life* (New York: Oxford University Press, 2001); and Timothy E. Quill and Margaret P. Battin, eds, *Physician-Assisted Dying: The Case for Palliative Care & Patient Choice* (Baltimore, MD: Johns Hopkins University Press, 2004).

105 See, for example: Daniel Callahan, letter, *New England Journal of Medicine* 331 (1994): 1656; Daniel

Callahan and Margot White, "The Legalization of Physician-Assisted Suicide: Creating a Regulatory Potemkin Village," *University of Richmond Law Review* 30 (1996): 1–83.

106   *Planned Parenthood v. Casey* 505 U.S. 833 (1992) at 851.

107   See editorial written shortly after the Oregon initiative passed: Derek Humphry, William K. Kaula and Geoffrey N. Fieger, "To the Editor," *New York Times*, December 3, 1994, 14.

108   *Lee v. Oregon*, 869 F. Supp. 1491 (D.Or. 1994).

109   *Lee v. Oregon*, 891 F. Supp. 1429 (D.Or. 1995).

110   *Lee v. Oregon*, 107 F.3d 1382 (9th Cir. 1997).

111   21 U.S. 702 (1997) and 521 U.S. 793 (1997).

112   See: Sonia Suter, "Ambivalent Unanimity: An Analysis of the Supreme Court's Holding," in *Law at the End of Life: The Supreme Court and Assisted Suicide*, ed. Carl E. Schneider (Ann Arbor: The University of Michigan Press, 2000).

113   Timothy Egan, "The 1997 Elections: Right to Die," *New York Times*, November 6, 1997, A22.

114   These documents and related materials have been brought together in a very useful volume: Susan M. Behuniak and Arthur G. Svenson, eds, *Physician Assisted Suicide: The Anatomy of a Constitutional Law Issue* (New York: Rowman & Littlefield, 2003).

115   Arthur L. Caplan, James J. McCartney and Dominic A. Sisti, eds, *The Case of Terri Schiavo: Ethics at the End of Life* (Amherst, NY: Prometheus Books, 2006).

116   Claudia Rowe, "Ex-Governor Seeking Death with Dignity—Booth Gardner Devotes His Final Days Fighting to Legalize Physician-Assisted Suicide," *Seattle Post Intelligencer*, May 18, 2007, http://www.seattlepi.com/local/316298_gardner18.html.

117   Daniel Bergner, "Death in the Family," *New York Times*, December 2, 2007, http://www.nytimes.com/2007/12/02/magazine/02suicide-t.html.

## 4  Taking Life: Lynching and Capital Punishment

1   Examples abound: Justice Brennan's oft-quoted comment in *Furman v. Georgia*: "The calculated killing of a human being by the State involves, by its very nature, a denial of the executed person's humanity." See: Robert M. Cover, "Violence and the Word," *The Yale Law Journal* 95 (1986); Charles L. Black, Jr., *Festschrift*: 1601–1629; Albert Bandura, "Moral Disengagement in the Perpetration of Inhumanities." *Personality and Social Psychology Review* 3 (1999): 193–209; Dov Cohen and Richard E. Nisbett, "Self-Protection and the Culture of Honor: Explaining Southern Violence." *Personality and Social Psychology Bulletin* 20 (1994): 551–567.

2   See, in particular: Donald Black, *The Behavior of Law* (New York: Academic Press, 1976).

3   NAACP, *Thirty Years of Lynching in the United States (1889–1918)* (NAACP, 1919); Arthur F. Raper, *The Tragedy of Lynching* (Chapel Hill: University of North Carolina Press, 1933); Ralph Ginzburg, *100 Years of Lynchings* (Baltimore, MD: Black Classic Press, 1962); Stewart E. Tolnay and E.M. Beck, *A Festival of Violence: An Analysis of Southern Lynchings, 1882-1930* (Urbana, IL: University of Illinois Press, 1995); and W. Fitzhugh, ed., *Under Sentence of Death: Lynching in the South* (Chapel Hill: North Carolina Press, 1997).

4   James Elbert Cutler, *Lynch-Law: An Investigation into the History of Lynching in the United States* (Montclair, NJ: Patterson Smith, 1905, reprinted 1969), 2–3.

5   *The Longview, Texas Times Clarion*, quoted in James W. Marquart, Sheldon Ekland-Olson and Jonathan R. Sorensen, *The Rope, The Chair, and the Needle* (Austin: University of Texas Press, 1994), 7.

6   See Robert L. Zangrando, *The NAACP Crusade Against Lynching 1909–1950* (Philadelphia, PA: Temple University Press, 1980).

7   *Congressional Record*, 65 Congress, 2 Session, LVI (April 19, 1918), 5362.

8   Cited in the NAACP's *Thirty Years of Lynching: 1889–1918*, 5.

9   See, for example: "For Action on Race Riot Peril," *New York Times*, October 5, 1919.

10   Firsthand reports of the events in Phillips County come from newspaper accounts, the trial record, and the writings of Walter White, who traveled to Arkansas to investigate. More reports come from a subsequent Supreme Court decision released in February, 1923. For contemporary summaries, see: "The Real Causes of Two Race Riots," *The Crisis* 19 (1919): 56–62; *Moore v. Dempsey*, 261 U.S.

86 (1923); and Ida B. Wells-Barnett, *The Arkansas Race Riot* (Chicago, 1920). For later, well-documented histories, see: Richard Cortner, *A Mob Intent on Death: The NAACP and the Arkansas Riot Cases* (Middletown, CT: Weskean University Press, 1988); Grif Stockley, *Blood in Their Eyes: The Elaine Race Massacres of 1919* (Fayetteville: The University of Arkansas Press, 2001); and Robert Whitaker, *On the Laps of Gods: The Red Summer of 1919 and the Struggle for Justice That Remade a Nation* (New York: Crown Publishing Group, Random House, 2008).

11  *A Man Called White*, 1948, reprinted by Viking Press and University of Georgia Press, 1995, 48.

12  See Stockley, *Blood in Their Eyes*, ch. 3.

13  *A Man Called White*, 48.

14  See Chronology of Events in Stockley, *Blood in Their Eyes*.

15  *Moore v. Dempsey*, 261 U.S. 86 (1923): 87.

16  Stockley, *Blood in Their Eyes*, xiv.

17  *Moore et al. v. Dempsey*, 261 U.S. 86 (1923): 88.

18  See: Cortner, *A Mob Intent on Death*; Whitaker, *On the Laps of Gods*.

19  See Walter F. White, "'Massacring Whites' in Arkansas," *The Nation* 109 (1919): 715–716.

20  Cited in Stockley, *Blood in Their Eyes*, 197. For further detailed accounts of the measures used see Whitaker, *On the Laps of Gods*, ch. 9.

21  Whitaker, *On the Laps of Gods*, 175.

22  Whitaker, *On the Laps of Gods*, 176.

23  *Slaughter-House Cases*, 83 U.S. 36 (1873), *United States v. Cruikshank*, 92 U.S. 542 (1875), *Hodges v. United States*, 203 U.S. 1 (1906), and *Frank v. Magnum*, 237 U.S. 309 (1915).

24  For an interesting account of the sometimes contentious connection between the NAACP and the Arkansas lawyers, see Whitaker, *On the Laps of Gods*, ch. 10; Stockley, *Blood in Their Eyes*, ch. 6.

25  *Moore et al. v. Dempsey*, 261 U.S. 86 (1923).

26  Whitaker, *On the Laps of Gods*, 312.

27  These and the statistics that follow come from the records kept by the Tuskegee Institute.

28  See: http://users.bestweb.net/~rg/lynching_century.htm and http://www.ojp.usdoj.gov/bjs/glance/exe.htm.

29  See: James W. Marquart, Sheldon Ekland-Olson and Jonathan R. Sorensen, *The Rope, The Chair, and the Needle* (Austin: University of Texas Press, 1994). In the same town in 1916, Jesse Washington, a 17-year-old black farmhand, was tortured, mutilated, and burned alive before the mayor and a large crowd in the "Waco Horror."

30  The electric chair had been first adopted in New York in 1890. By 1920, fifteen states had carried out executions in an electric chair. In 1924, Florida and Georgia passed similar laws to the one in Texas.

31  "Midnight Appeal Causes Pause in Harvest of Death," *Austin American Statesman*, February 8, 1924, 1.

32  Jacquelyn Dowd Hall, *Revolt Against Chivalry: Jessie Daniel Ames and the Women's Campaign Against Lynching* (New York: Columbia University Press, 1974), 130.

33  Hall, *Revolt Against Chivalry*.

34  Quoted in Hall, *Revolt Against Chivalry*, 162.

35  Quoted in Hall, *Revolt Against Chivalry*, 194.

36  The incident became an oft-told and well-documented story. See *Powell v. Alabama*, 287 U.S. 45 (1932); Dan Carter, *A Tragedy of the American South* (Baton Rouge: Louisiana State University Press, 1979); James R. Acker, *Scottsboro and its Legacy* (Westport, CT: Praeger Publishers, 2008); Aretha, *The Civil Rights Movement*, http://www.pbs.org/wgbh/amex/scottsboro/sfeature/sf_trial.html.

37  *Powell v. Alabama*, 287 U.S. 45 (1932).

38  Important among these decisions was *Norris v. Alabama*, 294 U.S. 587 (1935). The case was argued on February 15 and 18, 1935, and decided on April 1, 1935. It held that the systematic exclusion of blacks from juries was a violation of equal protection provisions in the Constitution.

39  This and quotes that follow, unless otherwise specified, come from Mamie Till-Mobley and Christopher Benson, *Death of Innocence: The Story of the Hate Crime That Changed America* (New York: Ballantine Books, 2003), chs 11 and 12.

40  Stephen J. Whitfield, *A Death in the Delta: The Story of Emmett Till* (Baltimore, MD: Johns Hopkins

University Press, 1988); Till-Mobley and Benson, *Death of Innocence*. For a summary, see: http://www.pbs.org/wgbh/amex/till/timeline/timeline2.html.

41   Two days after the *Look* article appeared, *The California Eagle* began a five-part story that ran from January 26 through February 23. See also *Life Magazine* photos: http://www.life.com/image/52757602/in-gallery/23001/civil-rights-emmett-tills-murder.

42   Quoted in Amos Dixon, "The Truth, the Whole Truth," *The California Eagle*, January 26, 1956.

43   Personal correspondence, November 21, 2009.

44   Michael Meltsner, *Cruel and Unusual: The Supreme Court and Capital Punishment* (New York: Random House, 1973), 72–73.

45   For a detailed account of this case see: Eric W. Rise, *The Martinsville Seven: Race, Rape, and Capital Punishment* (Charlottesville: University of Virgina Press, 1998).

46   Personal correspondence, November 21, 2009.

47   http://www.deathpenaltyinfo.org/executions-us-1608-2002-espy-file.

48   Anthony Amsterdam quoted in Nadya Labi, "The Man against the Machine," *New York University Law School Magazine* (2007): 11–19.

49   http://www.ojp.usdoj.gov/bjs/glance/tables/exetab.htm.

50   Jack Greenberg, *Crusaders in the Courts: Legal Battles of the Civil Rights Movement* (New York: Twelve Tables Press, 2004), 474.

51   *Rudolph v. Alabama*, 375 U.S. 889 (1963).

52   Greenberg, *Crusaders in the Courts,* 474.

53   Marvin E. Wolfgang, Arlene Kelly and Hans C. Nolde, "Comparison of the Executed and the Commuted Among Admissions to Death Row," *Journal of Criminal Law, Criminology, and Police Science* 53 (1962): 301–311.

54   http://diglib.princeton.edu/ead/getEad?id=ark:/88435/hd76s005t.

55   Michael Meltsner, *Cruel and Unusual: The Supreme Court and Capital Punishment* (New York: Random House, 1973), 87.

56   *Furman v. Georgia*, 408 U.S. 238 (1972).

57   Maxwell v. Stephens, cert. denied, 382 U.S. 944 (1965).

58   Michael Meltsner would later write, "Lawyers often fight hard for such tactical advantages, knowing that their adversary may be too overwhelmed by bulky documents, or simply too lazy to dispute the facts." Meltsner, *Cruel and Unusual,* 97.

59   Meltsner, *Cruel and Unusual,* 100.

60   Cited by Meltsner, *Cruel and Unusual,* 101.

61   Personal correspondence, September 7, 2009.

62   *William L. Maxwell, Appellant, v. O.E. Bishop, Superintendent, Arkansas State Penitentiary*, United States Court of Appeals Eighth Circuit: 398 F.2d 138. As he continued outlining the court's decision, Judge Blackmun took note of two recent Supreme Court decisions, released just months before in April, *United States v. Jackson*, 390 U.S. 570 (1968) and in June, *Witherspoon v. Illinois*, 391 U.S. 510 (1968). They had already begun to reshape the capital punishment landscape. Nevertheless, he was not persuaded and rejected the appeal.

63   *William L. Maxwell, Appellant, v. O. E. Bishop, Superintendent, Arkansas State Penitentiary*, United States Court of Appeals Eighth Circuit: 398 F.2d 138.

64   Oral argument, May 4, 1970, *Maxwell v. Bishop*, 398 U.S. 262 (1970).

65   *Witherspoon v. Illinois*, 391 U.S. 510 (1968).

66   Citing *Witherspoon v. Illinois*, 391 U.S. 510 (1968).

67   Meltsner, *Cruel and Unusual,* 235–236.

68   *McGautha v. California*, 402 U.S. 183 (1971); *Crampton v. Ohio*, 402 U. S. 183, 210–211 (1971).

69   Greenberg, *Crusaders in the Courts,* 483.

70   Anthony Amsterdam, personal correspondence, September 7, 2009.

71   This and following quotes come from: Arthur J. Goldberg and Alan M. Dershowitz, "Declaring the Death Penalty Unconstitutional," *Harvard Law Review* 83 (1970): 1773–1819.

72   I would like to add here a special note of thanks to Tony Amsterdam and Michael D'Amelio for their kindness in digging up and providing these documents, which by 2009 were beginning to gather a great deal of dust.

73 *People v. Anderson*, 100 Cal Rpt. 152 (Cal. 1972).

74 Meltsner, *Cruel and Unusual*, 287.

75 *Furman v. Georgia*, 408 U.S. 238 (1972).

76 Meltsner, *Cruel and Unusual*, 289.

77 Greenberg, *Crusaders in the Courts*, 487.

78 *Gregg v. Georgia*, 428 U.S. 153 (1976), *Proffitt v. Florida*, 428 U.S. 242 (1976), *Jurek v. Texas*, 428 U.S. 262 (1976), *Roberts v. Louisiana*, 428 U.S. 325 (1976), and *Woodson v. North Carolina*, 428 U.S. 280 (1976).

79 *Coker v. Georgia*, 433 U.S. 584 (1977) and *Lockett v. Ohio*, 438 U.S. 586 (1978).

80 Oral argument in *Jurek v. Texas*, 428 U.S. 262 (1976), March 30, 1976.

81 See Norman Mailer, *The Executioner's Song* (Boston, MA: Little, Brown, 1979).

82 See: *Godfrey v. Georgia*, 446 U.S. 420 (1980); *Beck v. Alabama*, 447 U.S. 625 (1980); *Adams v. Texas*, 448 U.S. 38 (1980); *Hopper v. Evans*, 456 U.S. 605 (1982); *Enmund v. Florida*, 458 U.S. 782 (1982); and *Pulley v. Harris*, 465 U.S. 37 (1984).

83 Blackmun was dissenting from the Court's decision not to review a case from Texas. *Callins v. Collins*, 510 U.S. 1141 (1994).

84 See, for example, Edwin Brochard, *Convicting the Innocent; Sixty-Five Actual Errors of Criminal Justice* (New Haven, CT: Yale University Press, 1932); Hugo A. Bedau, "Murder, Errors of Justice, and Capital Punishment," in *The Death Penalty in America: An Anthology*, ed. Hugo A. Bedau (Garden City, NY: Anchor Books/Doubleday, 1964), 434–452.

85 *McCleskey v. Kemp*, 481 U.S. 279 (1987).

86 David C. Baldus, Charles Pulaski and George Woodworth, "Comparative Review of Death Sentences: An Empirical Study of the Georgia Experience," *The Journal of Criminal Law and Criminology* 74 (1983): 661–753.

87 For example, Samuel R. Gross and Robert Mauro, *Death and Discrimination: Racial Disparities in Capital Sentencing* (Boston, MA: University Press of New England, 1989); Raymond Paternoster, *Capital Punishment in America* (New York: Lexington Books, 1991).

88 *Callins v. Collins*, 510 U.S. 1141 (1994).

89 Hugo Adam Bedau and Michael L. Radelet, "Miscarriages of Justice in Potentially Capital Cases," *Stanford Law Review* 40 (1987): 24.

90 Michael L. Radelet, Hugo A. Bedau and Constance Putnam, *In Spite of Innocence* (Boston, MA: Northeastern University Press, 1992).

91 http://www.innocenceproject.org/about/.

92 Tim Junkin, *Bloodsworth* (Chapel Hill: Algonquin Books, 2004).

93 http://www.deathpenaltyinfo.org/innocence-list-those-freed-death-row.

94 *Herrera v. Collins*, 506 U.S. 390 (1993).

95 http://www.tdcj.state.tx.us/stat/herreraleonellast.htm.

96 Gary Graham was executed on June 22, 2000. See: http://www.txexecutions.org/reports/222.asp and *Jet* July 10, 2000: http://findarticles.com/p/articles/mi_m1355/is_5_98/ai_63537150/. Most final statements are brief, but Gary Graham prepared a lengthy review of his case and those who had helped him. See: http://www.tdcj.state.tx.us/stat/grahamgarylast.htm.

97 *Furman v. Georgia*, 408 U.S. 238 (1972) and *Lockett v. Ohio*, 438 U.S. 586 (1978).

98 *Callins v. Collins*, 510 U.S. 1141 (1994).

99 By this time there was a growing mountain of research. See, for example: David C. Baldus, George G. Woodworth and Charles A Pulaski, *Equal Justice and the Death Penalty* (Boston, MA: Northeastern University Press, 1990), esp. ch. 12; Marquart, Ekland-Olson and Sorensen, *The Rope, the Chair, and the Needle*, 158–162, fn 8. See also: http://www.deathpenaltyinfo.org/.

100 John C. Jefferies, Jr., *Justice Lewis F. Powell, Jr.: A Biography* (New York: Charles Scribner's Sons, 1994), 451–452.

101 http://www.innocencenetwork.org/.

102 Carol S. Steiker and Jordan M. Steiker, "Sober Second Thoughts: Reflections on Two Decades of Constitutional Regulation of Capital Punishment," *Harvard Law Review* 109 (1995): 355–438.

103 http://www.law.northwestern.edu/wrongfulconvictions/aboutus/.

104 James S. Liebman, Jeffrey Fagan, and Valerie West.

105 See: http://www.deathpenaltyinfo.org/anthony-graves-becomes-12th-death-row-inmate-exonerated
-texas.

106 http://www.deathpenaltyinfo.org/execution-2010.

107 Ken Armstrong and Christi Parsons, "Half of State's Death-Penalty Cases Reversed," *Chicago Tribune*, January 22, 2000, 1.

108 http://www.northwestern.edu/observer/issues/2003-01-23/deathpenalty.html. This speech was widely reported. See, for example, Reynolds Holding, "Historic Death Row Reprieve Illinois: Gov. Ryan Spares 167, Ignites National Debate," *San Francisco Chronicle*, Sunday, January 12, 2003; "Guarding Death's Door," *Time*, January 14, 2003; Florence Template (Mac). http://dir.salon.com/story/news/feature/2003/01/14/ryan/index.html.

109 BBC, "Activists Hail Death Penalty 'Watershed,'" January 12, 2003, http://news.bbc.co.uk/2/hi/americas/2650021.stm.

110 *Batson v. Kentucky* 476 U.S. 79 (1986) was a "weak legal instrument" in reducing racial bias as it called for "deciphering racially motivated uses of [peremptory strikes]"; Melynda Price, "Performing Discretion or Performing Discrimination: Race, Ritual, and Peremptory Challenges in Capital Jury Selection," *Michigan Journal of Race & Law* 15 (2009): 57. *McCleskey v. Kemp*, 481 U.S. 279 (1987), declared racial disparities in the death penalty as an "inevitable part of our criminal justice system" and required that the defense present "exceptionally clear proof" that discrimination was carried out with a "discriminatory purpose" (see Stephen B. Bright, "Discrimination, Death, and Denial: The Tolerance of Racial Discrimination in the Infliction of the Death Penalty," 211–259 in Charles G. Ogletree, Jr. and Austin Sarat, *From Lynch Mobs to the Killing State: Race and the Death Penalty in America* (New York: New York University Press, 2006)).

111 The Justice for All Act of 2004 (HR 5107; Public Law No. 108–405).

112 Frank R. Baumgartner, Suzanna L. DeBoef and Amber E. Boydstun, *The Decline of the Death Penalty and the Discovery of Innocence* (New York: Cambridge University Press, 2008).

113 Jeremy Peters, "Death Penalty Repealed in New Jersey," *New York Times*, December 17, 2007.

114 Richardson's announcement was quoted widely. See: http://www.huffingtonpost.com/2009/03/18/new-mexico-bans-death-pen_n_176666.html http://www.huffingtonpost.com/2009/03/18/new-mexico-bans-death-pen_n_176666.html.

115 *Penry v. Lynaugh*, 492 U.S. 302 (1989).

116 In 2008, Johnny Paul Penry's death sentence was commuted to life.

117 *Atkins v. Virginia*, 536 U.S. 304 (2002).

118 *Stanford v. Kentucky*, 492 U.S. 361 (1989).

119 *Roper v. Simmons*, 543 U.S. 551 (2005).

120 All immediate quotes come from Justice Kennedy's announcement of the decision, March 1, 2005.

121 *Hodgson v. Minnesota*, 497 U.S. 417 (1990).

122 Quotes from Justice Scalia's verbal announcement of Justice Thomas', Chief Justice Rehnquist's, and his dissent.

123 There are numerous translations. The following quotes are taken from Robert France Harper, published by the University of Chicago Press, Callaghan and Company, Luzac and Company, 1904.

124 *Surah* 5: 32–33.

125 See, in particular, Donald Black, *The Behavior of Law* (New York: Academic Press, 1976).

All URLs correct when accessed at time of writing.

# Index